# The Vietnam Experience

# Thunder From Above

## Air War, 1941-1968

by John Morrocco
and the editors of Boston Publishing Company

Boston Publishing Company/Boston, MA

**Boston Publishing Company**

President and Publisher: Robert J. George
Vice President: Richard S. Perkins, Jr.
Editor-in-Chief: Robert Manning
Managing Editor: Paul Dreyfus

Senior Writers:
    Clark Dougan, Edward Doyle, Samuel
    Lipsman, Terrence Maitland, Stephen
    Weiss
Senior Picture Editor: Julene Fischer

Staff Writer: David Fulghum
Researchers: Kerstin Gorham (Chief),
    Sandra M. Jacobs, Christy Virginia
    Keeny, Denis Kennedy, Carole Rulnick,
    Ted Steinberg, Nicole van Ackere

Picture Editors: Wendy Johnson, Lanng
    Tamura
Assistant Picture Editor: Kathleen A. Reidy
Picture Researchers: Nancy Katz Colman,
    Tracey Rogers, Nana Elisabeth Stern,
    Shirley L. Green (Washington, D.C.),
    Kate Lewin (Paris)
Picture Department Assistants: Suzanne
    M. Spencer, Kathryn J. Steeves

Production Editor: Patricia Leal Welch
Assistant Editor: Karen E. English
Editorial Production: Sarah E. Burns, Pam-
    ela George, Theresa M. Slomkowski,
    Amy P. Wilson

Design: Designworks, Sally Bindari

Marketing Director: Jeanne C. Gibson
Business Staff: Amy Pelletier

**About the editor and author**

Editor-in-Chief *Robert Manning*, a long-time journalist, has previously been editor-in-chief of the *Atlantic Monthly* magazine and its press. He served as assistant secretary of state for public affairs under Presidents John F. Kennedy and Lyndon B. Johnson. He has also been a fellow at the Institute of Politics at the John F. Kennedy School of Government at Harvard University.

Author *John Morrocco*, a graduate of Boston College, has his M.A. in International History from the London School of Economics and Political Science and is a Ph.D. candidate at King's College of London.

Historical Consultants: *Vincent H. Demma*, a historian with the U.S. Army Center of Military History, is currently working on the center's history of the Vietnam conflict. *Lee Ewing*, editor of *Army Times*, served two years in Vietnam as a combat intelligence officer with the U.S. Military Assistance Command, Vietnam (MACV) and the 101st Airborne Division.

Picture Consultants: *Lou Drendel* has written and illustrated thirty books on modern military aviation, six of them on the air war in Vietnam. A commercial pilot, he served with the 82d Airborne Division prior to the Vietnam War. *Ngo Vinh Long* is a social historian specializing in China and Vietnam. Born in Vietnam, he returned there most recently in 1980. His books include *Before the Revolution: The Vietnamese Peasants Under the French* and *Report From a Vietnamese Village*.

**Cover Photo:**

A U.S. Marine F-8 Crusader, flying in support of U.S. combat troops in South Vietnam, bombs a Vietcong force outside of Da Nang in early 1966.

Library of Congress Catalog Card Number: 84-70448

ISBN: 0-939526-09-3

10  9  8  7  6
5  4  3  2  1

# Contents

# From Flying Tigers to Farmgate

Larry Guarino was in his early twenties when he first saw Hanoi. Looking down from his P-51 Mustang, the U.S. Air Force pilot had no opportunity to observe the European charm of the French colonial city. It was 1944 and Guarino was flying fighter escort for B-24 Liberators bombing Japanese bases in the occupied city. Twenty years later Guarino returned to Hanoi. This time he would stay for more than seven years.

When President Lyndon Johnson launched a systematic bombing campaign against North Vietnam in early 1965, Major Larry Guarino found himself on temporary duty at Korat air force base in Thailand. As operations officer for the 12th Tactical Fighter Squadron, he was soon planning missions and flying an F-105 Thunderchief against targets in Vietnam once again. On June 14 the odds finally caught up with Guarino. Shot down by North Vietnamese antiaircraft fire, he was captured by militiamen brandishing rifles and two-handed swords.

His hands bound behind his back, Guarino was taken from village to village and paraded past jeering peasants who pelted him with stones and kicked him to the ground. Finally handed over to a regular army unit, the flier was wrapped in blankets and thrown in the back of a covered truck. When he stepped into the light of day, Guarino found himself in a large, walled-in courtyard in downtown Hanoi. He was the eleventh American prisoner-of-war to arrive at Hoa Lo Prison, already being referred to by its inmates as the "Hanoi Hilton."

Striding up to Guarino, an NVA soldier shouted at him in English: "Why did you come here to murder my people? Now you are going to pay for your crimes." Guarino demanded his rights to proper treatment under the Geneva Convention. "Rights? You have no rights," the guard screamed. "You are nothing here but a criminal."

*Preceding page. American pilots of the "Flying Tigers," flying P-40 Tomahawks, return to base after strafing Japanese truck convoys along the Burma Road in April 1942.*

## Shifting allegiances

During Larry Guarino's twenty-year absence, the tides of nationalism and communism had transformed Southeast Asia. During World War II, Americans fought alongside Asian nationalist groups against Japanese forces. None were more famous than the Flying Tigers, led by General Claire L. Chennault. This small band of volunteer pilots helped to defend Chinese troops and their tenuous supply line along the Burma Road from Japanese air attacks.

By 1943, with the U.S. war effort reaching full stride, the Flying Tigers were absorbed into the 14th Air Force under Gen. Chennault's command. Operating from bases in unoccupied China, the Americans took the offensive against the Japanese, striking enemy bases throughout Southeast Asia, including those in Hanoi and Saigon. In late 1944 an American flier, shot down on a mission over Vietnam, found help from an unexpected source.

Parachuting into the jungle, a Lieutenant Shaw was found by a group of armed Vietnamese who called them-

*Smoke rises above Japanese installations near Saigon after an attack by planes of the U.S. Pacific Fleet on January 12, 1945.*

*A JU–52 Junker of the French air force bombs Vietminh positions ninety miles north of Hanoi on March 5, 1951.*

selves the Vietminh. He was escorted back to American lines in China at the instruction of their leader, a frail looking yet charismatic man calling himself Ho Chi Minh. The Communist-dominated Vietminh were among a number of nationalist groups that had been struggling for years to free their country from French rule.

When Japanese troops first arrived to occupy the French colony they had been greeted as liberators. But the Japanese were content to allow France to continue administering Vietnam while they siphoned off the economic resources of the country. Eventually regarding the Japanese as enemies, Ho Chi Minh sought to trade the Vietminh's services to the Allies in return for support of his movement.

At a meeting with Chennault, in which the American general thanked Ho for rescuing Lt. Shaw, the two men talked about assisting other downed airmen. Soon afterward, American agents of the Office of Strategic Services arrived in Ho's mountain retreat to train the guerrillas in operations against the Japanese. By the end of the war the

Vietminh were undoubtedly the strongest nationalist group in Vietnam. After the Japanese surrendered, Ho Chi Minh led his troops into Hanoi and proclaimed the independence of the Democratic Republic of Vietnam.

But the French were unwilling to relinquish their colony, and French troops began arriving in Vietnam. With the aid of the British, who were sent to disarm Japanese forces, French troops soon regained control over the southern portion of the country. After more than a year of fruitless negotiations and escalating military clashes, Ho retreated to his mountain sanctuaries and began guerrilla operations against the French.

During postwar conferences, the U.S., regarding Ho Chi Minh as a truly nationalist leader, had urged France to come to terms with the Vietminh. But as the Cold War intensified, Washington became increasingly concerned by Ho's Communist connections. Faced with the Soviet occupation of Eastern Europe and the success of Mao Tse-tung in China, U.S. leaders became obsessed with the expansion of communism. In May 1950, in the wake of the

*A French C–119 transport plane lies in ruins on the runway at Dien Bien Phu on April 20, 1954.*

outbreak of war in Korea, Washington authorized $164 million to help finance the French war effort in Vietnam. On August 3 members of the U.S. Military Assistance Advisory Group arrived in Vietnam to help coordinate the program.

In January 1951 the Vietminh initiated large-scale offensives against French positions in the Red River Delta. With this shift from guerrilla tactics to more conventional assaults, the French hoped to use superior artillery and air power to break the Vietminh. But the French air force consisted of an assortment of obsolete planes, including captured German JU–52 transports, surplus American C–47s and F–63 Kingcobra fighters, and British Spitfires. Overworked maintenance crews had difficulty finding spare parts to keep the aging planes flying.

As part of its military aid program, the U.S. delivered eight C–47s to the French that summer. Forty navy F–6F Hellcats arrived in December to replace the worn-out Spitfires. An additional ninety F–8F Bearcats landed early in 1951. The U.S. also gave the French large stocks of World War II surplus ammunition. The U.S. support proved decisive, allowing the French to double their air operations, forcing the Vietminh to retreat to their jungle strongholds. But Ho's guerrillas continued to mount hit-and-run raids, and for the next two years the war continued in a bloody stalemate.

The stalemate would be broken at Dien Bien Phu, an outpost in the northwest corner of Vietnam, which the French had fortified with 13,000 troops in late 1953. They hoped to lure the Vietminh into a pitched battle in which French firepower could annihilate a massed guerrilla force. Faced with growing antiwar sentiment at home and tired of the slow pace of the conflict, French leaders had agreed to negotiate with the Communists at a meeting of the big powers in Geneva in April 1954. A victory at Dien Bien Phu would strengthen France's bargaining position.

Ho Chi Minh also knew the diplomatic benefits of victory at Dien Bien Phu, however, and quickly turned the tables on the French, surrounding the outpost by January 1954 and committing nearly 50,000 troops to the siege. The battle began on March 13 with a furious Vietminh barrage that overran three vital French positions and shut down the airstrip, the camp's only link to the outside world.

French transport planes and twelve C–119 Flying Boxcars of the Civil Air Transport, secretly owned by the CIA and piloted by Americans, took over the job of supplying the camp with parachute drops. U.S. President Dwight Eisenhower sent 200 USAF technicians to help the French maintain the transports. But the drops became increasingly dangerous and inaccurate as General Vo Nguyen Giap's forces positioned antiaircraft guns in the hills surrounding the base.

Their confidence rapidly dwindling, the French formally requested direct U.S. air intervention in early April. For months President Eisenhower and his advisers had been mulling over just such an idea. Eisenhower, although opposed to committing the U.S. to another Asian land war like Korea, asked the chairman of the Joint Chiefs of Staff, Admiral Arthur Radford, to draw up contingency plans. Radford and the Pentagon offered Operation Vulture, which called for 60 B-29 bombers escorted by 150 navy fighters to hit Vietminh positions around Dien Bien Phu.

Many, including some of Radford's colleagues on the JCS, were skeptical of the plan, seeing it as the beginning of a potential spiral of intervention that could lead to another Korea. Senator Lyndon B. Johnson and other Congressional leaders agreed, rejecting the plan unless it was backed by America's allies. Although he told the world on April 7 that "the loss of Indochina will cause the fall of Southeast Asia like a set of dominoes," Eisenhower agreed only to supply the French with twenty-five unmarked B-29 bombers. He would approve Vulture only with Congressional backing, and that would not occur without the allies' approval.

Despite the additional B-29s and large quantities of U.S. ordnance, the Vietminh continued to tighten their grip on Dien Bien Phu, making the job of supplying the base even more treacherous. In late April, as the outpost hung on by a thread, the French made a final pitch for Operation Vulture. But with the British reluctant to back the plan, the French garrison was left to its fate as the Geneva Conference convened.

On May 6 James B. McGovern—better known as "Earthquake McGoon"—and Wallace A. Buford became the first U.S. casualties of the Indochina conflict. The two CAT pilots died while resupplying Dien Bien Phu when their C-119 crashed after being hit by antiaircraft fire. The next day the Vietminh launched their final assault. Within a few hours the French garrison surrendered.

## Under the American umbrella

After the humiliating defeat at Dien Bien Phu, the French gave in to the political settlement reached at Geneva that divided Vietnam in half at the seventeenth parallel, with the Vietminh occupying the northern portion while the French withdrew to the South. The introduction of any fur-

*Vietminh troops attack along the airstrip at Dien Bien Phu on May 7, 1954, the day the French fortress fell.*

ther military forces in either zone was prohibited. Finally, a country-wide election was to be held in July 1956 to reunify the country.

By then Ngo Dinh Diem had succeeded in ousting the French-supported government of Emperor Bao Dai and establishing a constitutional government of which he was overwhelmingly elected president in 1955. An anti-Communist nationalist, Diem refused to participate in any reunification elections. Instead he declared South Vietnam independent and turned to Washington for support.

Gradually, the Americans replaced the war-weary French as the protectors of the fledgling Republic of Vietnam. While President Diem consolidated his power, in 1955 the U.S. military advisory group began the difficult task of building an effective military force capable of withstanding Ho Chi Minh's avowed determination to extend his control over the entire country. USAF advisers assisted in formulating plans for an air force to be created from a small cadre of French-trained Vietnamese pilots and remaining French planes, including thirty-five C-47 transports, two squadrons of L-19s to act as aerial observers for army units, and twenty-five obsolete F-8 Bearcats that would provide the only source of close air fighter support.

In 1957 the USAF took over the task of training South Vietnamese air force pilots from the departing French. They discovered the young air officers were good fliers but relatively inexperienced in combat. The Americans also began upgrading logistical support for the VNAF, and runways at Tan Son Nhut and Bien Hoa near Saigon, as well as Da Nang in the north, were improved and extended to accommodate U.S. jet aircraft. But as the Americans struggled to fashion the VNAF into an effective fighting force, Hanoi began putting pressure on the South.

During the four years after the signing of the Geneva

# The CIA's Secret Airline

In April 1954 a group of C-46 transports landed at the French airfield in Haiphong. Twenty-four Americans dressed in brightly colored shirts and Bermuda shorts emerged from the planes carrying suitcases and crates of personal effects. The Americans looked more prepared for a holiday than the task at hand, flying supplies to the besieged French garrison at Dien Bien Phu. But the pilots were no strangers to combat.

The Americans were employed by the Civil Air Transport (CAT), which had been founded in 1946 by General Claire Lee Chennault, the former commander of the Flying Tigers. Purchasing war surplus C-46 and C-47 transports, Chennault hired American ex-servicemen to fly them. Like Chennault, they were colorful individualists who had become enamored of the Orient and found peacetime life dull.

One of Chennault's first contracts came from his World War II Chinese ally Chiang Kai-shek, who was engaged in a bitter civil war with Communist forces. CAT pilots flew supplies and ammunition to besieged cities and Chiang Kai-shek's troops in the field. They also carried agents of the newly created Central Intelligence Agency, which eventually provided money to keep CAT flying in China.

In 1949, when Communist victory appeared inevitable, the CIA advanced money to establish the airline in Taiwan, Chiang Kai-shek's followers' new home. The CIA considered the airline's presence in Taiwan an excellent cover for their growing clandestine operations in the Orient. Already part owned by the CIA in 1950 and helped by contracts to supply UN forces during the Korean War, CAT soon became the biggest and most profitable airline in the Far East.

In 1953 CAT became involved in the conflict between Vietminh guerrillas and French forces in Indochina. In November of that year, CAT transports helped the French air force airlift 16,000 men into Dien Bien Phu. By the following March, the garrison was completely surrounded by the Vietminh and cut off from the outside world. Although the French requested direct military support, the U.S. instead opted to provide limited covert support, commissioning CAT to assist the French to paradrop the supplies needed to hold the base. A squadron of C-119 Flying Boxcars, their U.S. Air Force markings painted out, was placed at CAT's disposal.

Situated in a narrow valley between two lofty ridges bristling with Vietminh antiaircraft batteries, Dien Bien Phu soon came to be referred to by CAT pilots as "the slot." With only two directions of approach and a limited drop zone, the lumbering transports were easy targets day in and day out.

CAT pilots maneuvered their C-119s through the treacherous crossfire of the slot at 5,000 feet while crewmen frantically kicked as many supplies as they could out the tail door. More cautious French C-47 pilots preferred to drop their parachute bundles from 10,000 feet, sometimes right on top of the American C-119s. Even more alarming to CAT pilots were the bombs that higher flying French fighter-bombers sometimes dropped right through the CAT flight formations. Because the CAT pilots were eventually forced to fly at higher altitudes to avoid the deadly ground fire, the parachute drops became increasingly less accurate. Nearly half the supplies dropped over the outpost fell into enemy hands as the Vietminh tightened their grip on Dien Bien Phu. On May 8 the beleaguered French fortress was finally overrun.

But the French defeat did not end CAT's operations in Indochina. By 1959 the airline had been taken over completely by the CIA. Renamed Air America, it became the CIA's private air force in its clandestine war against Communist forces in Southeast Asia. By the early 1960s, hundreds of Air America aircraft flew throughout the jungles of Laos and South Vietnam to supply the CIA's private armies of mercenary tribesmen and sabotage teams.

*After the Geneva Agreements of 1954, the U.S. gradually became the protectors of the new South Vietnamese regime. Here a U.S. adviser instructs a South Vietnamese pilot in an American-supplied T-28 Nomad.*

accords, Vietminh guerrillas who had remained in the South after the partition had promoted popular discontent throughout the South Vietnamese countryside. But in 1959 the Central Committee of Ho Chi Minh's Lao Dong party decided to escalate their destabilization campaign into an "armed struggle." Communist guerrillas, who Diem named the "Vietcong," or "Vietnamese Communists," began launching hit-and-run attacks on government installations and ambushing army patrols.

South Vietnamese military forces now found themselves battling increasingly large guerrilla units. USAF advisers urged greater participation by the VNAF, but with only one squadron of antiquated F-8 Bearcats, South Vietnam's air force offered little in the way of aerial firepower. The F-8 was an air-to-air fighter and could not carry large bomb loads. With spare parts hard to come by, the aging planes were in a constant state of disrepair. When a Bearcat piloted by the squadron commander mysteriously crashed in August, the superstitious Vietnamese became reluctant to fly them. President Diem grounded the

obsolete Bearcats and asked the Americans to replace them with jet aircraft.

Washington balked. Replacing former French VNAF planes with aircraft having greater offensive capabilities would violate the Geneva agreements prohibiting the introduction of more sophisticated weapons in either zone. Instead, President Eisenhower agreed to supply the Vietnamese with navy AD-6 propeller-driven fighter-bombers, later redesignated the A-1. The first six were delivered in early September 1959 and twenty-five more early the next year. A seven-man U.S. Navy advisory team, led by Lieutenant Ken Moranville, accompanied the first shipment to provide training and mechanical support.

Its high-power engine and heavier frame enabled the AD-6 Skyraider to carry a larger and more varied ordnance load than the lighter Bearcats. Disappointed at not receiving jets, Vietnamese military leaders were initially skeptical of the Skyraider's abilities. But any doubts were quickly dispelled when Lt. Moranville demonstrated it before VNAF officers at Bien Hoa.

Carrying a full load of bombs and rockets, Moranville made a few runs at a simulated target. "On one of the dives I simultaneously fired eight pods full of rockets, 152 in all," he recalled, "which really threw up the dust." Looping over the airfield, the navy lieutenant landed right in front of the line of VIPs, whose jaws were agape in awe of the Skyraider's capabilities.

Delivery of the new fighter planes had little immediate impact on the war. "In those days," Moranville recalls, "the war, for the most part, was a Monday-through-Friday, daylight-hours-only affair. We tried once to establish a weekend alert force, but it didn't get much business." Vietnamese pilots rarely flew on weekends or during afternoon siesta and never at night. Between August and October 1960, the 1st Fighter Squadron mounted only twenty combat sorties (a single plane flying a single mission).

In late 1960, the situation in Vietnam threatened to erupt into a major confrontation. Seeking to capitalize on a growing undercurrent of popular dissatisfaction with the Diem regime, the Communists accelerated the pace of the war. Ethnic southerners, who had regrouped to the North after the partition, were now returning to swell the ranks of the Vietcong. Large-scale raids were launched against government installations throughout the country and even threatened the capital of Saigon itself.

Asserting that the conflict was essentially a civil war, Ho Chi Minh announced the formation of a shadow government in the South, the National Liberation Front, in December 1960. Although the NLF included non-Communists, it was dominated by the Communists and controlled largely from Hanoi. Ho's strategy received a boost in January 1961 when Premier Nikita Khrushchev publicly pledged Soviet support for Communist-led wars of "national liberation."

Two weeks later, John F. Kennedy assumed office, determined to meet the new threat head on. "This is another type of war," he would later tell the graduating class at West Point, ". . . war by ambush instead of combat; by infiltration instead of aggression, seeking victory by eroding and exhausting the enemy instead of engaging him." To meet the challenge, Kennedy proposed ". . . a whole new kind of strategy, a wholly different kind of force. . . ."

## Jungle Jim and Operation Farmgate

Believing that strong, highly mobile units trained in counterinsurgency warfare were needed to match the guerrillas, Kennedy pressed U.S. military leaders to develop such forces for use in Vietnam. Foremost among these elite units were the army's "Green Berets," the Special Forces. Working in small teams, they were trained to operate in VC-controlled areas where they would recruit, organize, and lead local forces against the guerrillas. Not to be outdone, the air force offered its own version of the Green Berets for duty in Vietnam.

In the spring of 1961, the 4400th Combat Crew Training Squadron came into being at Eglin Air Force Base in Florida. Nicknamed "Jungle Jim," the squadron was assigned to instruct South Vietnamese pilots in unconventional air operations and provide support for counterinsurgency ground forces. Its 124 officers and 228 airmen, all volunteers, were trained and equipped to fly strike, reconnaissance, and airlift missions from makeshift runways in remote areas. Their picturesque uniforms were selected by General Curtis E. LeMay, the hard-nosed air force chief of staff.

One hundred fifty-five Jungle Jim commandos arrived at Bien Hoa on November 16 under the code name Operation Farmgate. The runway had been extended from 4,000 to 5,800 feet since Lt. Moranville's day, but the buildings were in such a dilapidated state that the men had to live in hastily erected tents. Their air fleet consisted of eight T-28 Nomad fighters, originally designed for training, four antiquated B-26 light bombers, and four redesigned World War II vintage SC-47 transports. The Farmgate pilots' primary task was to train South Vietnamese pilots. To assuage Washington politicians wary of openly committing American aircraft to combat in Vietnam, South Vietnamese markings were painted on all Farmgate planes. The eager American pilots, however, would soon see combat. With only a handful of fighter planes, the Vietnamese were consistently unable to respond to the growing number of army requests for air support. As a result, in December 1961 Admiral Harry D. Felt, commander in chief of U.S. forces in the Pacific (CINCPAC), proposed expanding Farmgate's role to include combat missions.

Secretary of Defense Robert McNamara approved Felt's request with one condition: A South Vietnamese trainee had to ride in the rear seat during any combat mission. State Department officials, opposed to any direct involvement by Americans in the fighting, protested the decision. A compromise approved combined crews for combat support missions but only when VNAF aircraft were unavailable.

Back seat combat training proved more of a political expedient than a practical one, and when an SC-47 crashed, killing eight Americans and the lone Vietnamese trainee aboard, reporters ridiculed the assertions that USAF personnel were engaged only in training. But McNamara continued to maintain the façade. Hiding behind a baffling and overlapping command arrangement, the reality of Farmgate combat operations was effectively kept from the American public.

## An uphill battle

While there were some excellent French-trained fliers, many of the new Vietnamese trainees were not keen on sitting in the back seat of a T-28 with a "gung ho" Farmgate pilot at the controls. One American recalled having

*An American pilot flies a twin-seated T-28 during an Operation Farmgate mission.*

to steal the shoes of the Vietnamese the day before a mission to prevent them from running off during the night.

Although the Vietcong preferred to launch their attacks under cover of darkness, the Vietnamese pilots rarely flew after dark. Daytime flying habits of the Vietnamese were also deemed rather unorthodox by the Americans. Some would prop cardboard panels on their wind screens to shield their eyes against the sun, severely reducing their view from the cockpit in the process. Relying on their intimate knowledge of the countryside, pilots rarely used their navigational instruments. They also flew without the aid of any air traffic control system until late 1961 when the Americans installed surveillance and air control radar equipment at three posts: Tan Son Nhut air base, later code named Paris Control, Da Nang, and Pleiku.

Vietnamese army officers' general ignorance of the tactical application of air power and even how a plane worked created further problems. There was one instance when a C–47 pilot refused to take off with a planeload of ARVN colonels because one engine's manifold pressure was dangerously low. The enraged colonels court-martialed the hapless pilot for insubordination.

In addition, because of shortages of parts, skilled mechanics, and experienced pilots, Lieutenant Colonel Nguyen Cao Ky's 1st Vietnamese Transport Group found themselves unable to meet army demands for airlifts of men and supplies. U.S. advisers were also shocked to find that 25 percent of the transport group's effort went toward ferrying VIPs around the country. To help meet the transport needs, the U.S. sent under Project Mule Train sixteen aging C–123 Providers, and the pilots to fly them, to Vietnam in December 1961. Modified into assault transports capable of carrying eight tons, the C–123s could operate from short and rough runways, which greatly enhanced air support capabilities for troops in the field. Thirty additional USAF pilots were also sent to help man the Vietnamese C–47s. Called the "Dirty Thirty" because of their unmilitary appearance, the Americans freed more Vietnamese transport pilots for combat training.

With all its problems, the VNAF sometimes seemed its own worst enemy but never so much as on February 26, 1962, when a pair of disgruntled VNAF officers flew their Skyraiders over Saigon in broad daylight and strafed and bombed the presidential palace. One plane was shot down, but the other escaped to Cambodia. President Diem, constantly fearful of plots against his life, immediately grounded all Vietnamese planes. When the ban was finally lifted, pilots were only allowed to carry 20MM ammunition, no bombs.

By June 1962, Farmgate had readied enough fighter pilots to man a second South Vietnamese fighter squadron. With forty-nine fighters now available, the VNAF had increased its sortie rate to 412 per month from 150 in January. They were, however, deemed capable of 1,029 per month by their U.S. advisers. More pilots and planes were

not the solution to the problems that plagued the VNAF: The root of the problem lay in a command and control system that lacked the coordination and flexibility needed to offset the VNAF's shortage of air units.

All Vietnamese air elements were controlled from the Air Operations Center at Tan Son Nhut, using the air control communications and reporting facilities of the Tactical Air Control Center. Requests from Air Support Operation Centers in each of the four military corps areas were forwarded to the AOC where they were evaluated in coordination with the Vietnamese Joint General Staff. Aircraft were then parceled out for missions in each corps.

Although the system looked good on paper, decisions on the use of air assets were not always based on sound military reasoning. With few of its senior officers placed in the army-dominated JGS, the VNAF carried little clout. Disputes over the allocation of air assets usually ended in the JGS deferring to the wishes of each corps commander. In Vietnam, where military control was equated to political power, the corps commanders jealously guarded their authority. They considered air units within their corps areas to be their own and were reluctant to allow them to be used in other corps zones.

Political considerations also reduced the effectiveness of the VNAF. President Diem's tendency to appoint only loyal supporters as corps commanders, sometimes regardless of their military abilities, indirectly left him as the sole arbiter of military operations. On occasion he would personally pass judgment on targets for air strikes.

Poor communications between ground troops calling in air support and the forward air controllers—FACs—who directed bombing runs from the air, only compounded the lack of cooperation between the South Vietnamese army and air force. When ARVN units met Communist forces, a control party on the ground would radio the positions of friendly and enemy troops to FACs, supposedly flying overhead in two-man L–19 observation planes. However, there were only forty-five L–19s available for duty and a shortage of trained forward air controllers, so FACs were not always on the scene when they were needed. Once the FAC arrived over a battle, communications with ground troops were unwieldy. FACs had to use two radios, one to communicate with ground troops and another for strike aircraft. And, often, they found themselves talking to an officer on the ground who knew nothing about air tactics.

After a bit of arm-twisting, the Americans were able to impress upon the Vietnamese the value of closer cooperation between air and ground units. General Paul D. Harkins, who had arrived in Vietnam in January 1962 to head the newly created U.S. Military Advisory Command–Vietnam (MACV), convinced his Vietnamese counterparts to initiate more aggressive, large-scale offensive operations. The strategy called for army sweeps to drive the guerrillas back to their base sanctuaries, then destroy them with

*An A-1 Skyraider of the South Vietnamese air force, flown by a rebellious pilot, pulls up into the sky over Saigon after attacking President Ngo Dinh Diem's palace on February 26, 1962.*

combined land and air assaults. Brigadier General Rollen H. Anthis, commander of the USAF's 2d Air Division, created in October 1962 to control USAF assets in Vietnam, doubted the VNAF's limited resources could fulfill the ambitious plan. Anthis pressed for a more efficient centralized control system for air assets within the country. But Gen. Harkins sided with his Vietnamese army counterparts who thought it too cumbersome.

Launched late in 1962, the campaign met with encouraging initial results. One of the first combined operations was aimed at a Vietcong stronghold seventy-five kilometers north of Saigon in War Zone D. VNAF Skyraiders blanketed the area with bombs and machine-gun fire prior to the assault. Following in their wake, five American-piloted C-123s and twelve VNAF C-47s dropped 500 paratroopers on the edge of the jungle stronghold. As the Vietnamese Rangers moved in on the VC, VNAF and Farmgate aircraft provided air support and blocked avenues of retreat with 500-pound bombs and rockets. In the three-week operation the Rangers killed sixty-two guerrillas, took ten prisoners, and discovered signs of further casualties from the aerial bombardment.

The arrival of three U.S. Army helicopter units in the country in January 1962 added greater mobility for Vietnamese offensive operations. The CH-21 Shawnee helicopters, with U.S. markings and flown by American pilots, could airlift Vietnamese troops in quick strikes against remote Vietcong concentrations. Results of these helicopter assault operations were so successful that Secretary McNamara ordered another two companies of CH-21s and a marine squadron of twenty-four UH-34D Choctaws sent to Vietnam.

Ideally, when flying into a known Vietcong "hotbed," the helicopter assault teams were accompanied by Farmgate T-28s, which scouted the terrain and strafed any concentrations of enemy fire on the flanks. But Farmgate units, already overburdened, were often unavailable for escort duty. The U.S. Army decided to provide its own air support and sent fifteen UH-1A and UH-1B Huey helicopters armed with two seven-tube, 2.75-inch rocket pods and twin .30-caliber machine guns mounted above each landing skid to work with the assault teams. Although forbidden to engage in offensive operations, the American crews were authorized to use "suppressive fire" in self-defense.

Along with the Huey gunships came six OV-1 Mohawk observation planes of the army's 23d Special Air Warfare Detachment. Powered by low-noise, turbo-prop engines, a Mohawk could swoop in over Vietcong jungle hide-outs, its specially fitted cameras clicking away. Accompanied by a mobile photo processing unit, the twin-seated observation planes provided rapid reconnaissance information.

Cruising in pairs as low as fifty feet above the ground, the Mohawks presented a tempting target to the Vietcong. But like the helicopter gunships, they were empowered to

strike back with their .50-caliber machine guns only when fired upon. Occasionally, by luring the VC into firing at them, they were able to engage in direct support of ground forces when strike aircraft were unavailable.

## Command and control

By the end of 1962, the army had deployed 199 aircraft in Vietnam compared to only 61 air force planes. Gen. Anthis questioned the increased size and combat role of army helicopters and fixed-wing aircraft, noting that it ran counter to the basic U.S. policy of building a Vietnamese military force capable of fighting its own war. But Gen. Harkins defended their role as a stopgap measure to buy time for the South Vietnamese military.

Air force and army clashes over air assets in Vietnam went far deeper than disagreements over U.S. policy objectives. They represented yet another round in the perennial dispute over the control of close air support. Army commanders were loath to place their aircraft under air force control, arguing that, like tanks and artillery, they were organically tied to ground forces. Air force commanders felt this posture threatened their role as the prime service branch for air warfare.

With the responsibility for coordinating all U.S. air operations within Vietnam, Gen. Anthis had unsuccessfully requested that army aircraft be placed under his control. Instead, army helicopters were controlled by U.S. Army corps advisers who deployed them according to the wishes of each Vietnamese corps commander. This ar-

*ARVN soldiers scramble toward CH-21 Shawnee helicopters. Starting in 1962, CH-21s were the first of the helicopters to be deployed to South Vietnam by the U.S., and they added significantly to the ability of ARVN troops to respond to guerrilla attacks.*

rangement reduced Anthis's ability to provide support by fixed-wing aircraft during helicopter assaults.

Although the widespread introduction of helicopters gave ground forces in Vietnam greater mobility than the more traditional airborne assaults using C-47 transports, they were more vulnerable to ground fire. Army commanders would soon learn that Huey gunships alone did not have the firepower necessary to protect transport helicopters when landing in heavily defended areas.

## Disaster at Ap Bac

On January 2, 1963, the 7th ARVN Division launched a helicopter assault on a suspected Vietcong stronghold near the village of Ap Bac, fifty-five kilometers southwest of Saigon. Learning of the plan only four days before, the USAF air liaison officer indicated that all available aircraft had already been committed to an airborne assault along the Cambodian border. Nevertheless, the attack at Ap Bac went on as planned with five Huey gunships providing close air support.

Instead of meeting the 200 guerrillas they expected, the men of the 7th Division landed in the midst of an entire Vietcong battalion. A reserve force, airlifted in to reinforce the pinned-down troops, was met by a storm of automatic-weapons fire from the surrounding tree line. One of the CH-21 helicopter transports was hit and plunged to the ground in flames. The Huey gunships made repeated strafing passes, but they were no match for the guerrillas' guns. One of the UH-1Bs was blasted out of the sky along with another CH-21 sent in to rescue the crew of the first downed transport.

A Vietnamese FAC, circling over the battle in his L-19, put in an emergency call for air support. Farmgate fighters were quickly diverted to the scene. Together with a B-26, fully armed with napalm, bombs, and rockets, they finally silenced the Vietcong fire. But confusion and hesitation among ground commanders surrounding the area allowed the guerrillas to slip away into the jungle.

A storm of criticism erupted after the disastrous engagement. Three American advisers had been killed and six others wounded; of the fifteen U.S. helicopters, five had been shot down and all but one of the remaining ten were badly damaged. American army advisers blamed the inefficiency and corruption within the Vietnamese military. Air force advisers, however, regarded it as a prime example of the need for a centralized control system for air operations. CINCPAC Admiral Felt ordered on January 9 that all future operations be coordinated with Vietnamese and Farmgate air units, telling General Harkins that "helicopters were no adequate substitute" for fixed-wing air support.

Anthis again tried to obtain authority over all air units in Vietnam, including helicopters. But Felt was unwilling to rule on such a touchy issue. Gen. Harkins was allowed to continue to let senior army and marine advisers in each corps area direct their own air units. This ongoing American dispute did little to impress upon the Vietnamese the importance of coordination between their own army and air units.

*The wreckages of a UH-1 Huey gunship (foreground) and a CH-21, shot down by VC gunners on January 3, 1963, during the battle at Ap Bac, lie in a rice field.*

*Rebels break through the walls surrounding President Diem's residence during the coup of November 2, 1963.*

## Aerial denial

American military advisers and their Vietnamese counterparts were in total agreement, however, on the concept of using their superior air power to carry the war to the Vietcong. Air strikes could destroy guerrilla bases and harass their supply lines in remote jungle areas. Known as interdiction bombing, such strikes had been carried out by the air force in World War II and Korea. All that was needed was timely and accurate intelligence, but in Vietnam, where the enemy consisted of fast-moving guerrilla units that lived off the land, that task proved more difficult.

In October of 1961, a detachment of four RF-101 Voodoo jets, from the 15th Tactical Reconnaissance Squadron at Okinawa, arrived at Tan Son Nhut airfield ostensibly to participate in an air show during South Vietnam's national day celebrations. They never left. Inquiring reporters were told the Voodoos had remained to "log some flying time." In fact, the four jets secretly began flying low-level photo reconnaissance missions. A month later, four more RF-101s joined them in Operation Able Mable, flying three patrols a day.

Their aerial photos provided excellent information on fixed installations, such as base camps and supply depots, but were less effective in spotting small groups of guerrillas who hid under the triple-canopied jungle by day and moved by night. Because of the time lag in processing and interpreting the photos, the camps were often empty by the time strike aircraft could be notified of a target.

To augment the reconnaissance effort USAF C-54 Skymasters were loaded with high-frequency direction finding equipment, personally designed by Gen. LeMay, to home in on VC radios. They uncovered a surprising number of radio signals but found it nearly impossible to pinpoint the locations of the low-powered radio sets that the guerrillas operated in short bursts. Instead, air units came to rely for their intelligence more and more upon army scouting reports, interrogations of Vietcong prisoners and defectors, local village chiefs, and government agents.

When timely and accurate information was available, interdiction bombing appeared to be highly successful. Simultaneous Farmgate-VNAF air strikes on fourteen separate targets in early 1962 were so devastating that the Vietcong reportedly suspected that spies in their midst had guided the aircraft to their hiding places. Aerial photos and army patrols uncovered splintered and smashed huts and the smoldering remains of stockpiles of ammunition and rice.

The most effective weapon in the VNAF's arsenal was napalm, a sophisticated version of gasoline "drop-tank" bombs used in the Pacific in World War II and further developed in Korea. For napalm, gasoline and phosphorous were mixed with an aluminum-based soap powder to create the jelly-like substance that was packed into canisters. On impact, a detonator ignited the phosphorous, splashing the burning mixture up to 100 feet in every direction. Clinging to anything it touched, the sticky napalm burned slowly with an intense heat—up to 2,000 degrees Fahrenheit.

Interdiction air strikes proved to be a two-edged sword. Whether because of faulty information or pilot error, the bombings sometimes inflicted heavy casualties among the civilian population. One such incident was personally brought to the attention of President Kennedy by Roger Hilsman, director of the State Department Bureau of Intelligence and Research.

In January 1962, aerial photos uncovered a guerrilla camp complete with a small munitions factory near the village of Binh Hoa, a few miles from the Cambodian border. Although the intelligence reports were five days old, the Vietnamese decided it was a target too inviting to be passed up. Early on the morning of the twenty-first, Farmgate T-28s and B-26s, led by Lieutenant Colonel Robert L. Gleason, hit the site with bombs and rockets.

With a Vietnamese FAC marking the target and an SC-47 transport overflying the canal that delineated the border with neutral Cambodia, Gleason felt sure he had not made any mistakes. But the only casualties of the barrage were five villagers, three of them children. Paratroopers sent in to mop up the remaining guerrillas found the camp empty. Villagers said the Vietcong had moved out an hour before the air strike. Two days later, the Cambodian government also charged that the planes had strayed across the border, killing one villager and wounding three others.

The Vietnamese minister of defense, who had watched the air strike from an orbiting C-47, shrugged off the protests, claiming the whole area was a "VC hotbed." But the repercussions of the incident were immediately felt in Washington, where officials began questioning the validity of interdiction bombing in a guerrilla war.

Unlike conventional wars, in Vietnam there were no set battle lines. Vietcong guerrillas wore no distinctive uniforms and mingled freely with the local population. They were difficult to identify by soldiers on the ground, almost impossible from a plane hundreds of feet in the air. Vague references to "groups of huts" or troop concentrations were often the only instructions pilots had to go on. Hilsman and others who saw the conflict as more political than military believed the key to victory lay in the ability of the Saigon government to win the allegiance of the South Vietnamese people. The high risk of civilian casualties appeared to outweigh the dubious results of interdiction

bombing and threatened to drive the people into the guerrillas' waiting hands.

American and Vietnamese military commanders realized the risks involved in aerial bombing but defended it as the only means available to deny the Vietcong sanctuary in their jungle strongholds. The strikes were thus continued, but stricter intelligence criteria and closer controls were imposed. If ground units could reach a target or if a province chief feared stray bombs might endanger his people, a request for an air strike would be denied.

At the order of Gen. Anthis, USAF intelligence officers worked with their Vietnamese counterparts to establish lists of areas known to be controlled by the VC. Once identified and delineated, the area would be designated a "free fire zone," in an attempt to create clear lines of battle where there had been none. Villagers would be warned by aerial leaflet drops and loudspeaker announcements and given an opportunity to vacate the area. Adm. Felt approved the plan and authorized the first such "aerial denial" operation to be launched on November 1, 1962, against the notorious Vietcong-controlled stronghold north of Saigon known as War Zone D.

Accurately gauging the effectiveness of such air attacks proved difficult, however. Aerial photos revealed little, and government patrols sent to assess the results often took days to reach the sites. By then the Vietcong had time to carry off their dead and wounded. To reduce their exposure to air attacks, the guerrillas dug tunnels or built log-covered bunkers reinforced with dirt banks. The shelters were impervious to anything but a direct hit.

## "We do everything over here"

In the summer of 1963, growing dissatisfaction with President Diem's administration threatened to paralyze the war effort. Demonstrations by Buddhist leaders, who accused the Catholic leader of religious persecution, erupted into full-scale riots when Diem resorted to force to quell the rebellious monks. Taking advantage of the civil unrest, the Vietcong stepped up their attacks.

With the situation rapidly deteriorating, a group of disaffected Vietnamese military leaders took matters into their own hands. With the tacit approval of Washington, they launched the coup on November 1 in which President Diem was assassinated. A revolutionary council of twenty-four officers led by General Duong Van "Big" Minh took over the government. But the resulting purges, including wholesale transfers of officers suspected of being loyal to Diem, paralyzed the war effort even further.

Capitalizing on the confusion, the Communists stepped up the pressure yet again on the new, unstable regime. Because Vietnamese aircraft were held on alert against a possible countercoup, Farmgate aircraft were forced to shoulder more of the burden. A record 298 strike sorties were flown by the Americans in November.

By the end of 1963, with 104 aircraft, mainly Farmgate A-1s and T-28s, and over 4,600 officers and men, the U.S. 2d Air Division's role had mushroomed far beyond its original mandate to advise and train the VNAF. Only by restricting the movements of American newsmen were officials able to keep the story of American pilots flying combat missions in Vietnam off the front pages back home.

It was not until mid-1964, after the letters of a Farmgate T-28 pilot who was killed in action were given to the press by his wife, that the American public became aware of the growing involvement of U.S. pilots. When the letters were published in May, Captain Edwin Gerald Shank's bitter commentary caused a minor sensation.

"I'll bet you that anyone you talk to does not know that American pilots fight this war," he wrote. "We—me and my buddies—do everything. The only reason the Vietnamese 'students' are on board is in case we crash there is one American 'adviser' and one Vietnamese 'student.' They're stupid, ignorant, sacrificial lambs, and I have no use for them . . . they're a menace to have on board. . . ."

Until his assassination, President Kennedy had been well aware of the alarming increase in the combat role being played by his "advisers." Despite glowing reports from MACV commander Gen. Harkins and McNamara, the day U.S. troops could be withdrawn to let the South Vietnamese fight their own battle seemed even further off than it had when Kennedy first took office.

Confronted with a fragile coalition government of South Vietnamese military commanders under increasing pressure from the Vietcong, Kennedy set his administration to picking up the pieces in Vietnam. The president sent McNamara to meet with U.S. military and diplomats in Saigon for a full review of the situation. But within twenty days of President Diem's demise, Kennedy was also felled by an assassin's bullet. Lyndon B. Johnson arrived in Washington on the plane that bore his predecessor's body to find a host of pressing problems. One of the most pressing before him was Vietnam.

*President Lyndon Johnson in the Oval Office. A few months after taking office he would confess to his press secretary that he had "the terrible feeling that something has grabbed me around the ankles and won't let go."*

# Taking the War to North Vietnam

When Lyndon Johnson assumed office, he pledged to continue his two predecessors' policy of support for South Vietnam, making it clear that he meant to hold the line in Vietnam until the new regime could stand on its own. But in December Robert McNamara returned from a visit to Saigon with a discouraging prognosis. The new government was "indecisive and drifting," he told the president. Although high-level U.S. military advisers in Saigon continued to recite a litany of statistics showing the progress of South Vietnam's fight with the Vietcong, McNamara found that junior officers in the field portrayed a much gloomier picture.

In December, U-2 reconnaissance jets from the Strategic Air Command had been stationed at Bien Hoa to conduct high-altitude overflights of North Vietnam and Laos. Their aerial photos revealed a vast network of narrow trails and mountain roads winding southward along the Laotian border. Originally hacked out of the

jungle during the war against the French, the routes were now being expanded as Hanoi increased its support of the war in the South.

During the first five months of 1964, an estimated 4,700 troops filtered their way through the web of roads and jungle paths, known collectively as the Ho Chi Minh Trail. Instead of ethnic southerners of previous years, the infiltrators were regular North Vietnamese soldiers. They carried sophisticated Chinese, Soviet, and East European-made weapons and ammunition.

The evidence confirmed General Curtis LeMay's belief that limited counterinsurgency operations against the VC were not enough. The air force chief of staff argued that the only way to insure the survival of South Vietnam was to strike at the source of the insurgency in North Vietnam. "We are swatting at flies," he complained, "when we should be going after the manure pile." American air power, LeMay argued, could strike at the root of the Vietcong's support without involving American ground forces. General Thomas S. Powers, commander of SAC, informed his boss that his B-52s could "pulverize" North Vietnam as well as destroy VC strongholds in the South.

President Johnson rejected LeMay's recommendations for all-out bombing. "I get anxious and look for the fire exits when a general wants to get tough," he told White House aide Jack Valenti. "LeMay scares the hell out of me." Johnson ordered his advisers to concentrate on more subtle ways to counter Hanoi's expanded role in the war.

In February, McNamara received the president's approval to initiate clandestine military operations against North Vietnam developed jointly by the Defense Department and the CIA. Known as OPLAN 34-A, it called for naval commando raids against North Vietnamese coastal installations, air drops of sabotage teams, propaganda broadcasts, and other "destructive undertakings" against the Hanoi regime. As Johnson had instructed, the program provided "maximum pressure with minimum risk." Although all 34-A activities were run from the Pentagon, the missions themselves were conducted by mercenaries and South Vietnamese nationals.

## Planning for a wider war

While they enthusiastically supported OPLAN 34-A activities, the Joint Chiefs of Staff thought that bolder actions were needed. "Currently, we and the Vietnamese are fighting the war on the enemy's terms," they wrote in a memo to Secretary McNamara. The generals outlined a ten-point program designed to seize the initiative, including aerial bombing of key North Vietnamese targets, using U.S. resources under Vietnamese cover.

*Preceding page. Their F-100 Supersabres parked on the flight line behind them, USAF pilots carry their flight gear back to the hangar at the Da Nang airfield in mid-1965.*

U.S. military leaders found a strong ally in Walt W. Rostow, chairman of the State Department Policy Planning Council. Drawing on his experience selecting bombing targets in Germany during World War II, Rostow argued that Hanoi's painstaking efforts to develop an industrial economy left North Vietnam highly vulnerable to air attacks. Even the threat that their newly built factories and power plants would be bombed could cause Hanoi's leaders to reconsider their goal of overthrowing the South Vietnamese government. "Ho Chi Minh has an industrial complex to protect," argued Rostow. "He is no longer a guerrilla fighter with nothing to lose."

Although they did not prescribe the same remedy as Rostow, a number of Lyndon Johnson's civilian advisers were beginning to feel that stronger actions were necessary if the Communists were to be defeated in Vietnam. The counterinsurgency programs now seemed to them inadequate against Hanoi's escalated support of the Vietcong. Secretary of State Dean Rusk began to see Vietnam as a military rather than a political problem. As a result, the secretary of defense became the prime mover in Vietnam policymaking.

After another trip to Saigon in March, McNamara returned with an expanded plan of action, centering on building the morale and fighting capabilities of the South Vietnamese. He also recommended that planning for bombing the North begin at once. In the event of a blatant VC terrorist act or North Vietnamese provocation that would attract the American public's attention to Hanoi's role in the war, McNamara wanted the U.S. prepared to launch retaliatory air strikes within seventy-two hours. He also wanted plans on the books to initiate a program of "graduated overt military pressure" within thirty days.

President Johnson approved McNamara's proposals and ordered planning to proceed. Wanting to keep his options open, Johnson saw the exercise as nothing more than contingency planning, insurance for the future. He was loath to do more for two reasons: First, his overriding concern was strengthening South Vietnam. He was convinced, as were most of his advisers, that escalating the war by direct air strikes might trigger Communist reprisals with which the Saigon government was "too fragile" to cope. Second, the president could not be sure how Hanoi's allies would react to an overt attack on their North Vietnamese comrades. Would Mao Tse-tung rush to Ho Chi Minh's rescue with thousands of Chinese troops as he had done when the U.S. intervened in Korea? Would the Soviets be willing to risk a confrontation over Vietnam with the U.S. that could lead to nuclear war? Johnson did not want to risk finding the answers unless it proved absolutely necessary. But LBJ's decision marked a critical turn in Washington's view of the war. American policymakers were beginning to believe that actions against the North could solve the problems in South Vietnam.

Working within the guidelines of McNamara's limited

*North Vietnamese President Ho Chi Minh inspects a steel mill at the Thai Nguyen industrial complex.*

proposal, the JCS began drafting blueprints for possible air strikes against the North. From U-2 reconnaissance photos they pinpointed ninety-four targets of military significance, mainly barracks areas, military supply depots, oil storage facilities, bridges, airfields, and other supply or staging areas for the war in the South. By May the chiefs had completed their work. Now all that was needed was a consensus on the operational details of the plan.

At a strategy session in Honolulu in June, military and political officials from Washington and Saigon met to discuss overall U.S. policy in Vietnam. Bombing was high on the agenda. The Joint Chiefs and the outgoing Commander in Chief, Pacific, Adm. Felt, made their pitch for "positive, prompt, and meaningful" actions. They proposed hitting all ninety-four targets in a twenty-day blitzkrieg of bombing designed to destroy Hanoi's will and ability to support the VC.

Sharing the president's concerns, a majority of the civilians present argued for a more cautious approach. Dean Rusk stated that air strikes should be conducted so as to "minimize the chances of a drastic Communist response." McNamara agreed. If massive bombing triggered Chinese intervention, intelligence reports estimated as many as seven U.S. Army divisions would be needed to prevent South Vietnam from being overrun.

A consensus developed around the idea of air strikes "designed to have more deterrent than destructive impact," as one of the participants noted. Faced with limited air strikes, gradually increasing in their scope and size and linked with threats of further escalation, Hanoi's leaders would be persuaded to cease their support of the Vietcong or face the full fury of American air power. With a program of gradual bombing the U.S. would exhibit its determination to stand by South Vietnam without risking a major escalation of the war. But they all agreed that any air strikes against North Vietnam would have to wait until South Vietnam was strong enough to withstand the inevitable counterescalation by the Vietcong. Dean Rusk also stressed the need to educate international and domestic public opinion to Hanoi's role in the war and the importance of America's stake there.

## Pierce Arrow

In the summer of 1964, Vietnam was still far from the concerns of most Americans. But the events that took place in the Tonkin Gulf on August 2 and 4 suddenly drew American and world attention to the conflict in Southeast Asia. While on an intelligence-gathering patrol off the North Vietnam coast, the U.S.S. *Maddox* was attacked on August 2 by Communist PT boats. It is possible that the North Vietnamese thought the U.S. destroyer was involved with South Vietnamese OPLAN 34-A naval raids against coastal installations that occurred nearby almost simultaneously. Also, it is likely that a second North Vietnamese PT boat attack, reported by the *Maddox* on the fourth, never took place. However, the incidents gave the Johnson administration its "smoking gun," apparent evidence of Communist aggression. Johnson and his advisers chose to retaliate. (For more on the Tonkin Gulf incident, see Chapter 7 of *Raising the Stakes*, another volume in "The Vietnam Experience.")

As the president informed the nation of his decision at 11:30 the evening of August 4, navy planes were already streaking toward the North Vietnamese coastline and their targets, four North Vietnamese PT boat bases and an oil storage depot. Commander Wesley McDonald, who had flown support for the *Maddox* during the August 4 "attack," found himself back in the cockpit of his A-4D Skyhawk after only a few hours' sleep. McDonald led a twenty-six-plane strike force from the U.S.S. *Ticonderoga* against the PT base at Phuc Loi and the oil depot in Vinh. After the Skyhawks dropped their bombs, the eight storage tanks were left in blazing ruins. Smoke billowed up to a height of 14,000 feet over the city.

Six F-8 Crusaders from the *Ticonderoga*, led by Commander R. F. Morhardt, strafed and bombed PT boat bases farther to the south at Quang Khe. Aircraft from the U.S.S. *Constellation* hit a second naval installation at Loc Chao. Twenty more planes from the *Constellation* were assigned to the northernmost target at Hon Gai.

Most of the inhabitants of Hon Gai were at work in factories or nearby coal mines that afternoon when the air raid sirens began blaring their shrill warning. A North Korean journalist happened to be sitting in front of his seaside hotel when the first jets came thundering in low over the bay. He later wrote:

Debouching unexpectedly from behind the hillocks and rocky islets, the Yankee planes poured down bombs and rockets.... Si-multaneously, the people's militia and the armed forces began their riposte. At the second dive, one saw one of the planes fall headlong into the sea, leaving behind a long trail of black smoke, and one heard the enthusiastic cheers of the people.

From the cockpit of his A-4 Skyhawk over Hon Gai, Lieutenant (j.g.) Everett Alvarez watched the splinters fly as he "walked" a stream of 20MM cannon fire across a North Vietnamese patrol boat. Pressing the attack until his gun was empty, Alvarez began pulling back up into the sky when his plane was hit by antiaircraft fire. Smoke began filling the cockpit as the A-4 shook violently. Fire warning lights glowed red on his instrument panel and the control stick froze. Alvarez radioed his flight mates that he was bailing out. His last words were: "I'll see you guys later." The twenty-seven-year-old navy pilot did not realize that he would be the "guest" of North Vietnam for eight years.

Operation Pierce Arrow, as the retaliatory air strikes were named, proved a great success. Besides the destruction of nearly 25 percent of the nation's oil stores at Vinh, half of North Vietnam's tiny torpedo flotilla had been sunk or damaged. But the price was high. In addition to the capture of Alvarez, the North Vietnamese had shot down another navy plane, killing its pilot, Lieutenant (j.g.) Richard Sather.

In the United States, the events in the Tonkin Gulf had a profound effect. Two days later, President Johnson sought and won the near unanimous backing of Congress for sweeping powers concerning the use of American forces in Southeast Asia. The so-called Tonkin Gulf resolution gave the president authority to use "all necessary measures" he deemed appropriate "to repel any armed attack against U.S. forces and to prevent further aggression."

## Moves and countermoves

Within days of the incidents in the gulf, additional American aircraft were dispatched to Southeast Asia. A third naval attack carrier group was deployed for duty in the western Pacific. Twelve F-102 Delta Dagger jet interceptors from the 509th Tactical Fighter Squadron (TFS) in the Philippines and the 16th TFS at Okinawa touched down at the Da Nang and Tan Son Nhut airfields on August 5. Eight F-100 Supersabres of the 615th TFS were sent to augment the small jet force already based at Da Nang.

Two days later a U-2 reconnaissance jet discovered that thirty-nine North Vietnamese Mig-15 and 17 jet fighters had been moved to Phuc Yen airfield near Hanoi from their training bases in southern China. Until then, North Vietnam's only air resources had been thirty training aircraft, fifty transports, and four light helicopters. General Hunter Harris, commander of the Pacific Air Force, immediately requested permission to destroy this new threat. A surprise air strike by F-100s, already on alert at Da Nang, would deal the North Vietnamese a "sharp lesson," he

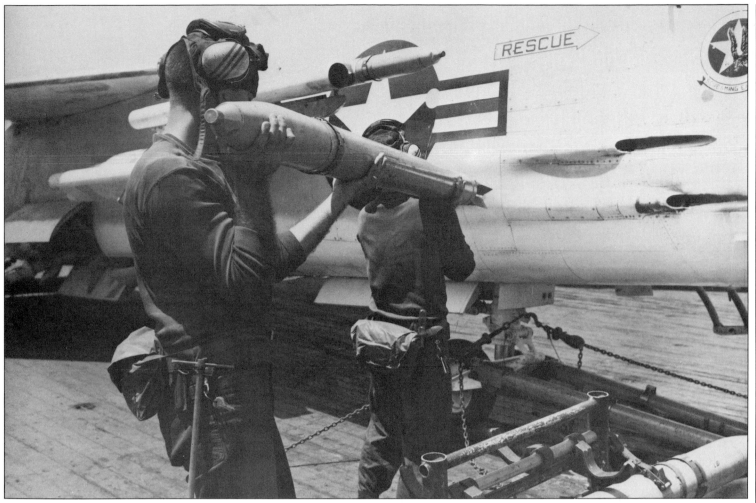

*Ordnancemen aboard the U.S.S. Ticonderoga arm an F-8 Crusader with a five inch Zuni rocket. F-8s from the Ticonderoga hit North Vietnam on August 4, 1964, in retaliation for the Gulf of Tonkin incidents.*

said. Admiral U.S. Grant Sharp, who had succeeded Adm. Felt as CINCPAC in July, passed the proposal on to Washington with his endorsement, but it was immediately rejected.

Despite his "blank check" from Congress, President Johnson wanted to keep the risks of escalation to a minimum. Although he warned that further attacks on any U.S. units would be met with a swift and forceful response, the president favored a short "holding phase." This would be followed by an increase in covert pressure against the North, including larger-scale air operations in Laos against Communist base camps and infiltration routes.

Since 1960 USAF Able Mable RF-101 reconnaissance jets based in Thailand had been flying over Communist-held portions of neighboring Laos. Navy RF-8 and RA-5Cs, with the code name Yankee Team, stationed aboard carriers in the South China Sea had joined them in the effort to monitor the Ho Chi Minh Trail. The low-flying, unarmed jets had encountered increasing ground fire as the North Vietnamese moved in light antiaircraft guns to keep the Americans at bay.

On June 6, 1964, when a Yankee Team plane had been shot down, General LeMay asked for permission to send armed escorts along with the unarmed photo planes. The State Department expressed concerns that such an action would jeopardize U.S. relations with neutral Laos, and LeMay was overruled. But after the Tonkin incidents, Washington reversed its decision. Eight F-105D Thunderchiefs of the 36th TFS were sent from Yokota, Japan, to Korat air base in Thailand to support the photo planes.

When the planes landed at the tiny air base the USAF captain in command could not believe his eyes. Neither could the incoming pilots. The base consisted of a runway and a few dilapidated wooden shacks with rusty tin roofs. The cluster of huts, with unpainted wooden slat walls and floorboards that barely touched, was soon dubbed "Camp Nasty" by the men of the 36th TFS.

When another plane went down on August 14, four Thunderchiefs from the 36th TFS were immediately launched to silence antiaircraft fire that was preventing rescue helicopters from reaching the downed American airman. Led by Captain Jack Stressing, the flight reached the spot to find the North Vietnamese guns strangely silent. Rolling in over what appeared to be a likely antiaircraft site, the two lead F-105s fired a few random bursts from their 20mm cannons to draw fire. Suddenly, all hell broke loose. Lieutenant Dave Graben's plane was quickly hit, a 37mm shell ripping a gaping hole in the tail of his Thunderchief. Captain Stressing told Graben to head for home, while the remaining two F-105s rolled in, raking the site with 20mm cannon fire and rockets. Graben was able to keep his Thunderchief on a stable course all the way back to Korat where he made a safe emergency landing.

Perhaps more significant than the stepped-up air operations over Laos was the dispatch of two squadrons of aging B-57 bombers to Bien Hoa air base in South Vietnam. With internal bomb bays and four additional bomb stations underneath their wings, the B-57 Canberras could carry a 6,000-pound payload and fly a combat radius of over 1,500 miles. Their deployment was a pointed reminder to Hanoi that it was not invulnerable to further air strikes. Communist forces quickly reacted to the threat.

Twenty-five minutes after midnight on November 1, Vietcong mortars opened fire on the overcrowded and poorly defended airfield at Bien Hoa. There was no mistaking what the guerrillas were after. Nearly eighty rounds fell squarely in the midst of the ramp where the twenty B-57s were parked in four rows. Explosions rocked the airstrip as the B-57s' fuel tanks caught fire. Five of the bombers were reduced to rubble and thirteen more damaged. Four American servicemen were killed and another seventy-two wounded in the attack.

## War gaming

The Joint Chiefs of Staff demanded a swift response. They recommended destroying the newly arrived North Vietnamese Mig jets at Phuc Yen airfield with long-range B-52 bombers already on alert at Guam. This would be followed by air strikes against all ninety-four targets on the JCS master target list.

From Saigon, Maxwell Taylor, the U.S. ambassador to South Vietnam, also recommended retaliatory air strikes. Although the former four-star general did not endorse the JCS plan, he did call for a limited reaction along the lines of Pierce Arrow. This marked a significant departure for Taylor, who had previously warned that the South Vietnamese were too weak to withstand the inevitable Communist reactions to further bombings.

But in Washington, Lyndon Johnson was in the final days of an election campaign. His opponent, Senator Barry Goldwater of Arizona, had seen the issue of tougher actions against the Communists stolen away from him by Johnson's firm response during the Tonkin Gulf incidents. The president had acted strongly but with restraint. Goldwater was portrayed as the trigger-happy cold warrior who was not afraid to use nuclear weapons.

Johnson was thus content to order additional B-57s to replace those damaged and destroyed at Bien Hoa. He

*The wreckage of USAF B-57 Canberra bombers, hit by VC mortars on November 1, 1964, litters the Bien Hoa airfield.*

*Lyndon Johnson on the 1964 presidential campaign trail in Nashville, Tennessee.*

refused to be pushed into a hasty decision by his generals. Instead he set up a special interdepartmental working group, under the direction of Assistant Secretary of State for Far Eastern Affairs William P. Bundy, to analyze and outline all the options available to him in Vietnam.

The Bundy working group, however, was unable to recommend any promising alternatives. The idea of pulling out of South Vietnam was dismissed outright. The U.S. had already invested its honor and prestige in the outcome. With South Vietnam teetering on the brink of collapse, the U.S. needed to achieve a stronger bargaining position if it hoped to reach a political settlement on favorable terms. Discussion quickly narrowed to the bombing plans formulated in the spring. To help assess the relative benefits and possible disadvantages of such a course of action, Washington's civilian and military leaders had already programmed a series of war games in the Pentagon in September.

Much to Gen. LeMay's dismay, the Red team representing Hanoi kept gaining the upper hand during the games. As the Blue team—the U.S.—escalated the bombing, the Red team would increase the pressure in South Vietnam or present a clever countermove. At one point, a Red team member announced that if his, Hanoi's, factories were

bombed, he would fill them with schoolchildren and dare the Blue team to continue the bombing.

As different players rotated between the three teams and played out a variety of scenarios, the Blue team gradually improved its situation. But when the games ended the results were inconclusive. A frustrated Gen. LeMay complained about the numerous civilian-imposed restraints that were factored into the war games. He believed that the U.S. should use every available resource against the North, even if it meant destroying "every work of man" in the country, to break Hanoi's will to continue the war. "We should bomb them back to the Stone Age," he said at the war game sessions. LeMay pointed out that during World War II the U.S. had dropped thousands of tons of bombs on German factories and cities and two atomic bombs in Japan, and he saw no difference in Vietnam. He urged swift, massive air strikes.

The Bundy group rejected LeMay's concept as too extreme. William Bundy pointed out that it risked escalating the war in a way that could lead to full-scale involvement of American combat troops as in Korea and "possibly even the use of nuclear weapons." Instead, the Bundy group favored a more limited course of action: a stepped-up program of covert pressures against the North, including U.S. air strikes on Communist routes in Laos, followed by "tit-for-tat" air reprisals to commence after the next Vietcong "spectacular," such as the attack on Bien Hoa. If this course failed to deter Hanoi, then the reprisal strikes could be gradually increased at a carefully controlled pace. Ultimately, they reasoned, Hanoi would be forced to negotiate on U.S. terms or face further punishment.

The Joint Chiefs were wary of this "progressive squeeze," as it came to be referred to in bureaucratic parlance. They were becoming increasingly nervous over growing civilian involvement in what they regarded as a purely military affair. Since Korea, military leaders had been wary of civilian theories of limited warfare, seeing danger in the belief that military power could be wielded like a scalpel to apply selective pressure without risking a wider war. The JCS thought a gradually escalating bombing campaign would merely grant the enemy more time to prepare its defenses. Instead of a "progressive squeeze," they urged instead a "full/fast squeeze" bombing program.

On the opposite end of the spectrum, Undersecretary of State George Ball was opposed to any bombing of North Vietnam. Ball's experience as codirector of the U.S. Strategic Bombing Survey after World War II, which found that Allied bombing had less impact on enemy war-making capabilities than had been originally thought, left him skeptical of military claims about the capabilities of air power to deter a determined adversary. He also dismissed the notion that limited air strikes could influence Hanoi's leaders to abandon the goal for which they had been fighting for over twenty years.

Ball argued that bombing North Vietnam would do nothing to help South Vietnam fight its own war. As long as Hanoi saw the possibility of victory in the South they would be willing to absorb substantial losses and costs from American air attacks. Hanoi would merely retaliate by committing even more troops to battle in the South, drawing the U.S. into a never-ending spiral of escalation.

But Ball found little support within the administration. Bolstering South Vietnam seemed the obvious answer. But pointing to past experience, the Bundy group's report confessed that progress in South Vietnam would take time and seemed "unlikely despite our best ideas and efforts." Something needed to be done immediately to reverse the declining situation. Actions directed against North Vietnam seemed the only course open.

By late November, President Johnson tentatively endorsed the Bundy group's recommendations over the protests of the Joint Chiefs. He agreed in principle to the concept of tit-for-tat air strikes but wanted everything possible done to strengthen the South Vietnamese first. In the meantime, Johnson ordered American air units to begin limited bombing against North Vietnamese supply routes and base areas in Laos. In an operation with the code name Barrel Roll, the strikes began on December 12, 1965, and within four months mushroomed into a full-scale campaign aimed at cutting infiltration down the Ho Chi Minh Trail into South Vietnam.

## Drifting toward defeat

While the Johnson administration was attempting to signal Hanoi of its determination to insure a strong and independent government in South Vietnam, Saigon's "revolving door" governments were presenting yet another picture. Between the assassination of President Diem and the end of 1964, leadership of the war-torn nation would change hands six times.

Throughout most of 1964 the dominant strong man in South Vietnamese politics was Gen. Nguyen Khanh. Although considered a ruthless political manipulator by American observers, Khanh was unable to unite South Vietnam's feuding political, military, and religious factions. In July, Khanh had tried to divert growing discontent with his regime by rallying the people behind the anti-Communist banner. On the anniversary of the partitioning of Vietnam, he publicly called for an invasion of North Vietnam. Taking up Khanh's rallying cry to "march North" was the commander of South Vietnam's air force. Air Vice Marshal Nguyen Cao Ky created a minor sensation when he publicly revealed that U.S. advisers were secretly training his pilots for bombing missions over the North. "We are ready," he boasted. "We could go this afternoon." U.S. officials rushed to deny his statements.

Immensely popular with his men, who imitated his flamboyant style and dress, Ky owed his rapid rise through the ranks to his support for General Khanh's successful bid for power in January. But unlike many senior Vietnamese officers who had achieved their commands as a result of political patronage, Ky proved an excellent leader. His appointment also automatically made him a key player in Saigon's turbulent political scene.

To the increasing frustration of the American command, South Vietnam's government lurched from crisis to crisis throughout the rest of 1964 and into the next year. But the war with the Communist guerrillas would not wait for South Vietnam to settle its internal problems.

On Christmas Eve, 1964, a bomb planted by the VC in a Saigon hotel being used as a U.S. bachelor officers' billet exploded, killing two and wounding fifty-eight Americans. Noting that the attack had been aimed specifically at U.S. soldiers, Ambassador Taylor joined Adm. Sharp and the Joint Chiefs in calling for an immediate response. To them, it was the Vietcong "spectacular" the U.S. had been waiting for to initiate reprisal air strikes. But after four days, President Johnson signaled his intent to let the incident pass. The State Department notified Amb. Taylor that air strikes might give the impression that "we are trying to shoot our way out of an internal political crisis."

In late 1964, spurred on by the instability of the Saigon government and bickering between the Americans and

*At Binh Gia, a U.S. Army Huey gunship hovers over ARVN troops killed by guerrillas on December 31, 1964.*

South Vietnamese, the Vietcong decided the time was ripe to mount a major offensive. They abandoned their hit-and-run tactics and began launching coordinated assaults against government-controlled hamlets and military outposts throughout the countryside. ARVN troops, rushing to the defense of these besieged outposts, were decimated by guerrilla ambushes along the roads.

With government troops reluctant to wander far from the safety of their fortified bases, the burden fell heavily on air reaction units. Preplanned strikes against VC strongholds and supply routes were canceled as aircraft were diverted to answer the record number of calls for air support. But VNAF planes were unavailable, held on alert by the South Vietnamese regime, fearful of rumored plots to overthrow it by force.

A major Vietcong victory in Phuoc Tuy Province, just east of Saigon, clearly revealed the declining state of affairs in Vietnam. On December 27 two VC regiments overran the government-controlled hamlet of Binh Gia. The next day U.S. Army helicopters, escorted by fifteen UH–1B

gunships, lifted in two Vietnamese Ranger companies to retake the hamlet. Using a tactic that had proven successful against the French, the guerrillas set an ambush for the inevitable reaction force. Machine-gun fire downed three of the choppers. One of the Ranger companies was able to fight its way out of the trap. The second was wiped out.

Another attempt to retake Binh Gia was mounted the next day. This time twenty-six helicopter transports ferried two South Vietnamese marine battalions into Binh Gia. Once again the landing force was met with heavy resistance from guerrilla positions in the surrounding rubber forests. Nine helicopters were lost during the operation.

One of the marine battalions, finding itself completely surrounded, radioed a USAF air controller overhead for help. Fighters were scrambled, but before they could reach the scene the senior Vietnamese commander, irritated because the request had not gone through the proper channels, ordered them back to base. Army helicopters were called in instead. But their machine guns and rockets failed to penetrate the thick rubber tree forest.

By the time fighter planes were diverted to the scene through the proper channels it was too late. The isolated battalion was overrun during the night, and more than half the men were either killed or captured.

The disaster at Binh Gia brought renewed air force criticism that army gunships just did not have the firepower to out-duel heavily armed and dug-in Vietcong units. Army advisers countered that fighter planes were never available when they needed them. During the month of January 1965, VNAF and Farmgate units flew 4,550 sorties but still failed to meet half of the requests they received. Of the forty-eight Farmgate A-1E and ninety-two VNAF A-1H Skyraiders, only sixty were available for duty on a daily basis because of maintenance problems and political infighting.

The magnitude of the VC victory at Binh Gia and continued guerrilla successes also worried General William Westmoreland, who had taken over command of U.S. forces in Vietnam in June 1964. He requested authority to employ USAF jets already in the country, such as the B-57s at Bien Hoa, in a combat role. The JCS secured White House approval for the request in late January, but the American jets could be used only in emergencies.

Washington had been stunned by the guerrilla offensives and the corresponding decline in the ability of the Saigon government to respond to them. William Bundy wrote Dean Rusk that the situation appeared likely to "come apart more rapidly" than he and his group had predicted in the fall. Rusk agreed that the situation seemed to be unraveling but stopped short of endorsing any further escalation. Secretary of Defense McNamara, however, believed the U.S. was "drifting" toward defeat in Vietnam and pushed bombing operations against the North as the only means available to reverse the decline.

## A "deliberate provocation"

Just after midnight on February 7, Vietcong sappers silently slipped past South Vietnamese guards manning the defensive perimeter at Camp Holloway near Pleiku, 384 kilometers north of Saigon in the central highlands. Undetected, they began attaching demolition charges to the twenty-seven planes and helicopters of the U.S. Army's 52d Aviation Battalion parked at one end of the air base's pierced-steel planking runway.

At 2:00 A.M. a series of deafening explosions shattered the night air as the homemade bombs were detonated. Simultaneously, a barrage of mortar fire slammed into the American advisers' barracks area adjacent to the runway. Fifteen minutes after it began, the shelling stopped, leaving five helicopters in ruins on the runway and eleven other choppers, four Caribou transports, and four scout planes seriously damaged. By the time the garrison could counterattack, the VC had melted back in the jungle.

*Presidential Special Adviser McGeorge Bundy and South Vietnamese leader General Nguyen Khanh inspect damage inflicted at the U.S. base at Pleiku on February 7, 1965.*

*While President Johnson ordered air strikes against the North in February 1965, Soviet Premier Aleksei Kosygin (center) was engaged in high-level talks in Hanoi. North Vietnamese Prime Minister Pham Van Dong is at his right.*

Simultaneously, another guerrilla team had raided the U.S. advisers' compound at II Corps headquarters, six kilometers to the northeast. When the final tally came in, it was discovered that 128 men had been wounded in the two attacks, and 8 Americans lay dead.

In Saigon, Westmoreland and Ambassador Taylor were roused from their sleep when news of the raids reached MACV headquarters. The two men were soon huddled in conversation with MACV staff members, poring over the incoming reports from Pleiku. Shortly afterward, they were joined by White House Special Adviser for National Security Affairs McGeorge Bundy, who was on the last day of a special fact-finding mission for the president. Convinced that the Vietcong would not have dared launch such attacks against American installations without instructions from Hanoi, Westmoreland characterized them as a "deliberate provocation." Ambassador Taylor agreed. Hanoi had thrown down the gauntlet. "This is the time we must strike back," Taylor told Bundy.

Known for his calculating pragmatism, Bundy had remained relatively silent during the debates on Vietnam. But in January 1965, according to Bundy's deputy, Chester Cooper, the White House adviser had begun pushing the president to make the hard choices he had been avoiding. Cooper said, "Either [Johnson] had to bite the bullet and

do something more or swallow his pride and get out."

Reviewing the lists of American casualties in Saigon that morning, removed from the antiseptic atmosphere and emotionless position papers of the White House, Bundy was now face to face with the grim reality of U.S. involvement in Vietnam. In his abrupt manner, he strode to the bank of phones in the conference room at MACV headquarters and demanded a direct line to Washington. Bundy crisply informed Deputy Secretary of Defense Cyrus Vance of their unanimous recommendation to initiate reprisal air strikes against North Vietnam.

First word of the raids at Pleiku reached the White House shortly after 3:00 P.M. on February 6. Upstairs, the president was meeting with some of his top political and military advisers when he was handed an advisory cable from Saigon. Johnson ordered American air units in Southeast Asia placed on alert and called a special meeting of the National Security Council for 7:45 P.M.

When the NSC members took their seats at the polished mahogany table in the cabinet room that evening, Lyndon Johnson made it clear that he had finally decided upon a course of action. Clutching the latest casualty reports from Pleiku in his hand, Johnson leaned forward in his chair and thundered: "I've had enough of this!"

The chairman of the JCS, General Earle Wheeler, and

Secretary of Defense McNamara outlined the options. Both urged that the preplanned reprisal air strikes be launched as soon as possible. The only hesitant voice came from Llewellyn Thompson, former U.S. ambassador to the Soviet Union, who questioned the timing of such a move. At that moment, Soviet Premier Aleksei Kosygin was engaged in high-level discussions with North Vietnamese leaders in Hanoi. Thompson suggested postponing the strikes until after Kosygin departed Hanoi to avoid risking greater Soviet involvement in the conflict. McNamara and others countered that any delays would lessen the impact of the raids.

Bolstered by the recommendation to retaliate from McGeorge Bundy and his advisers in Saigon, President Johnson canvassed each man present for his views. Only one did not favor the air strikes. Senate majority leader Mike Mansfield, worried that the strikes might heighten the risk of Soviet or Chinese intervention, advised his long-time friend and colleague to negotiate. Johnson's reply was quick and scathing. "We have kept our guns over the mantle . . . for a long time now. And what was the result?" he asked. "They are killing our men while they sleep. I can't ask American boys to go on fighting with one hand tied behind their backs."

With that, Johnson ended the discussion. Poring over Defense Department maps, the president personally selected four targets identified as infiltration staging areas to make it clear that the air strikes were being launched because of Hanoi's continuing direction and support of the war. In addition, he wanted VNAF Skyraiders to participate in the strikes in a show of allied unity. Reflecting on his decision in his memoirs, Johnson wrote that at the time he thought a swift, yet limited air strike "would convince Hanoi that we were serious."

## Operation Flaming Dart

One hundred and sixty kilometers east of Da Nang in the South China Sea, Rear Admiral Henry L. Miller received an urgent cable aboard his flagship, the U.S.S. *Ranger*, shortly after 6:00 A.M. on February 7. Just four hours after the first shell hit Camp Holloway, the commander of Task Force 77 was alerted to be prepared to launch Operation Flaming Dart. Crewmen and pilots aboard the task force's three aircraft carriers sprung into action. On the U.S.S. *Coral Sea* armorers dipped into the ship's magazines, fusing and bolting fins to high-drag, 500-pound "Snake-eye" bombs. Topside, sailors sweated and strained, lifting the heavy projectiles from their carts and attaching them to wing racks underneath the waiting aircraft. Fully fueled and armed, the jets were arranged on the warship's three-acre flight deck in the optimal launch sequence.

Below decks, pilots of the *Coral Sea's* Air Wing 15 assembled in their squadron ready rooms for final briefings.

In one of the rooms the "Blue Tail Flies" of Attack Squadron 153 ran down the check lists of target assignments and navigational instructions and calculations of weights, times, and fuel consumption with their skipper, Commander Pete Mongilardi. The forty-one-year-old squadron commander, tapped to lead the strike force, noted the excitement that rippled through the ship. "The long months of training and hard work," he later wrote, "were soon to be put to the test."

Four hours after the NSC meeting in Washington had ended, Adm. Miller finally received the long awaited "execute" order. After a last-minute briefing on weather en

route and over the target, the pilots ran to their jets. Swinging up into the cockpits, the fliers were strapped in and taken through a final systems check by their plane captains.

At 1:30 P.M. the launch began with the familiar rumble and thud of the carriers' steam-powered catapults, which shot the bomb-laden navy jets into the bright blue sky in rapid succession. In less than half an hour the entire eighty-three-plane strike force of A-4 Skyhawks and F-8 Crusaders was airborne.

Leveling off at 28,000 feet, the planes assembled in their respective squadrons and headed toward North Vietnam.

The young pilots, many on their first combat mission, chattered nervously to each other over their radios. Seventeen miles from shore, the force split in two. Planes from the *Ranger* peeled off to the west while Pete Mongilardi led the remaining forty-nine jets from the *Coral Sea* and *Hancock* toward their objective, the port city of Dong Hoi, twenty miles north.

Crossing the coastline at 500 knots, Mongilardi's strike force went "feet dry," navy slang for flying over land. But

*USAF pilots receive air medals at Da Nang following their Operation Flaming Dart mission on February 8, 1965.*

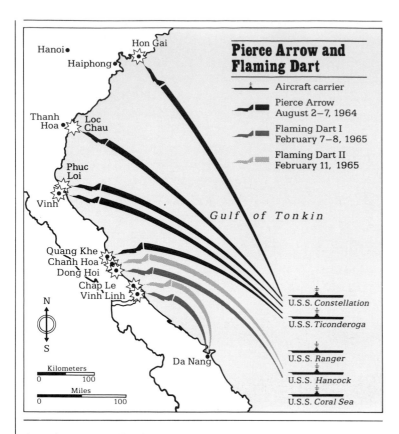

**Pierce Arrow and Flaming Dart**

⊥ Aircraft carrier

Pierce Arrow
August 2–7, 1964

Flaming Dart I
February 7–8, 1965

Flaming Dart II
February 11, 1965

Hanoi•
Hon Gai
Haiphong•
Thanh Hoa•
Loc Chau
Phuc Loi
Vinh
Gulf of Tonkin
Quang Khe
Chanh Hoa
Dong Hoi
Chap Le
Vinh Linh
N
S
Kilometers
0    100
Miles
0    100
Da Nang
U.S.S. *Constellation*
U.S.S. *Ticonderoga*
U.S.S. *Ranger*
U.S.S. *Hancock*
U.S.S. *Coral Sea*

they found the North Vietnamese countryside was not very dry at all. Rainfall had flooded the coastal plain, making it difficult for the pilots to pick out navigational landmarks. A dense cover of gray clouds forced the planes down to 300 feet, and Mongilardi wondered whether he would have to abort the strike. But as they passed their last landmark, the clouds broke over the coastal town.

Inching their throttles forward, Lieutenant Commander Ken Stafford's flight of four Crusaders fanned out and sped in ahead of the strike force at 600 knots. Dropping to 100 feet, they skimmed a small hill near their objective, an antiaircraft battery just west of the target. Stafford thought it strange that the guns had not started firing and held his fire. Streaking past he saw that the site was unoccupied. They had caught the North Vietnamese totally by surprise.

After gaining as much altitude as he could underneath the low clouds, Mongilardi pulled his Skyhawks into a shallow dive on the barracks complex below. Depressing the bomb release button, Mongilardi "pickled" his 250-pound Snake-eye bombs. The high-drag bombs, designed with spring-action fins to slow their momentum, were perfect for low-level bombing. They gave a pilot time to fly clear of the resulting explosion after he released them.

Wave after wave of Skyhawks pounded the complex with bombs and rockets. Slowly, the North Vietnamese guns came alive, sending crisscrossing streams of tracer bullets and bursting puffs of flak into the air. Within the womb-like confines of his pressurized cockpit, Mongilardi could hear the gunfire above the muffled roar of his engines.

Suddenly, one of the Skyhawks was hit. With flames dancing along his A-4's left wing, Lieutenant Edward Dickson pressed on with his bombing run. After releasing his bombs, he steered his smoking plane toward the safety of the ocean. Two miles off the coast, Dickson bailed out. Low-level clouds swallowed up the falling flier before his wing mates could be certain his parachute had opened.

Dickson's last ejection, during training in California, had been a harrowing one. His parachute never opened, but by luck he had landed in a forty-foot snow bank, unscathed. Fate was not as kind this time. Rescue teams scoured the sea for signs of Dickson's yellow life raft to no avail. Two days later his body was pulled from the water by North Vietnamese fishermen.

Over Dong Hoi the attack continued. At 3:42 the last Skyhawk pulled away from the blazing inferno below. In less than half an hour, the combined strike force had unleashed more than twenty-five tons of high explosives on the North Vietnamese barracks complex, plus a number of rockets and 20MM cannon fire. Touching back down on the carriers' decks, the pilots learned that theirs was the only successful mission that afternoon. The other three strikes— one by planes from the *Ranger* and two by U.S. and South Vietnamese air force units—had been forced to turn back because of bad weather.

## Sending the right signal

The next day, February 7, in Washington, the president convened another NSC meeting to discuss the results of Flaming Dart. Johnson ordered that only the aborted South Vietnamese operation be remounted to reinforce the joint nature of the raids. Obsessed with sending the "right signal" to Hanoi, President Johnson rejected any further American air strikes. He thought a South Vietnamese operation would make Hanoi realize that the reprisals were not linked solely to the raids at Pleiku but to a broader spectrum of Communist activities.

To defend against Communist countermoves, the president also approved the dispatch of a detachment of marines and an antiaircraft missile battery to Da Nang to beef up security at the U.S. air base there. He also ordered the immediate withdrawal of the more than 2,000 American dependents living in South Vietnam, fearing they might become the target of VC terrorist attacks.

The following day in Vietnam, twenty-four VNAF Skyraiders roared off the runway at Da Nang. At the head of the formation, resplendent in his black flight suit, lavender scarf, and white helmet with orange flashes, was Air Vice Marshal Nguyen Cao Ky. Escorted by six Farmgate A-1s acting as pathfinders and USAF F-100 Supersabres to suppress antiaircraft fire, Ky's prop-driven planes flew toward their target, a military complex at Chap Le. With their superior speed, the F-100s arrived first and began pounding the antiaircraft gun emplacements surrounding the old French base. Soon afterward the U.S.-piloted Farmgate planes reached the target. But Ky's force was nowhere to be seen.

Approaching Chap Le just as the American planes were swarming over the barracks complex, Ky abruptly changed course to avoid a collision. "Since there seemed little point in punishing the target further," Ky later remarked, "I found another target in the Vinh Linh area and we bombed that." But the target Ky had chosen, a military communications center, was also headquarters for an antiaircraft regiment.

"We came in very low, just over the treetops," he later told reporters. "Just before we reached the target we pulled up to release our bombs. That's when the flak hit us." Tracer bullets cut through the formation as the planes passed overhead. Four bullets punctured Ky's plane, one of them grazing the air vice marshal's side as he raised his arm to protect his face. Back at Da Nang, flowers and champagne were thrust upon the returning heroes.

North Vietnamese leaders assailed the raids as "brazen" acts of aggression by "American bandits," and Radio Hanoi urged the VC to step up their efforts. The guerrillas quickly obliged. On February 10 suitcases packed with 100 pounds of TNT were smuggled into the Viet Cuong Hotel in Qui Nhon. Without warning, the four-story building, which housed sixty-two U.S. enlisted men, disintegrated into a twenty-foot pile of rubble. Thirty-five hours later, the last survivor was pulled from the rubble. Twenty-one Americans had been wounded in the blast and another twenty-three killed.

## Flaming Dart II

The ball was now back in Washington's court, and the president lost no time authorizing joint U.S.-VNAF air strikes on two barracks areas just north of the DMZ. At 12:30 P.M. on February 11 in the Gulf of Tonkin, Adm. Miller launched ninety-nine planes from the *Ranger*, *Coral Sea*, and *Hancock* against an NVA complex at Chanh Hoa, four miles northeast of Dong Hoi. Two hours later, twenty-eight VNAF Skyraiders, led by Deputy Commander Colonel Nguyen Ngoc Loan and supported by twenty-eight USAF F-100s, restruck Chap Le.

Three navy jets, all from the *Coral Sea*, were lost during the raids. Two of the pilots were soon accounted for, but the third, Lieutenant Commander Robert Shumaker, was listed as missing. Shumaker had been one of the last pilots to leave the target area at Chanh Hoa that afternoon. Along with his squadron commander, Shumaker had been assigned to fly cover while an unarmed RF-8A reconnaissance jet streaked in low to take poststrike bomb damage assessment photos.

Breaking through the clouds at 500 feet, Shumaker aimed his F-8 Crusader toward an antiaircraft emplacement to draw its fire away from the photo jet. Unleashing

*Service revolver on his hip, Air Vice Marshal Nguyen Cao Ky talks to one of his pilots and a paratroop officer before leading the first VNAF strike north of the DMZ on February 8, 1965.*

a brace of Zuni rockets at the site, he banked left in a shallow climb, only to see another antiaircraft battery firing at him.

"I tried to evade them by going back into the clouds," he recalled. But by then it was too late. The Crusader took a hit in the tail, sending the plane into an uncontrolled, inverted dive. Shumaker called to his skipper to tell him he had been hit. But his commander, unable to see Shumaker's plane through the clouds, only heard "403," Shumaker's call numbers, over his headset. The thirty-one-year-old pilot had stopped midsentence. His plane already dangerously close to the ground, Shumaker realized "if I finished the sentence I'd never survive."

Reaching for the ejection handle, Shumaker quickly shot out of the inverted Crusader. He hit the ground a mere two seconds after the opening of his parachute,

*F–8 Crusaders are catapulted from the U.S.S. Coral Sea during Operation Flaming Dart II on February 11, 1965.*

which engulfed him in a cocoon of silk. Freeing himself, Shumaker stood up and felt a sharp pain in his back; he had fallen on his spine, fracturing a vertebrae. "I could still walk," he remembered, "but painfully." Knowing that he could not be far from the coast, Shumaker decided to hide until nightfall and then try to make his way to shore.

He had just settled in behind a cluster of bushes when he heard North Vietnamese soldiers approaching. Shumaker fingered his revolver as the group passed him by. Just as he thought he was out of danger, a straggler came trailing by armed with a Russian-made AK47 automatic rifle. "His eyes caught mine and before I could outdraw him he had me."

Thrown into the back of a blacked-out truck, Shumaker began an agonizing thirty-six-hour, 320-kilometer journey to Hanoi over primitive roads. His captors stopped along the way to exhibit the "Yankee air pirate" to jeering crowds who pelted him with stones. At one point he was forced to stand in front of a mock firing squad for ten minutes.

Shumaker's journey ended at the central prison com-plex in the heart of Hanoi. Covering a city block, the French-built prison was surrounded by a series of six-foot-thick concrete walls, fifteen to twenty feet high. Pieces of broken glass from old wine bottles had been embedded in the top of the wall to discourage escape. The structure was well known to Hanoi's leaders, many of whom had been imprisoned there during the struggle against the French colonial government. The Vietnamese had named it Hao Lo, which meant "fiery furnace." American prison-ers-of-war were to call it the "Hanoi Hilton."

In a room in the southeast corner of the prison, the North Vietnamese began interrogating their latest prize. Shumaker refused to give more than his name, rank, and serial number. When he asked his captors, "Where's Al-varez?" they would answer that the navy flier was in an-other prison "far away."

In fact, Ed Alvarez was being kept in a cell directly across the prison courtyard from Shumaker. For seven months Alvarez had been isolated from the outside world except for a short note from his wife, and he had begun to

*Navy Lieutenant Commander Robert Shumaker is marched through Dong Hoi after he was captured on February 11, 1965.*

wonder if he would ever be released. A devout Catholic, Alvarez had fashioned a small crucifix and passed the long days by praying and exercising.

In February, Alvarez learned of the two Flaming Dart strikes from an English-language press release given to him by his jailers. The report claimed that seven American planes had been shot down and a navy flier captured. It listed Shumaker's name and military I.D. number. A few days later, while exercising in the courtyard, Alvarez watched a black sedan pull into the prison. Thinking that the car might be carrying the recently shot down American, he yelled out, "Hey, Shumaker!" Although there was no response, Alvarez sensed he was not alone anymore. "Well," he thought, "the war's on. It's really on."

## Graduated and continued reprisal

Alvarez was right on the mark. Thousands of miles away in Washington, McGeorge Bundy had returned from his fact-finding mission to outline the situation in Vietnam. He was not encouraging. Pointing to the "astonishing" resiliency of the Vietcong despite heavy casualties, and their ever-expanding control of the countryside, Bundy noted there was growing uncertainty "as to whether a Communist victory can be prevented." Enemy successes, coupled with domestic unrest, were stretching the fabric of the war-torn country dangerously thin. The Vietnamese were "suspicious of our failure to use more of our obviously enormous power," said Ambassador Taylor, and the president's decision to evacuate American dependents only fueled speculation that the U.S. was preparing to negotiate a settlement of the conflict with Hanoi.

Bundy ruled out any negotiated withdrawal as merely "surrender on the installment plan," warning that U.S. prestige was "directly at risk in Vietnam." What was needed was forceful action to convince Hanoi that the U.S. was determined to "stay the course." He recommended a program of "graduated and continued reprisal" almost identical to the program advocated by his brother William Bundy's working group: Tit-for-tat air strikes would be directly linked to highly visible VC attacks. Succeeding reprisals would be tied to a more general catalog of Communist terrorism. This would eliminate the difficulty of finding specific targets to match specific guerrilla actions, yet still signal Hanoi that the strikes were directly connected to the level of Communist pressure in the South.

Assistant Secretary of Defense John McNaughton, who drafted the reprisal plan, wrote, "We must keep clear to both Hanoi and the world that our reprisals will be reduced or stopped when outrages in the South are reduced or stopped." Air attacks would begin at a low level and gradually increase. "The objective is not to 'win' an air war against Hanoi," McNaughton rationalized, "but to influence the course of the struggle in the South." Reprisal bombings would provide the sagging ARVN a needed shot in the arm and have a corresponding "depressing effect" on VC morale. Bundy and McNaughton rejected the Joint Chiefs' proposal of a swift, massive aerial blow. "We want to keep before Hanoi the carrot of our desisting," McNaughton reasoned, "as well as the stick of continued pressure."

Noting that "significant U.S. air losses," would necessitate American air strikes to neutralize North Vietnam's air defense system, McNaughton warned that the bombing campaign could escalate into a full-scale air war. But he reasoned this was an acceptable risk, especially when considered against the alternative of introducing American combat troops. "Measured against the costs of defeat in Vietnam," he wrote, "this program seems cheap. And even if it fails to turn the tide—as it may—the value of the effort seems to exceed its cost." In fact, McNaughton ambiguously placed the chances of success at somewhere between 25 and 75 percent.

In a separate cable from Saigon, Amb. Maxwell Taylor reinforced the Bundy group's proposal but with a different objective in mind. He tended to side with the JCS's view that bombing could erode North Vietnam's will to continue the war. Taylor believed a carefully orchestrated bombing program could present Hanoi's leaders with the specter of "inevitable, ultimate destruction" unless they agreed to cease their support of the Vietcong and agree to a settlement on U.S. terms.

Johnson pondered the consequences. The long-standing argument that a weak Saigon regime would not be able to withstand retaliatory Communist pressures if the war was extended to North Vietnam was now turned on its head. It was argued instead that bombing North Vietnam was the only way short of a massive influx of U.S. combat troops to prevent Communist victory in the South.

CIA sources had informed the president that Premier Kosygin had promised Hanoi substantial increases in foreign aid, including arms and other war-supporting materiel. Regular NVA units were being sent down the Ho Chi Minh Trail to bolster Vietcong forces who were already pushing the South Vietnamese to their limit. "It had become clear," Johnson later wrote in his memoirs, "that Hanoi was moving in for the kill."

On February 13 President Johnson announced his decision in a cable to Ambassador Taylor. "We will execute a program of measured and limited air action against selected military targets in North Vietnam remaining south of the nineteenth parallel. . . . These actions will stop when the aggression stops." The bombing was scheduled to begin in seven days under the code name Rolling Thunder. After nearly a year of strategy sessions and policy debates, the president had finally agreed to commit American air units against North Vietnam. As Johnson later told biographer Doris Kearns, he had decided "that doing nothing was more dangerous than doing something."

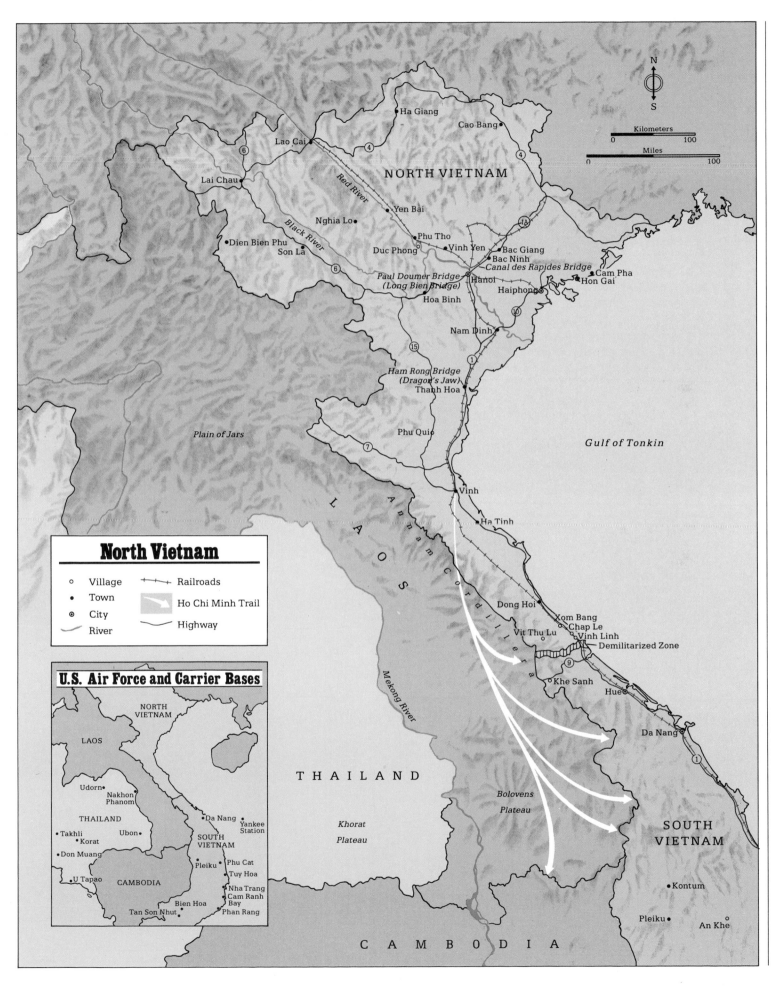

N

S

Kilometers
0 ——— 100

Miles
0 ——— 100

**NORTH VIETNAM**

Ha Giang

Cao Bang

Lao Cai

Lai Chau

*Red River*

Yen Bai

Nghia Lo

*Black River*

Dien Bien Phu

Son La

Phu Tho

Duc Phong

Vinh Yen

Bac Giang

Bac Ninh

*Canal des Rapides Bridge*

Cam Pha

Hon Gai

Paul Doumer Bridge
(Long Bien Bridge)

Hanoi

Haiphong

Hoa Binh

Nam Dinh

*Ham Rong Bridge
(Dragon's Jaw)*
Thanh Hoa

*Plain of Jars*

Phu Quio

*Gulf of Tonkin*

*Mekong River*

Vinh

Ha Tinh

L A O S

*Annam Cordillera*

Dong Hoi

Xom Bang

Chap Le

Vit Thu Lu

Vinh Linh

Demilitarized Zone

Khe Sanh

Hue

*Bolovens
Plateau*

Da Nang

**SOUTH
VIETNAM**

T H A I L A N D

*Khorat
Plateau*

Kontum

Pleiku

An Khe

C A M B O D I A

### North Vietnam

| | | | |
|---|---|---|---|
| ○ | Village | ┼┼┼ | Railroads |
| ● | Town | | Ho Chi Minh Trail |
| ◉ | City | | Highway |
| ∿ | River | | |

### U.S. Air Force and Carrier Bases

NORTH
VIETNAM

LAOS

Udorn

Nakhon
Phanom

THAILAND

Takhli
Korat

Ubon

Don Muang

U Tapao

CAMBODIA

Da Nang

Yankee
Station

SOUTH
VIETNAM

Pleiku

Phu Cat

Tuy Hoa

Nha Trang
Cam Ranh
Bay

Bien Hoa

Tan Son Nhut

Phan Rang

# On Line at Yankee Station

Aircraft carriers of the U.S. 7th Fleet, present off Vietnam since the mid-1950s, took an increasingly active role in the war as it heated up in 1964. Cruising 100 miles east of Da Nang, the "flat tops" of Task Force 77 had launched missions monitoring the Ho Chi Minh Trail since early 1964. The flights' code name was Yankee Team, and the cruising area of the carriers and their escort ships came to be called Yankee Station.

Among the three carriers "on line" at Yankee Station was the U.S.S. *Coral Sea.* With a crew of 3,500 men, its own repair shops, stores, dispensary, and closed-circuit TV station, the *Coral Sea* resembled a small, sea-going city. But everything aboard the ship, which measured longer than three football fields placed end to end, was geared toward a single purpose: maintaining and launching the approximately seventy-five aircraft on board.

The night before a mission, the command staff developed a strike plan while maintenance crews worked through the night to ready planes for the morning launch and ordnance men broke out their stores. By dawn the flight deck suggested the infield at the Indianapolis 500. Hundreds of crewmen, wearing jerseys whose color indicated each man's duties, scrambled to and fro making final pre-launch preparations. Below deck in their squadron ready rooms, pilots received plane assignments and all the details of the mission. The briefing complete, the pilots headed topside, climbed into their aircraft, and prepared to launch.

*Crewmen scramble out from underneath an F-4 Phantom after hooking it up to a catapult aboard the U.S.S.* Midway *on Yankee Station, 1966.*

*Above. Sailors watch a boxing match on the hangar deck of the U.S.S.* Coral Sea.

The success of a launch depended on the catapult that accelerated aircraft from zero to about 150 knots in less than 200 feet. If the hookup was bad or the catapult malfunctioned, the aircraft would dribble off the carrier, requiring the pilot to eject before the plane hit the water. For the most part, though, launches went smoothly: His plane hooked to the catapult, a pilot wound up his engines and waited for the "launch" sign from the catapult officer. When the catapult built up sufficient pressure, the catapult officer threw his hand forward. This signaled the catapult operator to punch the launch button, hurtling the aircraft into the sky.

More nerve wracking were recovery operations after a mission. Pilots had to land on a rolling deck that appeared only

*Left. A sailor aboard the* Coral Sea *works on the aft section of an A–4 Skyhawk fuselage, readying it for the next morning's launch.*

*Right. A crewman naps atop racks of bombs waiting to be loaded on the* Coral Sea's *aircraft.*

*Left. Two pilots in the squadron ready room review target information before a mission.*

as a speck on the ocean as they began their approach at 140 knots. Lining up with a beam of light reflected by a large mirror on the deck, the pilot guided his plane down. Just as his wheels slammed down on the deck, he pushed the throttle to full power so he could take off again should his tail hook miss or skip over the arresting cables. Usually, however, the tail hook snagged one of the four cables, bringing the aircraft to an abrupt halt and slamming the pilot forward into his shoulder harness.

For a pilot, service on an aircraft carrier meant the increased risks of takeoff

*Below. The Coral Sea's Combat Information Center, which tracks aircraft, "friendly" and enemy, directs the ship's course and collects all intelligence aboard the carrier.*

*Right. A red-jerseyed ordnance man wheels two 500-pound Snake-eye bombs with spring action tail fins across the flight deck.*

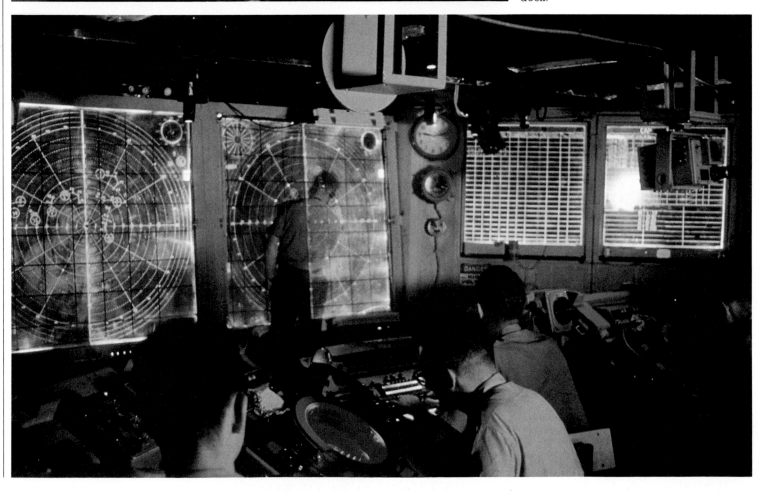

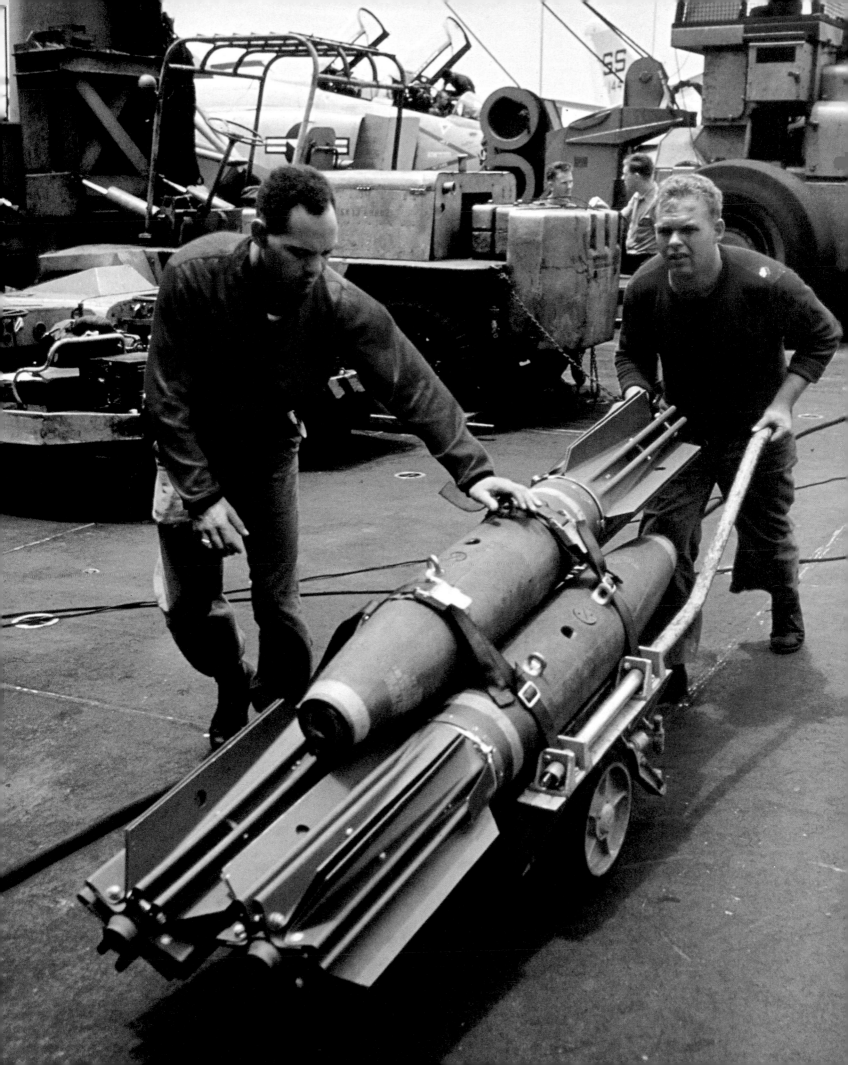

*Above. "Launch." An A-4 Skyhawk streaks past the Coral Sea's catapult officer.*

and landing, doubly hard jobs at night or during bad weather. For the crewmen, it meant hard, thankless work that seemed never to end: During 1965 the *Coral Sea* spent eleven months at sea, 80 percent of the time on line at Yankee Station. For all, it meant the anxiety of knowing that a small error could cause the loss of an aircraft and a pilot's death.

*Left. Steam released from the catapult after a launch swirls across the flight deck as the catapult crew (in green) and the plane captain (in brown) await the next aircraft.*

*Right. An F-4 Phantom starts its Rolling Thunder mission. The seated crewmen are plane handlers, who position the planes so they can be attached to the catapult.*

# Rolling Thunder

Twenty days after President Johnson's initial order was issued and only six days before U.S. Marines waded ashore at Da Nang, Operation Rolling Thunder got underway. On March 2, 1965, U.S. Air Force planes took off from bases in South Vietnam and Thailand in a massive, coordinated assault on an ammunition depot at Xom Bang, thirty-five miles north of the DMZ. The strike force consisted of forty F-100 Supersabres from Da Nang, forty-four F-105 Thunderchiefs now based at U.S. airfields in Thailand, and twenty B-57s stationed at Tan Son Nhut, as well as refueling tankers and other support aircraft. The addition of long-range B-52 bombers based in Guam, included in the initial strike plan, was canceled at the last minute. The president did not want to give the appearance of an all-out assault upon North Vietnam.

Leading the first F-105 Thunderchiefs that afternoon was the commander of the 67th Tactical Fighter Squadron, Lieutenant Colonel Robinson

Risner. The forty-year-old veteran had flown 109 combat missions during the Korean War, during which he had racked up eight Communist Mig "kills." Now Risner led his squadron's pilots, many on their first combat mission, in the air force's first major action against the North.

Until now the air force pilots had flown only a few missions in South Vietnam or Laos against little resistance. They were not accustomed to people firing at them. Nervous chatter filled the strike radio frequency as the uninitiated fliers underwent their baptism of fire.

## Over Xom Bang

When his Thunderchiefs closed in over Xom Bang, Risner could see a number of F-100s swarming over the target. They had been sent in first to soften up North Vietnamese defenses. To avoid overlapping with the Supersabres, Risner swung his formation wide of the target. Looping around in a slow 180-degree turn, he watched as the F-100s pounded antiaircraft batteries surrounding the ammo dump with rockets and 20MM cannon fire. Suddenly, one of the Supersabres burst into flames, hit by the burst from an exploding 37MM shell. Its pilot had no choice but to eject from the blazing aircraft. As the luckless flier drifted earthward, Robbie Risner led his fighter-bombers in on their attack run.

Orange tracers laced the sky as his lead flight of four Thunderchiefs swept in over the target. Within seconds Risner's wingman, Boris Baird, was hit, and as the fire light flashed its red warning on his plane's instrument panel, Baird pulled the ejection handle between his legs. There was so much noise and chatter in the radio traffic that no one knew he had been hit.

Captain Frank Tullo had just released his bombs when a strange apparition flashed before his eyes. For a split second he saw a man hanging from a parachute as he flew by. Recognizing the markings on the flier's helmet, the startled Tullo said to himself: "That's Boris Baird!"

When Risner realized his wingman had been hit, he immediately turned his flight around and began circling the smoking wreckage of Baird's aircraft. Switching his microphone to the guard channel, strictly reserved for emergency calls during rescue operations, Risner found the frequency awash with a roar of disjointed voices. Risner looked up to see the reason for the confusion. The precisely timed plan of attack had broken down completely. A second wave of Thunderchiefs from the 12th TFS had arrived before the first wave had completed its bombing runs. Planes were stacked up over the target like so many clay pigeons for the North Vietnamese gunners below. Normal radio discipline disintegrated as the inexperi-

enced pilots reported planes downed or on fire and frantically called for rescue helicopters.

As the senior officer on the scene, Risner decided to exert control. His voice boomed in over the radio and silenced all but essential communications. Ignoring the deadly ground fire streaming toward him, Risner directed incoming planes into the target, pointing out antiaircraft positions to avoid. "Without Robbie there," claimed one of the pilots, "it probably would have been a fiasco."

As the Thunderchiefs were finishing their last passes at the smoldering ammo dump, twenty B-57s appeared from the southeast. The bombers delivered their entire payloads in a single pass. Secondary explosions rocked the low-flying planes as they headed back over the target toward home. One of the B-57 pilots noticed some F-105s still darting around the area, "as if they didn't know what they were still doing there."

What he saw were Risner and two other Thunderchief pilots flying their vigil over Boris Baird, who had landed in thick jungle less than a mile from the target. As soon as he hit the ground, Baird hurriedly unharnessed his parachute

*Preceding page. A navy A-1 Skyraider takes off from the flight deck of the U.S.S. Ranger for an early Rolling Thunder operation against North Vietnam.*

*F-100 Supersabres receive a thorough inspection at Da Nang two weeks before they flew the first Rolling Thunder mission on March 2, 1965.*

and "ran like hell" away from the exploding ammo dump. Following standard operating procedure, immediately after ejecting Baird popped the handle on his seat releasing his survival kit, which was attached to him by a fifty-foot cord. It also automatically inflated a life raft farther down the cord. The raft had snagged on one tree and the survival kit containing his emergency radio, flares, and signal mirror on another; he landed in a third.

Without his emergency radio and flares, Baird realized his chances of being picked up were slim. He emptied onto the ground his maps and any other bits of paper he could find in the pockets of his flight suit and lit a small fire. Crewmen aboard a rescue helicopter circling nearby spotted the thin wisp of smoke. The chopper quickly swooped down and plucked Baird out of the jungle.

The F-100 pilot Risner had watched go down earlier in the attack was not as fortunate. Although rescue efforts failed, the pilot managed to elude his pursuers for seven days. But on March 9, Lieutenant Hayden Lockhart, Jr., became the first USAF pilot captured by North Vietnam.

Robbie Risner, low on fuel and his plane riddled with bullet holes, was forced to divert to the airstrip at Da Nang. The tired squadron commander was greeted by Gen. William Westmoreland and Lt. Gen. Joseph H. Moore, commander of the 2d Air Division. They were anxious to know how the raid had gone. "I guess we destroyed the target," Risner replied, "but as best I know we lost about seven airplanes." The two men stared at him in disbelief. If Risner was correct, North Vietnam's air defenses were far better than had been assumed.

At a press conference later that day, air force officials in Saigon announced that 120 tons of bombs had been dropped on the ammunition depot at Xom Bang, while a strike by nineteen Vietnamese Skyraiders had delivered 20 tons against the Quang Khe naval base thirty miles farther north. Allied aircraft were said to have destroyed 70 percent to 80 percent of both targets and faced only "light and not accurate" ground fire.

Lieutenant Colonel Robinson Risner, commander of the 67th Tactical Fighter Squadron, holding his survival kit.

But the pilots who flew the missions knew better. When the final tally came in later that evening, six planes were listed as lost with five of the pilots rescued. "We realized this wasn't going to be a pushover," recalled one of the pilots. "We were going to lose some people and some airplanes."

## Regularity and determination

A few days later Col. Risner and Captain William Hosmer, representing the 12th TFS, flew to Saigon for a formal debriefing. At this stage of the war there was no set command structure for air force units based in Thailand. In fact, the mere presence of the bases was kept under wraps at the request of the Thai government. Individual squadrons from various air wings stationed throughout the Pacific were rotated in and out on three-month tours of temporary duty. While in Thailand, they came under the operational control of the commander of the 2d Air Division, Lt. Gen. Joseph H. Moore, who was responsible for planning and implementing U.S. Air Force Rolling Thunder missions.

In the air-conditioned trailers at Tan Son Nhut airfield that housed 2d Air Division headquarters, Risner and Hosmer criticized the plan of attack that Moore's staff had provided them. It had been a "bad mistake," Risner argued, to send the strike force en masse over the target. Both agreed that the plan of attack put too many planes too close together for too long a time, giving North Vietnamese gunners time to find their range and altitude. "Let us control the damn thing and we'll do it right," Risner proposed.

Gen. Moore listened sympathetically to their arguments, but he was powerless to act on many of their requests. In their zeal to adhere to the president's wish for "limited" air strikes, Pentagon planners placed a number of restrictions on Rolling Thunder missions. Washington was to give commanders in the field specific instructions on what targets were to be hit, the day and often the hour of attack, the number of planes, the types and tonnages of weapons to be used, and sometimes even the direction from which pilots were to approach the target. If poor weather caused a strike to be canceled, it could not be rescheduled without consultation with Washington. In addition, South Vietnamese aircraft were to participate in each Rolling Thunder mission. But rival factions continued to jockey for control in Saigon and, since Ky's air force held the balance of power, it was constantly held on alert because of rumored coup plots. So the VNAF was often unable to meet scheduled strike dates, creating delays.

The second Rolling Thunder mission was scheduled for March 13, eleven days after the first strike. The directive called for one-time only US/VNAF strikes. No alternate targets were allowed, and the order stressed that in case of bad weather the strikes would be postponed until it cleared. This time rain and low cloud cover over North Vietnam kept U.S. planes grounded for two days. Finally, on March 15, more than 100 navy and air force jets struck the target, another ammo dump ninety-five miles southwest of Hanoi. The day before, 24 VNAF Skyraiders had hit a weapons installation on Tiger Island, a few miles above the DMZ off the coast.

Public pronouncements claimed success, but complaints about the limitations traveled up the command structure all the way to the chairman of the JCS, General Earle Wheeler. After ordering a study, Wheeler sent a memo to Secretary of Defense McNamara recommending that strike commanders be given more flexibility, especially with choice of weapons and timing of strikes.

A similar recommendation came from Army Chief of Staff General Harold K. Johnson in a report to President Johnson. During a fact-finding mission in South Vietnam, Gen. Johnson found the sporadic tempo of the air strikes "inadequate" to convey to Hanoi a clear sense of U.S. commitment. He echoed Gen. Wheeler's belief that the self-imposed restrictions on the strikes "have severely reduced their effectiveness."

On March 15 the president approved most of Gen. Johnson's recommendations. Targets would now be allotted in "weekly packages." During a given week, oper-

*A-4 Skyhawks from the U.S.S.* Coral Sea *fly north on a strike in 1965.*

ational commanders could decide on the precise day and time each target in a package approved by Washington would be hit. Simultaneous participation by VNAF forces was no longer required. Previously prohibited weapons, such as napalm, could be employed. According to the presidential directive, "the impression henceforth to be given is one of regularity and determination."

## Radar-busting week

Two primary targets were authorized for the first Rolling Thunder weekly package of March 19 to 25. The orders also authorized one U.S. and two VNAF "armed reconnaissance" missions—to seek out and destroy military targets along specified highway, railroad, and coastal routes. Only locomotives, rolling stock, military trucks, and "hostile" vessels could be hit, however.

Military commanders welcomed the easing of restrictions but believed they were still under too many constraints. Pointing out that the traditional purpose of armed reconnaissance missions was to disrupt the enemy's transportation system by constant harassment, Adm. Sharp argued that three missions per week were "completely insignificant" for the task. He said, "The North Vietnamese probably didn't even know the planes were there!"

Pilots on the large "Alpha" strikes against primary targets did not encounter that problem. Limited though it was, the North's radar system was efficient. Large formations of USAF planes flying from Thailand and USN aircraft heading inland from carriers at Yankee Station showed clearly on North Vietnamese radar screens. At the insistence of Adm. Sharp, the next weekly Rolling Thunder package of March 26 authorized strikes against nine radar sites below the nineteenth parallel. "Radar-busting week," as it came to be known, was a concession by Washington to the military.

Combined air force and navy strikes eventually knocked out all nine radar sites but not without considerable difficulty. One site proved particularly troublesome. Bach Long Vi (Nightingale) Island, 120 kilometers off the coast in the Gulf of Tonkin, provided the North Vietnamese with an excellent early warning radar site to monitor aircraft from Yankee Station. Seventy aircraft from the *Coral Sea* and *Hancock* hit the station on March 26 but failed to knock out the main antenna. Three days later seventy more planes were sent to finish the job.

When the strike force broke through the clouds, they met a barrage of flak streaming upward from antiaircraft emplacements that crisscrossed the tiny island. Four of the first six planes over the target were hit. One pilot was killed instantly. The pilots of the other three aircraft, all squadron commanders, were more fortunate. Pete Mongilardi, who had led the first Flaming Dart strike in February, took a hit in one of his wing tanks, which quickly began streaming fuel. Mongilardi managed to hook onto an aerial tanker that kept pumping fuel into his Skyhawk until he made it safely back to the *Coral Sea*. Commander Jack Harris, skipper of Attack Squadron 155, was forced to bail out of his plane into the sea. He had been in the water only a few minutes when, to his amazement, a USN submarine popped out of the sea, hauled him aboard, and submerged again.

The fourth pilot, Commander William Donnelly, felt a shell hit his F-8 Crusader. Climbing back into the clouds, the commander of the "Black Knights" of Fighter Squadron 154 checked his controls. Everything looked and felt good so he circled in an oval-shaped "race track" pattern, assembling his squadron for a second run.

As Donnelly began a rolling, 500MPH dive, his plane suddenly pitched earthward into a violent corkscrewing plunge. Fighting the stunning G-pressure of the uncontrolled spin, Donnelly reached for the ejection handles located above the headrest on his seat. Grabbing the handle with one hand, which pulled a protective curtain down over his face, he shot out of the aircraft. At that moment the gyrating Crusader happened to be upside down and already dangerously low. He felt the tug of his parachute a split second before he hit water.

Donnelly pulled the life raft from his survival kit and triggered the automatic inflation device. But during the violent ejection and landing he had dislocated one shoulder, injured his neck, and cracked six vertebrae, so it took him two hours to struggle aboard the raft. In the process he snapped the antenna off his emergency radio and punctured the raft. Every twenty minutes or so Donnelly had to blow air into the raft in order to keep it from sinking.

Drifting only a few miles offshore, Donnelly could see the effects of the strike. Not only had he and his companions knocked out the radar site, but they also set off a hidden ammo dump. "That island blew up all night long," he recalled.

Around midnight Donnelly heard the sound of a ship's propellers. Soon he could see a boat silhouetted against the fires still raging on Bach Long Vi, its searchlights playing on the water. Thinking it might be a U.S. destroyer looking for him, he pulled out his flare gun. He had squeezed the trigger halfway back when he said to himself: "You fool! It couldn't possibly be one of ours." Painfully crawling into the water and pulling the raft over his head, Donnelly tread water while the craft zigzagged around his position until dawn without spotting him. He later confirmed his suspicions; it was a Chinese destroyer.

Another day and night passed before Donnelly was spotted by a search plane from the U.S.S. *Hancock*. Within a few hours an air force HU-16 seaplane splashed into the sea nearby. "I could see the hatch opening," said Donnelly. "They were all carrying carbines pointed at me." He wondered if they thought he had been booby trapped by the North Vietnamese. Crewmen beckoned him to swim toward the plane. But after forty-five hours adrift the injured pilot was immobilized from overexposure and shock. A paramedic jumped in and swam rapidly out to Donnelly, attached a line to him, and hauled him aboard the plane. "Later on I found out why they were so concerned," Donnelly recounted. "I was sitting right in the middle of a school of sharks!"

# From isolated thunderclaps . . .

Although President Johnson had agreed to the easing of civilian controls on a tactical level, he continued to keep the selection of targets and the weight of Rolling Thunder strikes under careful personal scrutiny. Johnson said to journalists, "I won't let those air force generals bomb the smallest outhouse . . . without checking with me."

Military men chafed at the bit under the president's tight rein. Air force and navy commanders in Vietnam saw little logic in sporadic attacks against targets in southern North Vietnam of relatively minor military significance. They pressed for authority to strike more important targets farther north. But any such recommendations had to pass through an extraordinary chain of command before they were even considered.

Target recommendations for each weekly Rolling Thunder program were submitted by commanders of the 2d Air Division in Saigon and Task Force 77 at Yankee Station to CINCPAC headquarters in Honolulu. There, Adm. Sharp and his staff assembled the varying and sometimes conflicting air force and navy requests into a coordinated program and forwarded it to the Pentagon.

Military experts on the JCS staff and their civilian counterparts in John McNaughton's office of International Security Affairs then weighed the strategic implications of each target. State Department officials also considered the international political significance of each target. The final target requests of the Joint Chiefs were then sent to the White House.

Every Tuesday afternoon at one o'clock, a small group of senior administration officials gathered for lunch in the family dining room of the executive mansion. Seated at the mahogany table were Secretary of Defense Robert McNamara, Secretary of State Dean Rusk, and the president's special assistant for national security affairs, McGeorge Bundy. Surrounded by murals depicting the surrender of Cornwallis at Yorktown, Lyndon Johnson and his most trusted advisers masterminded U.S. strategy in Vietnam.

No other topic was examined in more detail by the "Tuesday lunch group" than the Rolling Thunder proposals of the JCS. Each target request, along with the comments of the various screening agencies, was graded on the basis of four criteria: military significance, the risks to pilots and planes, danger of civilian casualties, and the risk of widening the war.

Continually rejecting military recommendations for a bombing blitz against the North, Johnson at one point commented that "A total assault on the North would be rape rather than seduction." He saw the bombing as a political tool which, skillfully used, could signal U.S. resolve and convince Ho Chi Minh to give up without drawing the U.S. and Hanoi's allies—either the Soviets or the Chinese—into a larger war.

In hindsight, fears that Vietnam would mushroom into World War III were greatly exaggerated. But at the time, the threat seemed real to American officials conditioned by twenty years of cold war geopolitics. "I spent ten hours a day worrying about all this," Johnson later professed, "picking the targets one by one, making sure we didn't go over the limits."

Military commanders continued to believe that the signals were too weak to convince Hanoi of anything. Admiral Sharp, among others, complained that American offensive power was being wasted as "U.S. forces were not allowed to do more than peck at seemingly isolated random targets." Even some civilian members of the Johnson administration began expressing concerns over the effectiveness of the bombing. One of them was Ambassador Maxwell Taylor in Saigon. In a cable to Washington, the former head of the JCS said that Rolling Thunder should exhibit a "mounting crescendo" of air attacks to "progressively turn the screws" on North Vietnam. "I fear that to date Rolling Thunder in their eyes has merely been a few isolated thunderclaps."

Toward this end, military planners submitted fresh proposals to strengthen Rolling Thunder. The Joint Chiefs put forth a plan designed by Admiral Sharp. In his plan, CINCPAC called for an integrated strike and armed reconnaissance program designed to cut North Vietnamese lines of communication (LOCs) below the twentieth parallel. Primary targets would be bridges, ferries, and choke points along major highway routes and rail lines. Armed reconnaissance missions would be flown around-the-clock to blast backed-up truck and rail convoys and harass repair efforts.

In Washington, the Joint Chiefs expanded Sharp's proposal into a twelve-week program, which they submitted to Secretary of Defense McNamara on March 22. It recommended that the LOC-cut campaign be extended north of the twentieth parallel after three weeks to hit rail lines connecting Hanoi with Communist China. This would be followed by strikes against port facilities and industrial plants outside heavily populated areas.

Although McNamara rejected the twelve-week program, reflecting the president's wish to preserve maximum flexibility, the LOC-cut proposal was adopted in

*Shot down during a March 29 air strike, Commander William Donnelly spent two days in shark-infested waters awaiting rescue. Here Donnelly, applauded by fellow pilots, returns to the U.S.S.* Coral Sea *on April 4, 1965.*

principle. Senior administration officials, concerned by reports of the crumbling war effort in South Vietnam, were at that moment pondering sending in additional U.S. combat troops. Bombing North Vietnamese supply routes to reduce the flow of men and materiel reaching the Vietcong seemed a much cheaper alternative. The decision marked a turning point in the bombing campaign: targets were increasingly being chosen for military rather than psychological or political value.

## Flying into the Dragon's Jaw

The LOC-cut program began in earnest on April 3, when carrier-based aircraft struck the Dong Thoung Bridge sixty-five miles south of Hanoi. Flying in two waves, the navy planes destroyed the approach section and center lanes. Only one plane was damaged, but this time the damage did not come from antiaircraft fire.

Three North Vietnamese Mig-15s had pounced on an unsuspecting Crusader just as it pulled off the target, raking the F-8 with cannon fire. The Migs retreated just as quickly when challenged by the remaining Crusaders in the flight. Although Migs had been sighted during previous missions, this was the first time that North Vietnam's tiny air force had challenged American planes. It was not to be the last.

That same day forty-six Thunderchiefs, armed with 750-pound bombs and 250-pound Bullpup air-to-ground missiles, roared off runways in Thailand. Their target was the Thanh Hoa railroad and highway bridge, known to the Vietnamese as Ham Rong—the Dragon's Jaw. Located halfway between Hanoi and the northernmost entrances to the Ho Chi Minh Trail, the Dragon's Jaw was a vital link in North Vietnam's supply line to the South. The 56-foot-wide span stretching 546 feet across the Song Ma carried the country's only north-south rail track and main highway, Route 1.

Destruction of the bridge would be both a strategic and a psychological blow to the North. Completed after eight years of painstaking labor, the Dragon's Jaw represented the Hanoi regime's crowning technological achievement. Ho Chi Minh himself presided at its dedication in 1964. Comprised of two steel thru-truss spans resting on a massive reinforced concrete pier sixteen feet in diameter, the bridge was anchored on each bank by forty-foot-thick concrete abutments. Realizing that the bridge would be an obvious target for U.S. bombers, the North Vietnamese had positioned numerous antiaircraft batteries in the surrounding hills.

Flying in the lead Thunderchief that day was Lt. Col. Robbie Risner. In the last month, Risner had established a reputation as an aggressive squadron commander. He was respected by the young pilots in his command and his superiors in Saigon alike. As the senior and most experienced aviator among the four squadrons of the 18th Air Wing based in Thailand, he had become the de facto wing commander. "The man was fearless," recalled one pilot who flew with him. "He just exposed himself to flak as if it didn't exist." Risner had already been shot down and rescued once during an attack on a North Vietnamese radar site in late March.

Some thought his aggressiveness was unnecessarily risky and criticized the higher rate of aircraft downed in his squadron. But the "Fighting Cocks" of Risner's 67th TFS always got the job done. "We didn't go over there to preserve our lives and aircraft," Risner noted. "We went over there to destroy targets."

Cruising toward the Dragon's Jaw at 17,000 feet, the air force pilots could see a battle progressing ahead. F-100 Supersabres, sent in ahead of the strike force to neutralize the North Vietnamese antiaircraft batteries, were already drawing heavy fire. Angling down through the maze of orange and black flak bursts, Risner led the first wave in on the bridge.

Squeezing off one of his Bullpups, Risner guided it to the target by manipulating a small toggle switch inside the cockpit. Keeping his plane on the same flight path as the missile to maintain a steady line of sight between it and the target, Risner scored a direct hit. Rolling off to the left in a climbing turn, he glanced back to see what looked like popcorn bursts of flame as several more Bullpups from other planes slammed into the bridge. But as they swung in for a second pass, he could see no damage through the spiraling smoke. The second barrage proved no more effective than the first.

Now the second wave of Thunderchiefs from the 12th TFS, each armed with eight 750-pound bombs, joined the attack. One by one, the jets hurtled toward the bridge in forty-five-degree dives to release their bombs. But heavy crosswinds had buffeted the jets off their precisely calculated delivery path, sending many of the bombs bursting harmlessly against the far riverbank. The last flight in the strike force, led by Captain Carlyle "Smitty" Harris, scored several direct hits. But when the smoke cleared, the only damage to be seen was a few holes in the concrete roadway.

His fuel tanks punctured by shrapnel, Risner was forced to head for Da Nang before the strike was completed. When he touched down he heard that the Dragon's Jaw was still standing and two planes had been lost. After a new fuel tank was fitted underneath his F-105, Risner flew straight back to the squadron's base at Korat airfield in Thailand.

Landing with only a few hours of daylight left, Risner was surprised to find the airfield a beehive of activity. Bomb carts were strewn about the taxi ramp. Planes were being rearmed and refueled. When he asked one of the ground crew what was going on, he could not believe his ears. "We're going again," he was told.

Risner strode into the squadron's operations shack and

*A 250-pound Bullpup air-to-ground missile—like the one used by Robbie Risner against the Ham Rong Bridge—streaks toward North Vietnam.*

*The Ham Rong Bridge—the Dragon's Jaw—remains standing after being hit by USAF F-105 Thunderchiefs on April 3, 1965.*

reached for the scramble line to 2d Air Division headquarters in Saigon. "Are you out of your mind?" he bellowed into the telephone. With darkness falling he protested that their chances of hitting the bridge would be next to nil, while the chances of heavy losses in pilots and planes would be dangerously high.

Persuading headquarters to postpone the strike until morning, Risner requested the poststrike reconnaissance photos be sent to them immediately. One of the most exasperating problems faced by pilots in the early months of Rolling Thunder was the lack of up-to-date reconnaissance photos. During the prestrike briefing at Korat before the first Dragon's Jaw mission, the only photo available to Risner and his pilots had been an aerial view from an old *National Geographic* magazine. The photos did not show the massive central support underneath the bridge, and the pilots had mistakenly aimed for the center of the span believing it to be the weakest point. Not until they were over the target had they realized their mistake.

## A second try

The next morning Risner led his squadron against the Dragon's Jaw once again. This time the entire strike force of forty-eight planes was armed with 750-pound bombs. The smaller Bullpups were left at home for use against softer targets. Risner again was in the lead, but this time he had been ordered to fly high above the bridge and coordinate the mission.

Capt. Smitty Harris, given the dubious honor of being the first "down the chute" that morning, knew the North Vietnamese would be waiting for him. "We came in the same route, the same altitude, same tactics," he later recalled. "They could have looked at their watches and started shooting." Harris could see muzzle flashes erupting from the barrels of antiaircraft guns as he plummeted toward the bridge. At 4,000 feet he depressed the button on the top of his control stick and dropped the three tons of bombs attached to his wings. Leveling off at 1,000 feet, the lightened Thunderchief began surging skyward when a 37MM shell rammed into the fuselage.

Smitty Harris could feel the huge plane lose power. Instinctively, he turned the struggling jet toward the safety of the ocean. But it was a hopeless cause. Rapidly losing altitude and air speed, Harris had to bail out. During the ejection his left elbow caught on the edge of the cockpit, breaking his collarbone. Drifting earthward, Smitty saw that he was heading straight for a small village. Vainly trying to maneuver the chute with his good arm, he landed right in the middle of a crowd of farmers who overpowered him. Twenty-four hours later, Smitty Harris, who had passed up two weeks of R & R in Bangkok to be in on

the raid against the Dragon's Jaw, found himself in a cell at the Hanoi Hilton.

Helplessly watching Harris's plane disappear into the clouds, Robbie Risner was quickly forced to turn his attention to the battle raging below. A flight of four F–105s from Takhli AFB had arrived on the scene a few minutes early. To avoid bunching up over the target, he ordered "Zinc" flight to make a loose orbit outside the area before making its run. Minutes later, Risner heard an urgent call over his headphones, "Zinc lead, break! You have Migs behind you!"

Four North Vietnamese Mig–17s had evaded the F–100s flying combat air patrol over the target by coming in low through a thick layer of haze. Climbing undetected into the clouds, they burst down upon the Thunderchiefs from behind, cannons blazing. The warning came too late. The Migs knocked out the first two planes in one pass. Just as quickly as they appeared, the four Migs streaked away northward.

But the Americans learned two important lessons from the encounter. As in the unsuccessful skirmish with U.S. Navy planes the day before, the Mig pilots were using hit-and-run tactics. Secondly, with the poor visibility that morning it was doubtful whether the Russian-made Migs could have achieved their advantageous position without

*Although repeated U.S. air strikes crippled the Dragon's Jaw, shown here in 1967, it would not be felled until 1972.*

being directed by radar. It was evident that North Vietnam possessed ground control intercept radar capability.

Despite the Mig attack, the air force planes continued their assault on the Dragon's Jaw. One hundred and two tons of heavy explosives rained down on the bridge that morning. Numerous hits cratered the roadways and punched gaping holes through the central rail track. But the Dragon's Jaw remained standing, silently defying American might.

For three more years, U.S. aircraft would fly mission after mission against the bridge. By 1968 nearly 700 planes had been sent against the bridge, pounding it with more than 12,500 tons of explosives. The entire area around the bridge looked like a "valley on the moon," according to one navy official. Despite the attacks, American planes were able to render the bridge unusable for only short periods. North Vietnamese repair crews worked around-the-clock to keep traffic moving across the scarred, twisted structure. The Dragon's Jaw remained a symbol of North Vietnamese tenacity until 1972 when it was finally brought down by laser-guided "smart bombs."

Other targets were not so dramatically invulnerable. Bridges were key targets in Adm. Sharp's program to disrupt the enemy's supply system and also the most difficult to destroy. As the pilots soon found out, rockets were in-effective against the steel and concrete structures. The only effective way to destroy a bridge was to drop high-explosive bombs from directly overhead. Since a bridge provided a narrow target, low-level approaches and pin-point accuracy were required.

The North Vietnamese were quick to read American tactics, so early in the Rolling Thunder attacks key bridges bristled with antiaircraft defenses. Their gunners would simply pour everything they had into the air directly above the span, knowing that planes had to fly through the barrage if they were to hit their target. One pilot likened it to flying through an "exploding curtain of steel."

## The billion dollar carrot

In spite of the difficulties, American pilots had accomplished the goals of Adm. Sharp's program by the end of April. In four weeks, twenty-six bridges and seven ferries were knocked out of commission. Armed reconnaissance missions, expanded from three sorties per week to twenty-four per day, maintained the pressure on all military movement facilities. Hundreds of trucks, locomotives, and supply-laden boxcars trapped in the southern panhandle were destroyed. At a press conference, Secretary McNamara declared the objective of the campaign was "to

force the infiltration from railroads to trucks and from trucks to feet." He pointed out that the bombing had forced Hanoi to divert its limited resources from the battle in the South to keeping lines of communication open.

But as the bombing of North Vietnam intensified, so had the level of international and domestic criticism. On March 8, U.N. Secretary General U Thant publicly called for a reconvening of the 1954 Geneva Conference to negotiate an end to the escalating conflict. Even America's allies were getting edgy. Canadian Prime Minister Lester Pearson received a frosty reception in Washington after publicly suggesting a halt to the bombing as a prelude to peace talks.

At home, criticism of the administration's Vietnam policy began to take organized form. Informal discussion groups questioning U.S. involvement in Vietnam, called "teach-ins," began to spring up on college campuses across the nation. Some political figures, among them Senator Robert Kennedy, were privately urging the president to halt the bombing in order to start negotiations. As syndicated columnist Walter Lippmann wrote, it appeared the administration's Vietnam policy was "all stick and no carrot."

Lyndon Johnson had known that the decision to bomb North Vietnam would be criticized at home and abroad. The major escalation of the war had to be balanced by an exhibition of American willingness to negotiate a settlement. Not only would an assertion of the limited nature of the bombing be necessary to deflect dissent among allied nations and the American public, but also to assure Hanoi's protectors in Moscow and Peking that the U.S. sought no wider war. Toward these ends, on April 7 the president delivered a televised speech from Johns Hopkins University in Baltimore. Reiterating his willingness to engage in "unconditional discussions," Johnson offered North Vietnam a $1 billion economic development program if it would halt its aggression in South Vietnam.

But the speech failed to soothe either the fears of the president's critics or to evoke any positive signals from Hanoi. The media labeled Johnson's attempt to extend his cherished Great Society program into the realm of foreign policy the "billion dollar carrot." Radio Hanoi called it a blatant "bribe." Speaking before the National Assembly on April 8, North Vietnamese Premier Pham Van Dong rejected the offer and spelled out Hanoi's bargaining conditions: (1) the bombing must cease; (2) all U.S. troops must withdraw from South Vietnam; (3) the demands of the National Liberation Front, the political arm of the Vietcong, must be recognized by the Saigon government; (4) the reunification of Vietnam must be settled by the Vietnamese themselves without outside interference. Dong flatly asserted that only when these four points were met would Hanoi even consider formal discussions.

To Washington, Hanoi's four points were a request to sell out South Vietnam. Their strident tone also suggested that the bombing had done little to shake North Vietnam-

ese resolve. The latest intelligence speculated that only expanded bombing and/or a substantial increase in American combat troops would persuade Hanoi to negotiate on more favorable terms.

## Project Mayflower

In a memorandum to the president, Admiral William Raborn, the new director of the CIA, voiced these fears and advocated the extension of air attacks to economic and military targets. He cautioned that escalation should begin only "after any current possibility of serious negotiations have been fully tested" and suggested a bombing pause as a vehicle to test Communist intentions. Secretary of State Dean Rusk also endorsed the pause, if only "to meet criticisms . . . that we haven't done enough" in the search for peace.

Periodic pauses in the bombing, to allow for the possibility of negotiating with Hanoi, had always been an integral part of the pressures program against the North. But timing was considered essential. Any premature attempt might give Hanoi the impression that the U.S. was eager for a settlement at any price. After two months of sustained air attacks, Johnson felt that the time was ripe. On May 10 he cabled Ambassador Taylor in Saigon that he intended to initiate an unannounced bombing pause within the next two days. The purpose of the pause would be to "clear a path toward . . . peace or toward increased military action," depending on Hanoi's response.

The true nature of the bombing pause was not publicly announced. An elaborate scenario with the code name Project Mayflower called for a private communication to be sent to Hanoi the day the pause began, spelling out U.S. terms for negotiations. If the terms were rejected, Johnson would then be able to undercut his critics and justify further escalation of the bombing by publicly revealing Hanoi's unwillingness to negotiate even after a bombing halt.

The text of the secret message barely mentioned negotiations. It merely informed the North Vietnamese of a lull in the bombing for a "limited trial period." If a reciprocal reduction of Vietcong activity were not forthcoming, the president warned of further escalation.

At a press conference in Saigon on May 12, U.S. officials announced a temporary bombing halt, ostensibly "to observe the reaction of DRV rail and road transportation systems." At the same time, the U.S. ambassador to the Soviet Union, Foy Kohler, requested an urgent meeting with the North Vietnamese representative in Moscow. The North Vietnamese refused, stating any message should be delivered through the Soviet government.

Kohler found the Soviets unwilling to be a party to what they considered an "insulting" ultimatum. "I am not a postman," Deputy Foreign Minister Firyubin told the ambassador, "Deliver it yourself." Kohler tried once again, sending a hand-delivered note to the North Vietnamese. It was returned the next day, unopened. After five frustrating days, Johnson ordered the bombing resumed.

On May 18 more than 100 navy planes hit a petroleum storage facility at Phu Qui. The unannounced resumption caught North Vietnamese gunners napping. Pilots reported no casualties amid very light flak, while claiming destruction of 90 percent of the fuel dump.

## Gradual escalation reaffirmed

Gradual escalation remained the overriding theme of Rolling Thunder. Although a few scattered strikes were authorized north of the twentieth parallel in June, military and transportation facilities in the panhandle continued to be the primary targets of the large-scale Alpha raids. Armed recon missions, empowered to strike moving trucks, trains, and other "targets of opportunity," were increased to 200 sorties per week. The total monthly level of sorties rose from 3,600 in April to 4,000 in May.

Field commanders reported the raids were becoming less effective as the North Vietnamese began abandoning fixed military emplacements below the twentieth parallel and moving supplies at night along smaller roads and paths in the dense jungle. Commander Wesley McDonald, who took over as skipper of the *Coral Sea's* air wing in mid-1965, recalled the frustration of being ordered to go back and hit targets when "we knew nobody was there." Morale became an increasing problem as pilots were asked to risk their lives against targets they knew to be "absolutely worthless," according to McDonald. "We were going into harm's way for what was perceived to be little return on the dollar."

At the end of June, General John P. McConnell, who had replaced General Curtis LeMay as air force chief of staff, resubmitted a plan for a massive strike against all ninety-four targets on the JCS master list. He warned that the present slow pace of the bombing merely gave Hanoi "the opportunity and incentive to strengthen both their offensive and defensive capabilities." But by this time concern over the effectiveness of the bombing was overshadowed by a growing worry about the land war in South Vietnam.

In cables from Saigon, General William Westmoreland reported that large numbers of North Vietnamese regulars were appearing in the South to bolster the guerrilla forces. The American commander feared the Communists were massing for a bold strike, which the already battered ARVN would be unable to stop. Captured Vietcong documents later confirmed Westmoreland's suspicions. The spring offensive of 1965 was to be a "turning point" in the war, according to Communist strategists. Vietcong commanders and their counterparts in Hanoi had decided to concentrate their forces as a prelude to "dashing to win a decisive victory."

It is uncertain whether Hanoi's escalation of the ground war was a response to the bombing, as George Ball had predicted, or merely the result of long-range strategic planning. By mid-June, after Hanoi's defiant rejection of American negotiation attempts and with the Vietcong's spring offensive in full swing, it was obvious that Rolling Thunder had not provided the quick, inexpensive solution many had hoped it would. During the next months, a debate over basic U.S. strategy raged in Washington. Should the bombing be escalated? Should more combat troops be sent? Or both?

Gen. Matthew Ridgway had prophesied during the debate over Operation Vulture in 1954 that once American air units were committed in Southeast Asia, U.S. ground troops would inevitably follow. He had been right. Since the first contingent of marines waded ashore in early

*Secretary of Defense Robert McNamara (front) and Chairman of the Joint Chiefs of Staff General Earle Wheeler don the "Mickey Mouse" headgear of aircraft carrier launch crewmen aboard the U.S.S.* Independence *during their inspection tour of Vietnam in July 1965.*

March to protect the American air base at Da Nang, the number and role of U.S. troops in South Vietnam had gradually expanded. As the war effort continued to deteriorate, their role changed from a strictly defensive posture to a more aggressive one that found them in combat. In June Westmoreland asked for even more troops in a greater combat role.

Gen. McConnell argued that committing large numbers of U.S. troops to a ground war in the South should be considered only after a concentrated strategic air offensive against North Vietnam. He maintained U.S. air power could give ARVN the necessary support to keep the Communists at bay long enough for the bombing to destroy Hanoi's ability to continue the war. This could be accomplished by a greater effort against infiltration targets as well as the destruction of North Vietnamese port facilities, including the mining of Haiphong Harbor, and rail lines between Hanoi and China to reduce the level of supplies from outside sources.

In Washington, as Johnson's advisers debated further moves in the air or on the ground, one spoke out for an American withdrawal from Vietnam. George Ball warned of the grave risks of "bogging down" American soldiers "in a protracted and bloody conflict of uncertain outcome." If an unlimited infusion of troops failed to reverse the situation, there would be increased pressure to expand the bombing "as a reflex to a deep sense of national frustration." Ball argued that escalating the Rolling Thunder campaign would accomplish even less. Hanoi had already weighed the consequences of U.S. air attacks for more than six months and "is apparently ready to accept the likely costs."

But the overwhelming majority of Johnson's advisers rejected Ball's argument, believing an American pullout from Vietnam would lead her allies to question the reliability of U.S. commitments, especially in Western Europe. Dean Rusk warned that withdrawal would be seen as a sign of weakness. "The Communist world," he wrote the president, "would draw conclusions that would lead to our ruin."

On July 20, after returning from a trip to South Vietnam, Robert McNamara formally endorsed Westmoreland's troop request. He recommended to the president that an additional forty-four battalions be dispatched to Vietnam, bringing the total U.S. force level to 179,000 men by the end of the year. Although he had originally indicated his support for a corresponding escalation in the bombing, McNamara now changed his mind.

He warned Johnson that the benefits of an expanded bombing campaign might be offset by the greater possible risks of "confrontations" with the Soviet Union and China. McNamara doubted whether any bombing campaign could shake Hanoi's will as long as there was the possibility of victory on the ground in South Vietnam. Stressing that success could only be achieved by "denying the Viet-

cong victory," he proposed that the main objective of any bombing effort should be "to put a ceiling" on Hanoi's ability to support the guerrillas.

Basically, he called for a continuation of the strategy aimed at infiltration-related targets. Gradually increasing the size and scope of the campaign would "emphasize the threat" of future attacks, thus keeping the pressure on North Vietnam while minimizing the possibility of hardening Hanoi's negotiating stance. Containing the bombing to interdicting supplies outside the potentially sensitive zones around Hanoi and Haiphong would provide the U.S. with maximum effectiveness with a minimum of risk.

On July 27 President Johnson endorsed McNamara's recommendations. With his decision, Johnson relegated the air war against North Vietnam to a role secondary to the ground war in the South. For the next year, Rolling Thunder would continue its limited pressure on Hanoi.

A number of military men later argued that if there had been no restrictions on the use of air power in the North, the war could have been won in 1965. Adm. Sharp later said:

We had strong air forces on the spot. The logical course would have been to unleash that air power against the homeland of the aggressor. Instead we wasted our air strength against inconsequential targets while planning to commit still more of our men to the ground battle. We were denying ourselves the advantages of our immensely superior firepower and technology, fighting a war with one hand tied behind our backs.

Whether a decisive air offensive could have broken the will of North Vietnam in 1965 is highly debatable. Historically, air power alone had never won a war. Hitler's bombing blitz on London had not forced the British to surrender in 1940. Neither had the Allied air offensives against Germany and Japan. The latter succeeded only after the two atomic bombs were dropped on Hiroshima and Nagasaki. In North Vietnam, where U.S. goals were much more limited, the U.S. bombing blitz might have persuaded Hanoi to seek a negotiated settlement. But after twenty years of sacrifice and struggle, Ho Chi Minh's government appeared very close to its goal in 1965. It is uncertain whether intensive bombing alone would have been enough to force Hanoi's leaders to abandon their bid to unify Vietnam under their rule.

But in Washington, the decision not to implement a heavy, swift stroke against North Vietnam left an air of uncertainty on which military leaders were quick to capitalize in subsequent debates over the bombing. As Rolling Thunder failed to achieve its objectives, the generals attempted to shift the responsibility for failure onto the shoulders of those civilians who had refused to follow their professional advice. As a result, Washington policymakers would be forced gradually to accept military proposals that theoretically offered better results in order to avoid a public confrontation with military leaders, something that the politicians could not afford to let happen.

# Arsenal of the Sky

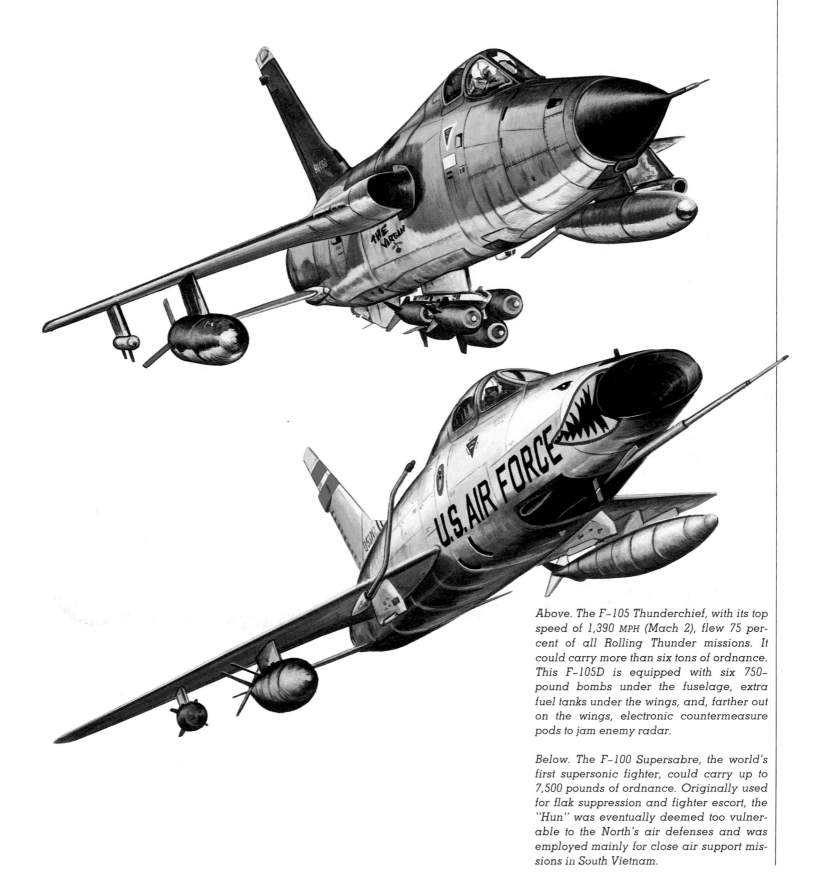

*Above. The F–105 Thunderchief, with its top speed of 1,390 MPH (Mach 2), flew 75 percent of all Rolling Thunder missions. It could carry more than six tons of ordnance. This F–105D is equipped with six 750-pound bombs under the fuselage, extra fuel tanks under the wings, and, farther out on the wings, electronic countermeasure pods to jam enemy radar.*

*Below. The F–100 Supersabre, the world's first supersonic fighter, could carry up to 7,500 pounds of ordnance. Originally used for flak suppression and fighter escort, the "Hun" was eventually deemed too vulnerable to the North's air defenses and was employed mainly for close air support missions in South Vietnam.*

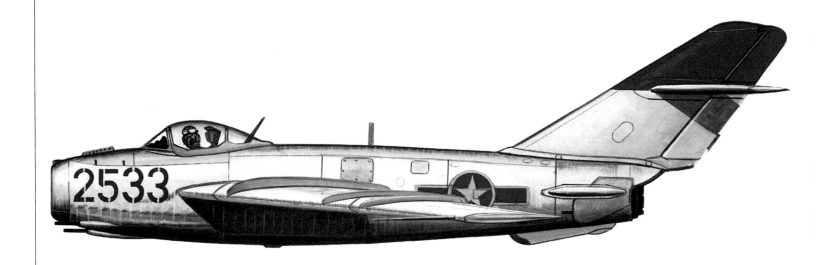

*Above. An F–4 Phantom, fitted with air-to-air missiles for anti-Mig fighter support for Rolling Thunder missions. Primarily designed as a fighter, the rugged F–4 also saw action in bombing and close air support missions. Although pilots considered the F–4 ugly, the twin-engine jet's supersonic speed and maneuverability made it a favorite. F–4s racked up 107 Mig kills during the war, more than any other aircraft.*

*Below. North Vietnam's Mig–17 carried the burden of attacking U.S. aircraft until delivery of the supersonic Mig–21 in 1966. Although not capable of supersonic speeds, the Mig–17's light weight and short wing span made it highly maneuverable. It was armed generally only with 23MM and 37MM nose cannons but could also carry air-to-air missiles.*

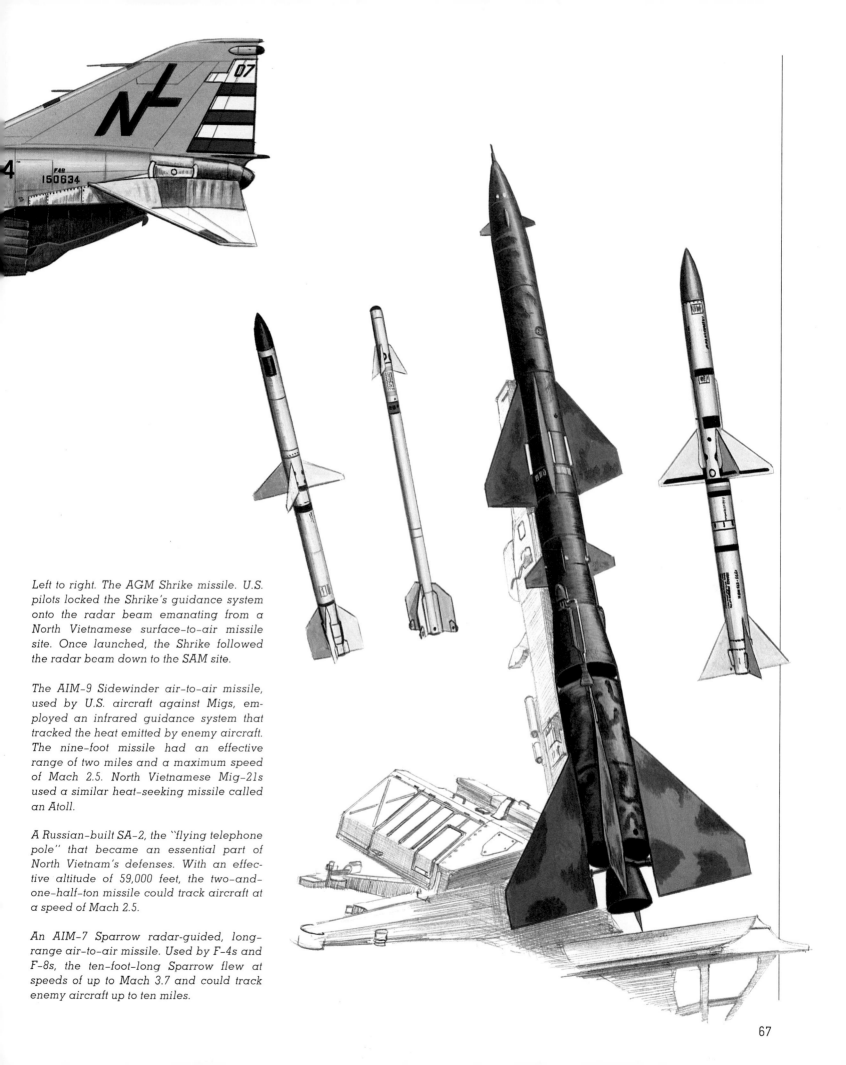

Left to right. The AGM Shrike missile. U.S. pilots locked the Shrike's guidance system onto the radar beam emanating from a North Vietnamese surface-to-air missile site. Once launched, the Shrike followed the radar beam down to the SAM site.

The AIM-9 Sidewinder air-to-air missile, used by U.S. aircraft against Migs, employed an infrared guidance system that tracked the heat emitted by enemy aircraft. The nine-foot missile had an effective range of two miles and a maximum speed of Mach 2.5. North Vietnamese Mig-21s used a similar heat-seeking missile called an Atoll.

A Russian-built SA-2, the "flying telephone pole" that became an essential part of North Vietnam's defenses. With an effective altitude of 59,000 feet, the two-and-one-half-ton missile could track aircraft at a speed of Mach 2.5.

An AIM-7 Sparrow radar-guided, long-range air-to-air missile. Used by F-4s and F-8s, the ten-foot-long Sparrow flew at speeds of up to Mach 3.7 and could track enemy aircraft up to ten miles.

*Above. The A-4 Skyhawk flew more missions in Vietnam than any other naval aircraft. While it was extremely durable, the lightweight A-4 could fly at only 685 MPH but made up for its lack of speed with maneuverability and a powerful punch. Used for both Rolling Thunder and close air support missions, the A-4 could carry up to 5,000 pounds of bombs and rockets. The Skyhawk depicted here is equipped with twelve 500-pound bombs and a center line 300-gallon fuel tank.*

*Below. The A-1E Skyraider in which Major Bernard Fisher won the Medal of Honor in March 1966 (see sidebar, page 82). Nicknamed the "Spad," the A-1 was ideally suited to close air support missions because of its endurance and heavy weapons load of up to 8,000 pounds, in addition to its four 20MM cannons. A-1s had a top speed of only 318 MPH but could remain airborne over targets far longer than their jet-powered cousins.*

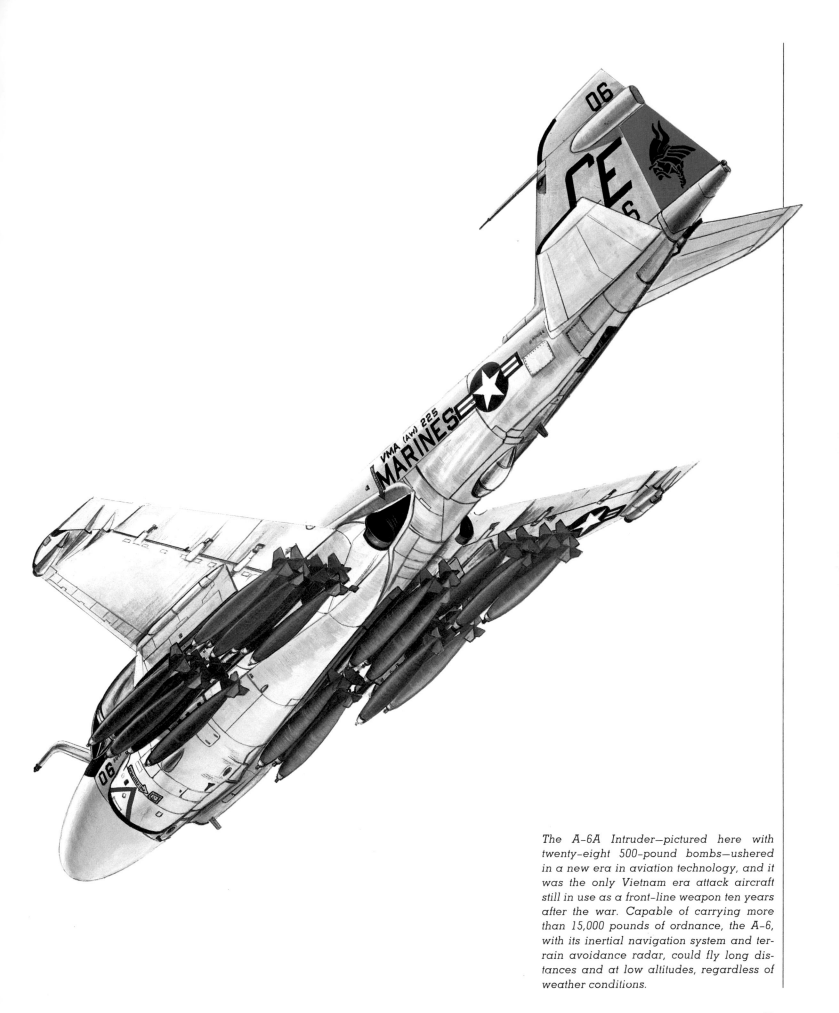

The A-6A Intruder—pictured here with twenty-eight 500-pound bombs—ushered in a new era in aviation technology, and it was the only Vietnam era attack aircraft still in use as a front-line weapon ten years after the war. Capable of carrying more than 15,000 pounds of ordnance, the A-6, with its inertial navigation system and terrain avoidance radar, could fly long distances and at low altitudes, regardless of weather conditions.

Above. The CH-47 Chinook, the most widely used transport helicopter in Vietnam. Although its large size prevented its use as an assault craft, the ninety-three-foot-long Chinook could carry thirty-three passengers or twenty-four litters for medical evacuation. It could also ferry howitzers and light tanks into the field.

The UH-1 helicopter, the "Huey," provided the U.S. with unprecedented air mobility in Vietnam. The "B" (pictured here) and "C" models could carry six men into battle; the larger "D" and "H" versions eleven. Many Hueys, armed only with a nose grenade launcher and M60 machine guns in each door, were used for transporting troops. Others were outfitted with rocket launchers and additional machine guns for use solely as gunships to provide cover for troop carriers. Hueys were also widely used in "dust off" missions evacuating casualties from the battlefield.

Shown here with experimental camouflage paint and a pair of external fuel tanks, the RF-101 Voodoo was the USAF's primary photo reconnaissance aircraft in Vietnam until 1967. The Voodoo's cameras, fitted into the nose cone, could photograph objects up to 50,000 feet away. Despite their supersonic speed, unarmed RF-101s were highly vulnerable to North Vietnamese Mig-21s, and in October 1967 they were replaced by even faster RF-4Cs with their more sophisticated cameras, infrared sensors, and side-looking radar.

# The In-Country Air War

On February 17, 1965, Major Howard F. O'Neal was greeted by the base commander at Bien Hoa airfield as he stepped from his silver B-57 jet bomber. The commander of the "Grim Reapers" of the 13th Bomb Squadron was surprised to see the base commander out on the flight line. "You ready to go fight a war?" he was asked. "Hell, yes," replied O'Neal. "The Grim Reapers are ready any time." The base commander implied they would be going that day. O'Neal took the news with a grain of salt. Since their arrival at Bien Hoa six months before, the men of the 13th and 8th Bomb Squadrons had been placed on alert several times but had not yet seen the real "shooting war." Instead they had been assigned to fly unarmed reconnaissance missions over the routes leading out of Saigon, on the lookout for VC roadblocks. In keeping with official policy, the only American pilots engaged in combat were Farmgate air commandos.

But this time, it was not just another false

alarm. After spending two days on alert, the two squadrons were ordered to hit a suspected concentration of guerrillas near Binh Gia, thirty miles east of Saigon, where ARVN troops had been badly mauled by the Vietcong a month before. Flying at the head of the eighteen-plane formation of B-57s were Major O'Neal and his bombardier/navigator, Major Frank R. Chandler. Over the target area they made contact with the FAC orbiting in his O-1 Birddog light observation plane. The FAC warned them that he had drawn heavy ground fire just before they had arrived. But the B-57s found everything quiet. Marking their target with a round of white phosphorus smoke rockets, the FAC scurried out of range as the bombers rumbled in on the attack.

O'Neal and Chandler peeled off from the formation and swooped in on their bomb run. "After dropping four 750-pounders we heard a big secondary explosion," Chandler recalled, "meaning we'd hit an ammo cache." American jets had flown their first combat mission in South Vietnam.

## A matter of military prudence

While Lyndon Johnson and his advisers pondered the decision to bomb North Vietnam during the early months of 1965, the war in the South had grown steadily worse. Noting the appearance of larger enemy units and their willingness to engage South Vietnamese troops in open battle, General William Westmoreland voiced his concern to Washington. After a VC force virtually annihilated two South Vietnamese battalions during the battle of Binh Gia in early January, Westmoreland repeated an earlier request for authority to use U.S. jets in a combat role "as a matter of military prudence."

Washington agreed but with reservations. American jets were only to be employed to thwart a "major" attack or to protect the lives of "numbers" of Americans and even then only when it could be established that the VNAF could not perform the task. It had not been long before the topsy-turvy political scene in Saigon gave Westmoreland the opportunity to implement the new directive.

On February 19, six days after President Johnson sanctioned Rolling Thunder, a coup attempt again paralyzed the South Vietnamese command. It was that same day that Westmoreland sent Maj. O'Neal's B-57s on their first combat mission. With Ky's planes involved in the duel for political control in Saigon, the VNAF was unable to mount any of its scheduled air strikes for over a week as Ky maintained his Skyraiders on "coup alert." Westmoreland plugged the gap with U.S. aircraft.

On the twenty-fourth, an ARVN Ranger battalion and its American advisers were ambushed by a large guer-

rilla force near An Khe. Westmoreland sent USAF B-57s and F-100s to the rescue. The jets pounded the Vietcong force, keeping them at bay, while U.S. Army helicopters swooped in and evacuated the 220 survivors.

In a press statement issued in Saigon that day, U.S. officials acknowledged the use of American jets in combat but tried to play down the move's significance. It was labeled as a reinforcing measure "in keeping with the announced U.S. policy of providing maximum assistance [to South Vietnam]." The episode was quickly overshadowed by the more dramatic opening of Rolling Thunder bombing raids against North Vietnam on March 2.

On March 6, Washington removed all restrictions on the use of U.S. aircraft for combat in South Vietnam. U.S. planes were made available to support ARVN forces whenever they were needed, at the discretion of Gen. Westmoreland. Although Farmgate training would continue, all A-1s not owned by the VNAF would be repainted with USAF markings and flown by American pilots, and no longer would there need to be a Vietnamese trainee aboard.

Within a few months, the air war in South Vietnam was to become a totally American operation. Applying the same logic they had used to rationalize Rolling Thunder, Washington officials saw the commitment of American aircraft to the battle in the South as another low-risk method of pressuring Hanoi to reconsider its aggressive aims. But they soon learned that they had seriously underestimated the Communists' determination and their ability to counter American air power.

## The build-up

Once the restrictions on the use of U.S. aircraft in Vietnam were lifted, American planes poured into the country. USAF tactical fighter and bomber squadrons were deployed to South Vietnam on temporary assignments that gradually became permanent. More F-100 fighter jets were sent to augment the force at Da Nang, and a new detachment arrived at Bien Hoa. In April, USMC F-4B Phantoms flew into Da Nang to provide air support for the U.S. Marines who had arrived the month before to protect the sprawling air base.

It became immediately apparent that additional airfields would be needed to accommodate the incoming aircraft. Of the three main operational airfields in South Vietnam only two, the former French air base at Da Nang and Tan Son Nhut in Saigon, were capable of handling jet aircraft. The asphalt runways at Bien Hoa were suitable for prop-driven planes, but jets needed concrete runways. All three of the airfields were in need of extensive repairs and modifications.

In a crash program, two 10,000-foot concrete runways were laid down at Bien Hoa, and those at Da Nang and Tan Son Nhut were extended and upgraded. Airfields at

*Preceding page. A U.S. Marine F-8 Crusader swoops low to bomb a Vietcong force that had mortared U.S. positions near Da Nang on January 25, 1966.*

*A landing signal officer aboard the U.S.S.* Constellation *"talks in" an F-4 Phantom during recovery operations.*

Pleiku and Nha Trang were made jet-capable. Construction of five more airfields at Cam Ranh Bay, Phan Rang, Phu Cat, Tuy Hoa, and Chu Lai was begun. While work was underway, Westmoreland requested that carrier-based aircraft be used temporarily in South Vietnam.

Navy jets from the U.S.S. *Midway* and *Coral Sea* flew their first close air support missions in South Vietnam in April. F-8E Crusader jets of the Marine Corps fighter squadron VMF-212 aboard the U.S.S. *Oriskany* joined in soon after. Westmoreland was so impressed with their performance that he asked that a navy carrier be assigned off the coast for operations solely in South Vietnam. Adm. Sharp agreed and Dixie Station was established 100 miles southeast of Cam Ranh Bay in the South China Sea. From there, incoming navy carriers launched their planes on close air support missions in the South before heading to Yankee Station farther north. This gave incoming pilots an opportunity to familiarize themselves with the terrain and weather without being harassed by antiaircraft fire before they flew in raids against the North.

By November the huge complex under construction at Cam Ranh Bay became operational, and USAF F-4Cs of the 12th Tactical Fighter Wing set up shop there. Construction at the other new air bases was also soon complete. By the end of 1965 more than 500 USAF aircraft and 21,000 pilots, crewmen, and support personnel were stationed at eight major air bases in South Vietnam.

USAF personnel developed their own tactical support apparatus as the Americans took over air support for ground troops. Although the façade of joint USAF-VNAF command was maintained, the Americans ran the show through a fragmented network of commands and a series of ad hoc arrangements combining preexisting command structures with new ones as the situation warranted. While the air wars in North Vietnam and Laos were run from Honolulu by Adm. Sharp, CINCPAC, through a variety of local field commands, tactical air operations in the South were under the control of Gen. Westmoreland, the MACV chief. If Westmoreland needed support from navy carrier-based planes, KC-135 aerial refueling tankers stationed in Guam, or transport aircraft of the Military Airlift Command based outside South Vietnam, he had to get approval from CINCPAC through each of the subordinate commands.

Management of U.S. air units in South Vietnam was left to Major General Joseph H. Moore, who was both MACV deputy for air operations and commander of the 2d Air Division. Moore had two direct bosses, MACV in Saigon and the 13th Air Force headquarters in the Philippines, of which the 2d Air Division was a component. Although he answered to Westmoreland concerning air operations in the South, Moore was also responsible for directing the in-

*A forward air controller scours the South Vietnamese countryside for signs of the enemy from his O-1E Birddog.*

creasing number of missions over the North and Laos flown by units based in Thailand. Moore's staff was rapidly transformed from a force of less than thirty officers to a major field command.

In his dual role, Gen. Moore often found himself confronted with conflicting demands from his two superiors, with the 13th Air Force and Gen. Westmoreland frequently requesting the same aircraft for different missions. Gen. Westmoreland's continued refusal to place army air units under Moore's control only added to his problems. The fact that the two commanders had been friends since high school, however, probably helped reduce tensions between the two feuding service branches.

Air force assets in South Vietnam were divided between the four corps tactical zones. A Direct Air Support Center in each corps, manned by USAF and VNAF personnel, coordinated air support for the corps' ground forces. Each of these centers reported requests for air strikes to the Tactical Air Control Center in Saigon, which theoretically assigned air units to each task.

ARVN corps commanders jealously guarded their assigned air units, however, making long-range planning and the shifting of planes from one zone to another to meet emergency situations a lengthy and complicated process. Another complication was the U.S. Marines' independent role in I Corps. Like army aircraft, marine planes were outside of the control of Moore's network.

While these conflicting and confusing command arrangements prevailed at the top, the real control of air support operations lay in the hands of a single pilot, the forward air controller. Those pilots roamed over the battlefield in single-engined, light observation planes. Flitting around the countryside in their Cessna O-1 Birddogs, FACs were the eyes and ears of U.S. fighter pilots in South Vietnam. From the cockpits of their unarmed aircraft, FACs searched the countryside for the enemy, marked their location, and directed fighter-bombers on bombing runs. Their presence could make the difference between life and death for embattled ground troops.

Under the new guidelines given General Westmoreland, American FACs were no longer required to carry a South Vietnamese observer aboard to approve the calling in of an air strike. Observation planes on loan to the VNAF were repainted with U.S. markings and flown by USAF pilots. Another four squadrons of O-1s arrived in early spring to bolster the effort.

## A pair of good eyes and guts

A majority of the Birddog pilots were converted jet jockeys accustomed to flying at supersonic speeds. In the O-1s they found themselves puttering above the treetops at a maximum speed of 115 miles per hour. Unlike their former fighter pilot comrades, who lived in air-conditioned huts in well-defended base areas in South Vietnam or Thailand, the FACs were assigned to live with the ground troops. They operated from small, dirt airstrips that were attacked regularly and shared the dangers of the ground soldiers. The transition was a bit abrupt for some, but air force FACs quickly found pride in their jobs and earned the respect of army troops and fighter pilots alike. "You've got to hand it to those guys," said one Skyraider pilot. "Nothing between them and the VC but air. No armor, no guns, no bombs. Just a light plane, a pair of good eyes, and guts."

Each army battalion was assigned a FAC as an aerial observer. Patrolling the same territory day in and day out, FACs came to know every inch of the terrain below. "Those FACs can tell if the grass is bent one way or another," remarked a B-57 pilot. Once a target was located, a FAC began coordinating an air strike. Using one of his three radio frequencies, FM, AM, and UHF, he first called the Direct Air Support Center for his corps area to get approval for the strike. The request was then flashed to the Tactical Air Control Center at Tan Son Nhut, which dispatched fighters as needed. If it were an emergency, a FAC could call in any plane that happened to be nearby.

When the fighters arrived, a FAC really began earning his pay. Simultaneously in touch with a fire support controller on the ground and the orbiting fighters, he became ringmaster. He had to determine the exact locations of friendly and enemy forces below, then mark them and direct the fighters to the right target. His only weapons were canisters of colored smoke.

Swooping in as low as possible for precision, a FAC fired a round of white phosphorus with a small rocket or hand-held grenade to mark the enemy positions. He could also identify the positions of friendly troops or civilians in the area with different colored smoke. When a FAC could not make out the enemy position, he had to rely on the fire support coordinator on the ground.

Captain John R. Gilchrist, a veteran of 178 FAC missions, recalled one incident where he was attempting to direct a strike against a Vietcong machine-gun nest that had pinned down ground patrols on either side only forty yards away. The fire support coordinator on the ground could tell Gilchrist only that the weapon was "under a big tree." Gilchrist remembered, "I saw no less than about 2,000 trees from where I was."

Picking out a likely candidate, Gilchrist passed on his selection to the strike flight of four A-1Es. He asked the lead pilot to make a strafing run with "the shortest possible burst of 20mm cannon fire" at the tree. If it was the right one he could get confirmation from the ground coor-

*A FAC pulls up after marking enemy positions near Pleiku with a white phosphorous ("Willie Peter") smoke rocket.*

77

dinator. If not he could be sending in the Skyraiders to fire on friendly troops. "He rolled in and I held my breath," said Gilchrist, "and I'm sure that the guys down there ducked their heads. I was quite relieved when I heard, 'That's the one!' The fighters then did away with the gun position. All this was within 100 feet of friendly units, the personification of close air support."

On preplanned air strikes, FACs played a game of cat and mouse with the guerrillas to avoid tipping them off. Usually they would arrive at the briefed area half an hour ahead of time. "We mosey around and then move on down the road," said one FAC. "When the time is right, we move back into the target area and—zapp!—in goes the smoke and in come the fighters."

Guerrillas hated the "death bringers" that circled overhead. They were reluctant to fire first on the unarmed planes, knowing it would only reveal their position. But once they knew they had been spotted, the Vietcong unleashed a barrage of small-arms fire. Since accuracy was crucial, when it was time to fire their marker smoke, FACs would zip in precariously low in spite of the bullets that zinged around them. Many FACs returned from a day's work to find a number of nickel- and dime-sized holes in their O-1s.

## Aerial arsenal

FACs controlled a deadly arsenal of aircraft and weaponry. Basic to their inventory were the tried and trusted general purpose bombs employed since World War I. Ranging in size from 250 to 2,000 pounds, they came in a variety of shapes depending on the amount of drag one wished to impose on a plane's air speed. With high explosives making up half their total weight, general purpose bombs were mainly used for their blast effect against "hard" targets, like bunkers or bridges.

Against concentrations of enemy soldiers, fragmentation bombs were used. Only 14 percent of the weight of these bombs was comprised of explosives; the fragmentation of their metal casing gave the bombs their destructive effect. When the charge was detonated it sprayed shrapnel in all directions. An even more lethal antipersonnel weapon was the cluster bomb unit (CBU), engineered to burst 500 feet above the ground, dispersing 600 individual bomblets over the target. Each bomblet—about the size of a golf ball—contained two ounces of explosives which, when detonated, sent 300 steel pellets (180,000 pellets per bomb) ripping through the air.

Rockets and missiles were also available in a wide

*Napalm canisters burst on Vietcong structures south of Saigon in 1965. To spread the fire over the greatest area, napalm was dropped at low dive angles by aircraft flying as low as 100 feet.*

An A-1 Skyraider of the 1st Air Command Squadron swoops in over gutted Vietcong warehouses near Ban Me Thuot to release canisters of napalm.

variety of sizes, shapes, and destructive power. Heavyweight, five-inch air-to-ground Zuni rockets were especially good against small structures. Smaller 2.75-inch rockets, which could be fired individually or in salvos, were also used in the South. They came with three types of warheads: armor-piercing, fragmentation, and white phosphorus for marking targets.

Napalm, for all of its eventual controversy, remained the favorite weapon of fighter pilots and ground troops alike. The fiery substance could penetrate the thick jungle foliage and, since napalm created no shrapnel, it could be used for support very close to friendly troops. Napalm also exerted a devastating effect on VC morale.

Delivering this vast array of ordnance was a mixture of USAF jet fighter-bombers, old and new. B-57 Canberras provided the sole complement of medium bombers. F-100D Supersabre fighter-bombers, developed in the late 1950s, were used extensively for air support in the South. Representing the latest in aerial technology was the F-4 Phantom II, which entered operational service in the early 1960s. Designed to operate as a fighter and a bomber, the Phantom combined the capability for Mach 2 speed—or twice the speed of sound—with a hefty ordnance capacity. A typical F-4 load included eighteen 750-pound bombs or eleven 150-gallon napalm canisters or fifteen 2.75-inch

air-to-surface rockets. Phantoms were standard issue in all three service branches. A-4 Skyhawks from carriers at Dixie and Yankee Station and the USMC base in Chu Lai were also available for ground support.

The most effective weapon for close air support in South Vietnam was an old straight-winged plane with a "fan on the front." In 1960 prop-driven A-1 Skyraiders became the principal fighter aircraft of the VNAF and the USAF 1st and 602d Air Commando Squadrons. Vietnamese pilots sometimes called it *trau dien,* or "crazy water buffalo." American fliers dubbed it the Spad, after the famous World War I fighter. Rugged and reliable, the Skyraider could take an incredible amount of punishment. Its landing gear, originally designed for carrier operation, held up remarkably well on even the most primitive runways. With a liberal amount of armor plating, the Skyraider was virtually impervious to small-arms fire.

Although capable of a maximum speed of only 300 knots, the A-1 possessed greater maneuverability and endurance than its jet-powered cousins. Flying in tight circles at low altitude, a Skyraider could remain directly over its target. A jet swept by so fast it would end up a mile away before it could make a wide turn to circle back. Requiring less fuel, Spads could stay at work for over four hours while fuel-guzzling jets came and went. Sometimes

*AC-47 gunships fire on a target at night. The gunship's three machine guns each fire at 6,000 rounds per minute; one of every five rounds is a tracer, which forms the pattern in this time exposure.*

referred to as a "flying dump truck," the Skyraider could carry more than four tons of napalm, rockets, and bombs on fifteen separate attachments underneath its wings and fuselage. The entire payload of an F-100 could be carried under just one A-1 wing. Four 20MM cannons, housed inside its wings, gave the Skyraider an added edge in strafing attacks.

Its vast spectrum of firepower and superior staying power made the Skyraider ideally suited for close air support. It was so effective that it was chosen to provide air cover for downed airmen and rescue helicopters. A pilot who flew these specialized Rescue Combat Air Patrol missions came to be known by the RESCAP call sign, "Sandy." By the end of the war Sandies had assisted in the rescue of more than 1,000 downed fliers.

Another propeller-driven plane that proved its versatility in Vietnam was the venerable C-47 "Gooney Bird." In addition to its role as a cargo and troop transport, the C-47s came to play another important role. To counter the guerrillas' favorite tactic of night attacks, the South Vietnamese sometimes needed air cover around the clock. Fuel-hungry jets could not provide the sustained endur-

ance or firepower necessary for nighttime defensive operations.

Major Roland W. Terry, of the USAF Aeronautical Systems Division, set about adapting an aircraft to provide maximum firepower for a sustained period at night. At the Special Air Warfare Center at Eglin AFB in Florida, Terry mounted rapid-fire, 7.62MM Gatling guns in the windows and cargo door on the left side of a C-47. By maneuvering the plane in a constant, banking left-hand turn, using a mark on the left side of the wind screen as a sight, Terry found that he could keep the guns trained on one area as the planes circled.

He fashioned two experimental gunships, named AC-47s, and they were sent to Vietnam in December of 1964. Stocked with a supply of flares and able to remain airborne for long hours on combat alert, the AC-47 gunships were excellent for nighttime base defense. The attacking guerrillas could be pinpointed or exposed to the flare light. Then the AC-47s' three miniguns would go to work.

American combat aircraft had arrived in the nick of time. With the help of U.S. close air support, the South Vietnamese barely managed to stave off the VC spring offensive, which began in February. But the pressure continued unabated as more troops and materiel poured down the Ho Chi Minh Trail. Intelligence reports confirmed the presence of at least one entire NVA battalion in the South.

ARVN forces were still reeling from the spring onslaught when the guerrillas took advantage of the monsoon rains to launch another offensive in May. As the scattered attacks began to take shape, it became apparent that the VC were attempting to isolate provincial and district military headquarters by cutting key roads and communication lines. The Communists then concentrated their forces against the isolated installations while setting ambushes for relief forces.

## Holding the fort

Battered ARVN units threatened to collapse under the mounting pressure. Gen. Westmoreland warned the JCS in June that "enemy strength was increasing at a pace that ARVN simply could not match." Noting that five South Vietnamese battalions had been wiped out by the Vietcong, the American commander told the Joint Chiefs that the U.S. force in Vietnam would have to be increased to forty-four combat battalions to stabilize the situation. The

number of U.S. troops in South Vietnam had been gradually increasing since their arrival in March. The president had authorized the deployment of another 18,000 men in April. But Johnson was hesitant to commit large numbers of ground troops to the war.

While Washington debated his request, Westmoreland employed U.S. air power to neutralize the VC offensive. The American commander and his South Vietnamese counterparts decided on a policy of trying to hold out at each besieged garrison as long as possible. This would extend the length of time the guerrillas would be exposed to American air power, which would be dispatched to the scene to inflict the maximum numbers of casualties.

One of the biggest battles occurred ninety-five kilometers north of Saigon in Phuoc Long Province, where 300 montagnard irregulars, a 100-man Regional Forces company, and 15 U.S. Green Berets defended a small Special Forces camp at Dong Xoai. Three heavily armed Vietcong regiments launched their attack against the camp just after midnight on June 10. Outnumbered and outgunned, the surprised defenders buckled under the swift onslaught; it seemed only a matter of time before they would be overrun. Within an hour, two VNAF Skyraiders could be heard droning overhead. But even in the glow of flares dropped

*ARVN assault troops advance into heavy VC machine-gun fire during the battle for Dong Xoai in June 1965.*

by a C-47 flareship, the Skyraiders were unable to penetrate the low clouds that hung over the camp.

Just before dawn, two USAF A-1s from Bien Hoa arrived to find the area still socked in by clouds that dipped as low as 500 feet. With the desperate voices of the camp's defenders ringing in their headphones, Captains Richard Y. Costain and Doyle C. Ruff decided to throw away the rule book. Despite the decreed 1,000-foot minimum safety altitude for delivering 250-pound fragmentation bombs, the two pilots broke between the clouds and the ground on low and level bombing runs. Costain and Ruff dropped twenty-four bombs in a series of passes through a hail of automatic-weapons fire. Still the VC kept coming and soon were pouring over the walls. The camp's defenders asked the pilots to strafe the area. Swooping down in low-angle dives, their 20MM cannons blazing, the two Skyraiders sprayed 1,500 rounds at the attackers.

The guerrillas gained control of the camp as dawn broke. The remaining defenders, withdrawing to one blockhouse in a corner of the camp, pleaded desperately for more air support. Additional USAF and VNAF Skyraiders rushed to Dong Xoai, along with F-100 Supersabres. They were joined by B-57s diverted from armed reconnaissance missions over North Vietnam. Creeping in under the low clouds, the Canberras hit buildings in the town where the Vietcong had positioned automatic weapons to keep at bay any aerial relief force. Flying in behind the B-57s, the A-1s strafed and rocketed VC positions.

# Hundred-to-One Chance

In the air-conditioned Officer's Club at Pleiku, an unframed photograph of a sandy-haired air force pilot hung over the bar. It seemed an incongruous spot for a picture of a thirty-nine-year-old Mormon who did not drink anything stronger than milk. But the soft-spoken Skyraider pilot was held in high esteem by his fellow airmen of the 1st Air Commando Squadron. Major Bernard F. Fisher was the first USAF pilot in Vietnam to win the nation's highest military award—the Medal of Honor.

Bernie Fisher earned his fame in the A Shau Valley, the site of a U.S. Special Forces camp, manned by 375 montagnard irregulars and their twenty U.S. Army Green Beret advisers. On March 9, 1966, the North Vietnamese attacked the outpost near the Laotian border with a force of 3,000 regulars.

Thick clouds, blanketing the valley from 8,000 feet down to as low as 200 feet, made air support of the camp nearly impossible. But Bernie Fisher, en route to a prescheduled strike over Laos, was diverted to A Shau to see what he could do. Finding a gap in the clouds, he spent the day strafing the attackers from his twin-seated A-1E and leading other Skyraiders through the clouds to defend the camp.

During the night, a second Communist assault overran the camp's tiny airstrip and breached the barbed wire perimeter of the outpost itself. By dawn the defenders radioed that they could not hold out much longer without air support. But the North Vietnamese had prepared a lethal reception for any aerial relief force. Overnight they had transformed the mile-wide valley, which U.S. pilots had begun to call "the tube," into a deadly flak trap. More than twenty small-caliber antiaircraft guns and hundreds of automatic weapons were positioned high atop the two ridges that flanked the valley.

The next day Fisher once again found himself diverted to A Shau along with his wingman, Captain Francisco "Paco" Vasquez. Fisher's luck held. Finding another "hole" in the clouds, he and Vasquez plunged through followed by two other Skyraiders of the 602d Air Commando Squadron piloted by Major Dafford W. "Jump" Meyers and Captain Hubert King.

Fisher led the four planes down "the tube" on their first strafing pass. It did not take long for the North Vietnamese gunners to find their range. A burst of machine-gun fire shattered Capt. King's wind screen, missing him by inches. Unable to see through the cracked canopy, King pulled back up through the clouds and out of the valley.

Hurtling through the gauntlet of fire, Fisher and the remaining two Skyraider pilots "hosed down" the valley walls with their 20MM cannons. But as they banked around for a second pass, "Jump" Meyers felt his plane lurch beneath him. What felt like 37MM rounds had slammed into his plane. Smoke began filling the cockpit as Meyers's engine sputtered, sparked, and then stalled out completely.

"I've been hit and hit hard," he radioed. "Roger," answered Bernie Fisher, "you're on fire and burning clear back past your tail." Realizing that he was too low to bail out, Meyers knew his only chance was to try and crash land. "I'll have to put her down on the strip," he told Fisher.

Peering through the curling smoke, Meyers glided his Skyraider toward the emergency airstrip below with Fisher talking him down. Seeing Meyers was heading in too fast to stop on the short strip, Fisher told him to pull up his landing gear and belly the plane in. Meyers had jettisoned his bombs but had been unable to drop his center line fuel tank, which exploded on impact in a billow of flames.

Careening down the runway, Meyers's Skyraider left behind a trail of fuel before it finally ran off the runway and skidded to a stop. A horrified Fisher watched as the "flame just followed him right down, caught up with him and the A-1 turned into a huge ball of fire." For nearly a minute, Fisher could not detect any sign of life below.

But Meyers had escaped the A-1 be-

American planes continued to pummel the exposed guerrillas through the morning as a relief force of four battalions prepared for a helicopter assault. One of the battalions landed right in the middle of a Vietcong reserve force two miles north of the town and was cut to pieces. Vietnamese Rangers, supported by U.S. Skyraiders and F-100s, finally battled their way into the town to relieve the garrison.

Friendly casualties sustained during the battle for Dong Xoai were high, with more than 416 killed and 233 missing, including many civilians caught in the crossfire. The South Vietnamese uncovered at least 300 VC bodies and estimated that another 300 had been killed during the air strikes, which had rained more than 1,000 tons of bombs,

incendigel, rockets, and .50-caliber machine-gun rounds down upon the guerrillas. During 644 sorties over Dong Xoai, the U.S. lost two UH-1 helicopter gunships to enemy ground fire. Another thirteen gunships, five F-100s, and thirteen A-1s were damaged.

According to Gen. Westmoreland, American air power had "turned the tide of battle." One of the wounded Americans evacuated from Dong Xoai put it more succinctly: "I owe my life to the air force."

## Airpower on the offensive

American air power was virtually all that stood between victory and defeat in the summer of 1965. Without ade-

fore it blew up. Frantically unbuckling his seat harness and stripping off his parachute after touchdown, Meyers prepared to make a break for it. Sliding back the side window, he spotted an opening in the sheet of flames. Climbing out onto the right wing, Meyers ran to the edge and tumbled to the ground. Picking his way through a jumble of expended shell casings, rocket pods, and empty fuel drums, he jumped into a weed-filled ditch on the side of the runway nearest the camp.

Fisher made a low-level pass and was relieved to see Meyers waving to him from his hiding place. After radioing for a rescue chopper, Fisher and Vasquez began strafing North Vietnamese troops who began taking an interest in the crashed Skyraider. They were quickly joined by two more A-1Es piloted by Captains Denis B. Hague and Jon I. Lucas. But after ten minutes, the rescue helicopter was still twenty minutes away.

Meyers was in trouble. Despite the strafing attacks, North Vietnamese soldiers were closing in on his hiding place. "There was at least a company of enemy troops on the top of the bank, but they couldn't see me," he recalled. "I think they thought I was dead."

Convinced that the North Vietnamese would get to Meyers before the rescue chopper arrived, Fisher made a daring decision. He was going to land and pick up Meyers himself. "I'm going in," he radioed the other three pilots.

His chances were slim. The runway was a mass of torn and jagged pierced-steel planking, mortar shell holes, and cluttered with debris, not to mention being surrounded by enemy guns. "I gave him

a hundred-to-one chance of pulling it off," Capt. Lucas remembered.

With Vasquez, Hague, and Lucas maintaining a continuous pattern of strafing runs to keep the North Vietnamese pinned down, Fisher began his approach. A gust of wind kicked up a cloud of dust that momentarily threw off his bearings. When the dust cleared, the Skyraider's wheels touched down, but Fisher saw he was too far down the runway to stop. Dodging and weaving through the wreckage, Fisher gunned his engine and sailed back into the sky. Bringing the Skyraider around, he tried again from the opposite direction.

Running in at 100 feet through a hail of ground fire, Fisher touched back down on the scarred strip. Pulling up the flaps and hitting the brakes as hard as he could, Fisher skidded down the length of the runway, stopping just short of a cluster of fifty-five-gallon fuel drums stacked at the end of the airstrip. Quickly turning the plane around, he taxied back down through the obstacle course. Oblivious to the bullets zinging past him, Fisher brought the Skyraider parallel to Meyers's position and set his parking brakes.

Waving frantically from the ditch, Meyers could not believe what was happening. "It never occurred to me that somebody would be crazy enough to put an A-1E down on that strip." Although they were out of ammo, the other three Skyraiders continued to buzz enemy troops around the runway. The mere sound of their engines was enough to keep the soldiers' heads down.

Crawling from the ditch, Meyers

sprinted toward the idling Skyraider. Fisher had just unbuckled his harness and slid back his canopy to climb out and look for Meyers when he caught a glimpse of something moving in his rearview mirror. "I looked in the mirror and saw two little red, beady eyes trying to crawl up the back of the wing." Meyers's eyes, red from exposure to smoke, "looked like neons" to the startled Fisher.

Clambering across the wing to the edge of the cockpit, Meyers began crawling in head first. Grabbing the seat of his pants, Fisher gave him a helping hand. Landing in the unoccupied seat in the twin-seater, Meyers said to Fisher, "You dumb son of a bitch! Now neither of us will get out of here!"

Fisher did not stop to argue. Ramming the throttle forward, he danced the plane around shell holes and debris. After absorbing nineteen bullet holes, the Skyraider sailed down the runway and surged skyward. Meyers, his scorched flight suit reeking of smoke and caked with mud, gave his rescuer a hug as they climbed out of the valley. "We couldn't help turning to each other and laughing all the way to Pleiku," said Fisher.

The other three Skyraiders made it safely back to Pleiku also. Ground crewmen counted eight bullet holes in Lucas's plane and twenty-two in Vasquez's. Despite their valiant attempt, the camp at A Shau fell later that day after sixty-nine of the survivors were airlifted out by marine helicopters. But at Pleiku there was rejoicing over Fisher's daring rescue. Meyers offered him a year's supply of whiskey for saving his life. But the teetotaling Fisher settled for a camera instead.

*The effects of defoliation, used by the U.S. to deny the Communists their jungle sanctuaries. Above. An unsprayed mangrove forest. Right. This forest was hit with defoliants three years before the picture was taken.*

quate ground forces, the allies relied on their advantage in aerial firepower. Usually when the Vietcong struck, U.S. planes raced to the rescue with tons of bombs, napalm, rockets, and cannon fire.

For pilots, close air support operations were probably the most satisfying missions they performed. Flying high above the battlefield, insulated in their womb-like cockpits, they often had no way of knowing how effective their bombing or strafing attacks were. Supporting other Americans and South Vietnamese on the ground gave pilots a sense that they were accomplishing something in the war. "You could hear them on your radio," recalled one B-57 bombardier/navigator, "and they tell you: 'We need you.'" Occasionally a pilot returned to base to find an army man waiting to thank him for saving his life.

But close air support missions and strikes flown in answer to requests from FACs or ground commanders accounted for less than half of all air combat missions in South Vietnam. The rapid build-up in U.S. aircraft also provided the means to take the offensive against the Vietcong. Sixty-five percent of all combat air operations were

preplanned strikes against guerrilla strongholds and supply routes. Such "spoiling attacks" denied the Communists safe havens where they could train and rest troops, store ammunition and food, and plan offensive operations. Air commanders relied on aerial reconnaissance or intelligence reports to pinpoint their targets. The air force also expanded the practice, begun in the early 1960s, of establishing "free fire zones."

With the approval of province and district chiefs, air intelligence officers marked off areas that were known to be controlled by the Vietcong or uninhabited by friendly civilians. Once a free fire zone was established, suspected targets in the area could be attacked from the air without advance clearance from local officials. They came to be used as dumping grounds for pilots returning from missions who had to unload their unexpended bombs and rockets before landing.

U.S. officials gave their assurances that free fire zones were indeed free of friendly civilians, but stories of friendly casualties continued to appear. One of the great problems of the Vietnam War was that it was difficult and often im-

possible, whether on the ground or in the air, to separate the guerrillas from the local populace. At times whole villages were evacuated to create free fire zones. Villagers were warned to leave the area by aerial leaflet drops or loudspeaker announcements from an orbiting helicopter. They were told that if they did not, they would be considered "hostile" and would suffer the consequences. Sometimes this was a matter of interpretation. Free fire zones often contained hamlets that local officials wrote off as Vietcong strongholds, reasoning that the villagers were VC sympathizers and therefore the enemy. To try and shake the image of indiscriminate bombing, the Department of Defense renamed the areas "Specified Strike Zones" and tightened up criteria for their establishment.

## Operation Ranch Hand

Aerial defoliation was also used to uncover guerrilla sanctuaries and isolate the VC from the local population. President Kennedy had authorized an experimental program of aerial spraying of herbicides alongside roads, rail lines, and outside military bases to deny the Vietcong use of the thick jungle to conceal troop movements and ambushes. Three C–123s, fitted with 1,000-gallon chemical tanks and

spray bars under their wings, had begun spraying in 1962 under an operation called Ranch Hand.

As the war widened in 1965, aerial spraying increased dramatically, and Ranch Hand flights were employed in tandem with offensive air operations. The C–123s began spraying suspected guerrilla strongholds hidden under triple-canopied jungle growth. Herbicides were also used against crops believed to be grown for or by the Vietcong.

Ranch Hand C–123s dispensed a variety of color-coded herbicides. Agent Orange, introduced early in 1965, proved the most effective and was used most extensively. An average 11,000-pound load could be dispersed over a 300-acre area in about four minutes. Within days the leaves started turning brown. Entire trees died in only five to six weeks. Over the door of the Ranch Hand ready room at Tan Son Nhut hung a plaque bearing the inscription: "Only You Can Prevent Forests."

Herbicide spraying became extremely controversial. Critics equated the practice to the use of poison gas in World War I, and the Vietcong and Hanoi exploited it for its propaganda value. Local peasants did not comprehend the purpose of herbicide spraying. All they knew was that their crops were being destroyed. Vietcong claims that the chemicals were poisonous led to widespread fear among the people, which sometimes resulted in defections of whole villages to the Vietcong.

Washington believed the advantages of the program outweighed the political disadvantages, assuring critics that the sprayings were as safe as dusting crops with insecticides and that the defoliants were dispensed under restrictions that also applied in the U.S. More than 157,000 acres in South Vietnam were sprayed in 1965 alone, 42 percent for crop destruction. By 1967 Ranch Hand operations reached their peak—more than 1.5 million acres were treated that year.

It was not until 1967 that moral and ecological objections to the use of herbicides forced the Pentagon to reassess the program. Scientific studies claimed that 2,4,5-T, the actual defoliant chemical in Agent Orange, produced harmful side effects in humans. As the objections of the scientific community grew, the Pentagon began gradually reducing herbicide operations.

Years after the Vietnam War, scientists were still trying to determine the toxic properties of Agent Orange. Soldiers and civilians who were exposed to the herbicide reported recurring side effects ranging from skin rashes to birth defects in their children, and many filed lawsuits against the government and manufacturers of Agent Orange. But in the mid-sixties, Ranch Hand pilots flew their defoliation missions oblivious to such concerns.

## Counterinsurgency from 30,000 feet

Even with the creation of free fire zones and the aid of Ranch Hand defoliation efforts, Westmoreland found that bombing Vietcong strongholds with tactical fighter-bombers was "relatively ineffective." For one thing, it was difficult to assemble sufficient numbers of planes to make the strikes worthwhile. For another, constant calls for emergency air support hampered any coordinated efforts. Also, the guerrillas countered the effect of interdiction strikes by dispersing their camps over large areas. These frustrations caused Westmoreland to ask for more firepower, and he requested authority to use B-52 jet bombers.

Although the B-52 Stratofortresses of the Strategic Air Command were designed primarily for long-range nuclear deterrence, their crews began extensive training in the delivery of conventional bombs in 1964 for possible use in Vietnam. The B-52F was modified with external bomb racks to carry twenty-four 750-pound bombs in addition to the twenty-five loaded in its internal bomb bay. According to the SAC commander, General Thomas S. Powers, successful tactical tests of the B-52 proved that SAC had "the capability to deliver conventional weapons . . . on short notice, accurately, and from bases far beyond the reach of any limited war opponent."

Impressed by SAC's newfound capability, the JCS and Secretary McNamara agreed to dispatch a force of B-52s to Guam for possible use over Vietnam. In June of 1965 the

B-52s were released for combat missions, but only in South Vietnam. Thirty of the eight-engined, swept-wing B-52s from the 2d and 320th Bomb Wings roared off the runway at Anderson AFB in Guam on June 18 in their first combat mission; its code name was Arc Light. It proved an inauspicious debut. Two of the giant bombers collided while refueling from KC-135 aerial tankers and plunged in flames into the South China Sea. Only four of the twelve crewmen were rescued. Another of the jets was forced to turn back with mechanical problems.

The remaining twenty-seven B-52s thundered over South Vietnam and swept in high above the jungle northwest of Saigon. Their target was a long-time VC stronghold called the "Iron Triangle." Intelligence indicated the guerrillas were massing there for an offensive operation. In one pass, the B-52s carpeted the jungle stronghold with more than a million pounds of high explosives. American

officials claimed the strike destroyed nearly forty barracks buildings, a communications center, and 25,000 pounds of rice. In addition, an enemy tunnel complex was ripped apart. The Arc Light mission, asserted a U.S. spokesman, "demonstrated that there were no inviolable VC zones."

There were some who questioned the logic of using the B-52s against guerrillas. Noting that only two Vietcong bodies had been discovered on the site of the attack, some journalists criticized the costly $20 million mission. A *Time* magazine correspondent equated it to "using a sledgehammer to kill gnats."

But Westmoreland and the air force defended Arc Light as an invaluable method of keeping the Vietcong off balance. Five more Arc Light missions were flown in July and within months the B-52 strikes became a daily occurrence over South Vietnam. Although he admitted that a lack of

hard intelligence made it difficult to gauge the effectiveness of Arc Light, Westmoreland cited evidence of increased enemy desertion rates and a general lowering of morale. Another MACV official indicated that the B-52 strikes had forced the VC to keep on the move, making them more visible.

The SAC B-52s held a semi-independent status in the command structure. Targets were recommended by army units and the 2d Air Division on the basis of intelligence and aerial recon reports. Westmoreland then selected from those recommendations and passed them on to SAC headquarters in Omaha, Nebraska, which retained operational control of its bombers. Second Air Division head-

*A scene that was to become common. Bomb craters scar an area in the Mekong River Delta after an early Arc Light strike by B-52 Stratofortresses in 1965.*

quarters was disgruntled by this further fragmentation of its command, but SAC retained control, acceding only to the degree of setting up an advance SAC liaison office in Saigon.

Arc Light strikes employed a carpet bombing technique, which had been used during World War II. Bombs were released in a set pattern designed for maximum coverage of the target area. In a matter of seconds a flight of six B-52s could scatter 150 tons of bombs, saturating an area the size of the mall in Washington, D.C., from the Potomac to the Capitol Building. Early in 1966 a number of B-52Ds were modified to carry an even deadlier bomb load of 108 500-pound bombs, 27 tons of high explosives.

Carpet bombing could change the face of the earth. A B-52 mission left behind miles of solid lines of craters. From the ground, the devastation was awesome. Uprooted trees littered the landscape. Matted undergrowth had been blown away like so many tumbleweeds, sometimes to reveal scorched buildings and collapsed tunnel networks.

Ground troops sweeping targets after a strike often uncovered large supply caches but rarely discovered enemy bodies. The Vietcong practice of carrying off their dead and wounded made it virtually impossible to gauge enemy casualties. This left in question the military effectiveness of Arc Light missions, but reports of "trails of blood, used bandages, and the smell of death" lingering in bombed areas led U.S. officers to believe that the B-52s were indeed hurting the guerrillas. Releasing their bombs from 30,000 feet, the B-52s were invisible and almost inaudible. "They wedded surprise with devastating powers," said Westmoreland, who called B-52s "the weapon the enemy feared most." Indeed, one VC prisoner described Arc Light strikes as "the chain of thunders!"

Encouraged by initial reports, Arc Light operations expanded rapidly. By the end of 1966, SAC B-52s had flown nearly 800 missions, dropping more than 130,000 tons of bombs against targets in South Vietnam. By 1968 they were flying almost 60 sorties a day.

Not all Americans were confident or impressed with Arc Light operations. Retired air force chief of staff, Gen. Curtis LeMay, thought them an "anomaly," pointing out that B-52s were not being employed in the role for which they had been designed, long-range strategic bombing operations against the enemy's homeland. Washington officials, however, were hesitant to expose the B-52s to North Vietnam's air defenses. The loss of one of the multimillion dollar bombers would present Hanoi with a propaganda coup. Instead the U.S. was sending tactical fighter-bombers, designed to provide air support for ground troops, for the different mission of striking strategic targets in the North. This represented a reversal of the traditional roles of strategic and tactical aircraft. The air force was using smaller planes to hit bigger targets in North Vietnam while employing its huge bombers against smaller targets in the South.

Relying on often sketchy intelligence reports or outdated aerial reconnaissance photos, B-52s would blanket an area with bombs in hopes of destroying a few bamboo huts full of rice and ammunition. Gen. McConnell, the air force chief of staff, admitted that the chances of a success were only about fifty/fifty. "Sometimes we bomb where there is no real enemy, no real target. But it's better to take a chance than to leave them untouched." This kind of reasoning dramatized the dependence of U.S. tactics in Vietnam on aerial firepower instead of ground troops. The practice fit well with Washington's early objective of denying the Vietcong victory without risking American lives. But could air power alone do the job?

## Air mobility comes of age

With the backing of the Joint Chiefs, Westmoreland's forty-four battalion troop request was finally approved after an intense debate in Washington. On July 28 President Johnson announced the deployment of an additional 50,000 men to Vietnam. Initially, the Americans had adopted an "enclave strategy," taking over the defense of coastal towns and rice-producing areas, freeing ARVN for offensive operations. But as the South Vietnamese continued to crumble, U.S. troops were put on the offensive. "We had to forget about enclaves," Westmoreland later wrote in his memoirs, "and take the war to the enemy."

Among the first American units deployed to Vietnam was the army's 1st Cavalry Division (Airmobile), under the command of Major General Harry W.O. Kinnard. With its 16,000 men and more than 400 support aircraft, the 1st Cavalry represented the latest concept in airmobile tactics, which the army had been developing since the Korean War.

Expanding on the airborne parachute assault tactics of World War II, army commanders had begun testing the concept of highly mobile air cavalry units. The first such test group, the 11th Air Assault Division, was activated at Fort Benning, Georgia, on February 15, 1963. Under the command of General Kinnard, the division was molded into a completely air mobile, self-sustaining fighting force. Its UH-1D Huey helicopters could ferry one-third of its entire complement of infantrymen into battle in one airlift. Originally nicknamed the "slick ship," because it was unarmed, or "slick," the UH-1D soon carried two M60 machine guns mounted in its cargo doors. Additional firepower for the airborne armada came from UH-1B gunships, which provided aerial artillery for the division. Once the infantry established itself on the ground, CH-47 Chinook cargo choppers were to follow with back-up troops and heavy artillery. Each Chinook could lug a 105MM howitzer and its ammunition and crew wherever it was needed. Rounding out the division's aircraft were a half dozen armed OV-1 Mohawk observation aircraft and a number of OH-13 light observation helicopters.

*Flares dropped by U.S. Air Force planes illuminate the Special Forces camp at Plei Me, besieged by Communist forces on October 19, 1965. During the seven-day battle, U.S. planes dropped 1 million pounds of bombs in support of the base.*

In July 1965 the unit was redesignated the 1st Cavalry Division (Airmobile) and was ordered to prepare for combat duty. The 1st Cav arrived in Vietnam in early September. Gen. Westmoreland immediately deployed them to An Khe in the central highlands, where intelligence had discerned increased enemy activity.

For years the central highlands, with dense jungles, fields of shoulder-high elephant grass, and forbidding mountain ranges, had been a safe haven for the guerrillas. Allied ground forces had only been able to hold isolated outposts along the region's few roads. One of the outposts was the Special Forces camp at Plei Me, forty kilometers southwest of Pleiku near the Cambodian border.

On October 19 a large force of heavily armed troops hit Plei Me under the cover of a fierce mortar barrage. For six days the camp's 400 montagnard defenders and twelve

Green Berets held on with the support of U.S. fighter planes (see sidebar, next page). An ARVN relief column finally battled its way through a series of ambushes to relieve the camp on the twenty-sixth.

What was initially thought to be an isolated Vietcong attack turned out to have been the first move of an offensive. Captured enemy documents and interrogations of prisoners revealed that three NVA regiments had infiltrated across the border and set up headquarters in the Chu Pong mountain area along the Ia Drang Valley in preparation for an attack to gain control of the central highlands and cut South Vietnam in two.

General Westmoreland decided to launch a preemptive counteroffensive of his own. On October 27, the day after the siege at Plei Me was lifted, General Kinnard received his orders: The 1st Cavalry was to "find, fix, and destroy" the enemy in the central highlands.

# Rescue at Plei Me

### by Kevin Generous

At 2:00 A.M. on the pitch-black morning of October 22, 1965, U.S. Air Force Captain Melvin Elliott of Glendale, Arizona, flew his A–1E Skyraider at 10,000 feet over North Vietnamese ground units surrounding Plei Me Special Forces Camp in South Vietnam's central highlands. Elliott and his wingman had rendezvoused with a C–123 flareship and were awaiting the arrival of an army CV–2 Caribou cargo ship on an aerial resupply mission to besieged Plei Me. Although the primary mission of Elliott's 1st Commando Squadron—based in Bien Hoa, 325 kilometers south—was to train South Vietnamese pilots in the propeller-driven fighter-bombers, when necessary the squadron flew close air support for isolated Special Forces camps in the mountains near the Laotian border. During his ten months in South Vietnam, Captain Elliott had racked up over 200 such combat missions.

Three days before, 2,200 troops of the North Vietnamese Army 33d Regiment had assaulted Plei Me in the initial phase of a dry season offensive designed to expand Hanoi's control over the strategic central highlands before American combat forces arrived in strength. However, Plei Me, a dusty border camp 345 kilome-

ters from Saigon, was proving to be a tough nut to crack; the NVA failure to overrun quickly the crude triangular fortress would soon turn the tactical initiative over to the newly arrived U.S. Army 1st Cavalry Division (Airmobile). By late November, the 1st Air Cav would engage and defeat three NVA regiments—including the 33d—in the bloody battle in the Ia Drang Valley.

This was Elliott's second trip over Plei Me. Following the initial North Vietnamese assault, Elliott had led a flight of four Skyraiders in support of the twelve American Green Berets and 450 montagnard irregulars inside the Plei Me compound. After seeing North Vietnamese infantry hurl themselves in human waves against Plei Me's walls, Elliott was only mildly surprised by the camp commander's desperate instructions to the Skyraiders: "Bomb our perimeter . . . use napalm if you have it." The Skyraider pilots obliged, dropping their canisters within yards of the defenders—at times from altitudes of only 100 feet—temporarily breaking up the Communist attack.

Now, on Elliott's second mission three days later, the situation at Plei Me was still critical. NVA mortars and rockets had zeroed in on the camp's dirt airstrip, preventing resupply or reinforcement by helicopter. With ground reinforcements bogged down by a North Vietnamese ambush thirty kilometers east, resupply consisted of parachute drops by CV–2 Caribou aircraft. Elliott grew impatient as he circled over Plei Me for ninety minutes awaiting the nightly Caribou run. And, with his fuel tanks nearly empty, Elliott discovered the Caribou mission had been scrubbed. The captain radioed the C–123 flareship of his intention to drop his load of two 750-pound napalm and six cluster bomb unit canisters—standard ordnance for night missions—on enemy positions and head back to base at Bien Hoa.

Even with the sky lit by flares, Elliott "could only see the outline of the compound—nothing else" as he eased his

heavy plane into a strafing run, firing 20MM cannon bursts from his four wing-mounted cannons. As the thirty-six-year-old pilot pulled the Skyraider out of its low-level run and away from the target he thought, "God, it's awfully bright." Glancing to his left, Elliott saw his entire left wing erupt in flames, caused either by a well-directed antiaircraft burst or, perhaps, by leaking hydraulic fluid ignited from the muzzle blast of his own guns.

"I'm on fire," the captain told his wingman, who was still a mile behind Elliott starting his own run. Realizing his chances of limping to the nearest base, thirty miles away at Pleiku, were nil, Elliott radioed, ". . . will attempt to maneuver over the compound and bail out." But the flames rapidly burned off the wing's surface panels, searing through the control cables. Wrestling in vain with the controls, the veteran pilot realized "there was nothing left of the ailerons." As the heavy airplane slowly began rolling over on its back, Elliott slid back the canopy and sent his last transmission to the nearby C–123: "Mayday, mayday . . . on fire and abandoning aircraft."

Popping open the seat harness, Elliott felt the wind blast tear off his flight helmet as he dropped like a stone from the stricken aircraft. Clearing the plane's tail, Elliott opened his chute at 800 feet, conscious only of his extremely low altitude and the bright glow of a newly dropped flare.

Elliott's parachute snagged on a tree, leaving him dangling thirty feet above the jungle floor. "I swung over, caught a vine, and climbed to the ground," he said. In his haste to avoid capture, he abandoned the survival gear strapped to his parachute harness, taking only a .38 pistol with five rounds, a battery-operated strobe light, and a two-way radio. Elliott's maps and M16 rifle—with all his extra ammo—had gone down with the Skyraider. His most prized possession by far, however, was his survival radio. Elliott realized that he had been lucky on this mission: Normally, A–1 pilots in Elliott's squadron were not guaranteed two-way radios. Because of an acute shortage, pilots were usually issued only homing beacons.

The downed flier contacted his wingman, who protectively stayed overhead until, perilously short of fuel himself, he flew off in the direction of Plei Me. Thus oriented, Elliott intended to walk into the relative safety of the compound. After hiking through dark jungles seeking the besieged camp, the pilot suddenly found himself in the center of "the biggest damned gunfight I'd ever heard." Amid whizzing bullets and crumping mortars, Elliott scrambled for refuge inside the top of a thick tree blown down by mortars. There he burrowed in for the night.

At dawn the next day, U.S. Army Captain William Rainey circled Plei Me at 1,500 feet in a single-engine O–1 Birddog. A FAC with the 219th Aviation Company in Pleiku, Rainey's job was to direct tactical air strikes over the camp and provide observation of enemy troop movements a safe distance away from NVA antiaircraft guns. Rainey also flew general utility missions and performed aerial radio relays for outlying Special Forces camps like Plei Me. In fact, Rainey had the distinction of flying the last aircraft off Plei Me's dirt airstrip only hours prior to the North Vietnamese attack. That morning, the small O–1's powerful radios were routinely monitoring frequency 243.0—the air emergency channel.

"Birddog, Birddog . . . this is Elliott, over," crackled the radio. Although engaged in his FAC duties, Rainey heard the desperate message. "You could tell he was talking at a whisper," Rainey recalled. He heard the transmission twice more before realizing that the message was directed at his aircraft. Rainey answered Elliott, quickly fixed his position, and rocked his wings in recognition. "We're going to get you out," Rainey assured the downed flier.

Over the next twelve hours, the FAC helped direct the air force pilot across the scarred landscape, from crater to crater, skirting the fierce firefights waged around Plei Me. At times the Green Berets inside Plei Me compound witnessed Elliott scampering near the jungle's fringe to reach a pickup zone southwest of the camp perimeter. An attempt by the Green Berets to link up with the pilot failed because of heavy North Vietnamese gunfire.

Shortly after dark Elliott heard the distinctive sound of a U.S. Army Huey helicopter combing the area. Emerging from the jungle and standing on an exposed trail, Elliott held up the bright strobe light. The chopper circled once in the darkness, then turned on its spotlight. Elliott could see a rope dangling from the Huey's door. Just as rescue appeared imminent, an enemy machine gun erupted, its tracers stabbing toward the hovering chopper. Both man and machine "got the hell out of there," recalled Elliott, who dove back into the jungle.

Lying still in the bush, with one arm flung over his face, Elliott heard an investigating North Vietnamese patrol along the trail. A crisscrossing search beam passed perilously close—within twenty feet—to the camouflaged pilot. The patrol reversed direction and swung the beam again close by, then receded into the jungle. Elliott spent a second night nestled at the base of a giant tree.

The familiar sound of a twin-engine C–47 greeted Elliott at dawn. Scanning the sky, the captain spotted an AC–47 Spooky gunship, its gunports open, about to fire on the area. Elliott "tore around that tree like a squirrel," putting it between himself and the gunship. But the AC–47 fired only a few rounds and departed. Elliott later discovered that engine trouble had aborted its mission.

By afternoon the flier had raised another O–1, whose pilot insisted on marking Elliott's position with smoke grenades. "You really don't need to do that," said Elliott, who feared that the smoke would only attract the NVA. But the O–1 pilot

missed his mark and soon departed. Elliott hunkered down to await the chopper that he had been told was "en route," only to be informed shortly afterward that his rescue chopper had been "diverted to a higher priority." By now Elliott's situation was no longer unique; other U.S. pilots had been downed near Plei Me as more U.S. aircraft had been committed to the camp's relief.

Discouraged for the moment at not being "a higher priority," Elliott washed up in a creek and felt better. As he continued to walk through the jungle, his heart nearly stopped as a 150-pound wild boar suddenly charged out of a bamboo thicket. Running in the other direction, Elliott found a patch of tall elephant grass and passed the time eavesdropping on his squadron mates' radio chatter as the Skyraiders flew past to drop napalm on nearby North Vietnamese emplacements.

Elliott's turn for rescue at last arrived. A twin-rotored U.S. Air Force HH–43 Husky rescue helicopter lumbered over the clearing escorted by two Huey gunships firing their rockets. Nearly blown over by the terrific prop wash, scratched up and punchy from his thirty-six-hour ordeal, Captain Elliott climbed onto the Husky's wheel and was hauled aboard the chopper for the short trip to Pleiku.

After his recovery, Elliott was whisked away to 1st Special Forces Group headquarters in Nha Trang for detailed debriefing. There he was asked by a curious intelligence officer whether he "was scared at any time" while surrounded by a full regiment of North Vietnamese regulars in pitched battle.

"Only for about thirty-six hours," Elliott replied wearily.

Kevin Generous, a defense policy analyst in Washington, D.C., has researched and written extensively on America's early involvement in the Vietnam War, including the battle of the Ia Drang Valley in 1965.

# Air cavalry at Ia Drang

Kinnard's helicopters immediately began moving westward from Plei Me in pursuit of the NVA troops who were withdrawing to their border retreats. OH-13 observation helicopters, with their Plexiglas bubble canopies, scoured the jungle for signs of the force. UH-1B gunships followed, ready to pin down any exposed units until the slicks could ferry in infantrymen.

The reconnaissance effort paid off on November 15 when Captain William P. Gillette in his OH-13 spotted movement along the Tae River, five miles west of Plei Me. Within a few minutes, an airborne rifle platoon was landed nearby and began a sweep of the area. They stumbled upon and captured a regimental-size hospital hidden in a dry creek bed.

Later that afternoon the North Vietnamese counterattacked. The ensuing skirmish was fought at such close quarters that orbiting gunships were unable to provide supporting fire for fear of hitting their own men. After reinforcements were airlifted in, the North Vietnamese retreated, leaving seventy-six dead behind; another fifty-seven were taken prisoner.

Sporadic skirmishes continued during the next two weeks. On the fourteenth, the 1st Battalion, 7th Cavalry, was ordered to sweep the hills at the base of the Chu Pong Mountains to cut the enemy's escape route into Cambodia. The battalion commander, Lieutenant Colonel Harold G. Moore, chose as a landing zone a clearing no more than 110 by 220 yards. He gave the landing zone the code name X-Ray.

Lieutenant Colonel John R. Stoner, the USAF's air liaison officer with the 1st Cav, coordinated a prelanding strike by artillery and air units. To cover the troopers' landing, half an hour before the assault an artillery barrage and UH-1B gunships plastered LZ X-Ray and a few other decoy sites. Seconds after the barrage ended, Major Bruce P. Crandall led sixteen slick ships into the still-smoking LZ. The airlift commander settled his chopper down in the tall elephant grass. M16s in hand, Colonel Moore and his men jumped out of Crandall's helicopters, spraying the nearby tree line with gunfire to counter any attempted ambush. There was no return fire.

Not until that afternoon did Col. Moore realize what he was up against. Ground reconnaissance patrols sent out by Moore had run into a large enemy force moving down from the Chu Pong Mountains into the Ia Drang Valley. Realizing he had run into a superior force, Moore ordered his men to regroup at X-Ray and form a defensive perimeter. Halting the airlift, he then called in air support. For the next three days the 1st Cavalry, closely supported by U.S. air power, found itself engaged in the bloodiest slugging match of the war up to that time.

UH-1B gunships saturated the area outside X-Ray with rocket barrages. More support came from USAF Sky-raiders on alert nearby. Carrying two tons of ordnance apiece and equipped with radios that could monitor army command and fire support frequencies, the A-1s began bombing and strafing the enemy. The pilots had to be accurate; often they dropped their bombs within 110 yards of friendly troops. The platoon leader of a surrounded unit said, "Those planes came in as close as we wanted them to. At times I could reach up and almost touch them. . . . They saved our necks."

During the battle, B-57s, F-100s, and F-102 Delta Daggers joined the air assault, as did navy and marine F-4 Phantoms. Col. Stoner in his role as air liaison officer was hard pressed to manage the overwhelming numbers and diverse types of aircraft. Planes arrived faster than his FACs could find targets. "In several instances," said Stoner, "the pilots pleaded to strike prior to receiving approval from the ground commander."

At night the air strikes continued with the aid of C-47 flareships. Ground troops marked their perimeters with trip flares, enabling FACs on the ground to direct air strikes throughout the night within thirty yards of friendly foxholes. During the battle, UH-1Ds kept a life line open to the embattled troopers at X-Ray, ferrying in fresh troops and ammunition as well as evacuating the wounded.

On the morning of the fifteenth, the North Vietnamese launched a ferocious attack on Moore's shrunken defensive perimeter. Hand-to-hand fighting broke out in places as the enemy threatened to overrun the landing zone. But with the support of fixed-wing fighter-bombers, Huey gunships, and artillery fire, Moore's men held firm. USAF fighters flew more than 350 sorties during the battle. B-52s were also called in—the first time they were used in direct support of ground troops. Stratofortresses flew a total of 98 sorties during a five-day period, at times dropping their bombs as close as three miles to friendly troops.

Just after midnight on the sixteenth, a relief unit landed a few miles away and fought its way into X-Ray, securing the LZ for good as the enemy withdrew into the hills. After a few more isolated skirmishes, including a bloody battle at an LZ called Albany, the operation was ended on the twenty-sixth. In its thirty-five-day sweep, the 1st Cavalry had driven the enemy from the central highlands back across the border into Cambodia.

General Westmoreland proclaimed the operation "an unprecedented victory." Estimates of enemy casualties ranged from 1,500 to 3,000 killed in action. American KIAs were placed at 240. Of fifty-six aircraft hit by enemy fire, only four were shot down. "The army had a true cavalry again," Gen. Kinnard proclaimed.

Helicopter assaults, coordinated with artillery and air strikes, were to become the backbone of General Westmoreland's "search and destroy" tactics in South Vietnam. The U.S. commander considered the key to victory not in holding territory but in defeating Communist forces whenever and wherever they could be found. Large-scale of-

*Small, medium, large: OH–13 observation helicopters (front), UH–1 Slicks (middle), and CH–47 Chinooks (rear) sit on the "Golf Course" chopper pad at An Khe, the 1st Air Cavalry Division's main base, in early 1966.*

fensive operations followed in 1966 as the Americans took the war to the enemy.

## A change in strategy

Stymied in their attempt to "tip the balance" in the South by initiating conventional large-unit actions, Hanoi's leaders were forced to reassess their strategy. The continued influx of U.S. aircraft and combat troops had altered the complexion of the war. At Ia Drang, they had learned that they could not compete in a pitched battle with the Americans' overwhelming superiority in firepower. At Hanoi's insistence, Communist forces in the South returned to the guerrilla tactics that had proven so successful against the French. Theirs would be a strategy of protracted war aimed at wearing down the Americans. Hanoi believed the U.S. would grow tired of a long and bloody conflict.

Operating in smaller units from their bases along the Cambodian border, the Communists avoided pitched battles when the odds were not in their favor. The appearance of the recon planes and prestrike aerial bombardments that always preceded American offensive sweeps gave them ample time to melt away into the jungle. When retreat was impossible they learned that U.S. firepower could be nullified if they swiftly engaged the Americans at close quarters, which also produced high U.S. casualties.

While sidestepping American sweeps, the Communists launched full-scale attacks at times and places of their own choosing. NVA troops scored a major victory in March 1966 when they captured a Special Forces camp in the A Shau Valley. Intensive attempts to rescue the outpost with close air support failed.

So effective were the enemy's efforts at avoiding American air power that late in 1965, a House subcommittee began looking into the effectiveness of tactical air operations in Vietnam. Committee Chairman Representative Otis G. Pike, a former marine pilot, noted:

Over twenty different models of American aircraft, undisturbed by enemy aircraft, roam the skies of South Vietnam at will, subject only to the danger of ground fire from conventional small arms.

Pike wondered, "Why [was] our air power unable to find and destroy the Vietcong in South Vietnam?"

Unlike Pike's experience in World War II, however, there were no front lines and no easily identified areas of enemy occupation. The guerrillas usually operated in remote areas, living off the land. They emerged from their jungle hide-outs only when they were sure they held the advantage.

In addition to the natural cover of the jungle, weather was the guerrillas' ally. From May to October, the southeast monsoon blanketed the country with heavy rains and thunderstorms reducing visibility and hampering air operations. "It was always tough to spot the guerrillas in the jungles," said one pilot, "and once the rains started they were invisible."

Perhaps the most frustrating characteristic of the Vietcong was their impressive ability to adapt to the massive American air build-up. Like their North Vietnamese comrades, the guerrillas became adept at defending against air strikes with camouflage and other ruses that hindered aerial recon efforts. One Defense Department analyst explained that air strikes were targeted "against places where the enemy *might* be, but without reliable information that he *was* there."

Arms, ammunition, food stores, and other supplies were broken up into small caches, which were buried throughout the countryside. At main bases buildings were dispersed over a wide area, and deeper bunkers and tunnels were built to reduce their vulnerability to air attacks. Entire munitions factories and hospitals were built underground.

With their extensive intelligence network, the guerrillas frequently received advance warning of planned interdiction strikes. Communist agents, posing as civilian workers, infiltrated U.S. air bases to gather intelligence on bombing plans and monitor flight activities. Even Arc Light operations, conceived thousands of miles away in Guam, were not immune to Hanoi's intelligence penetration.

"We normally had advance warning as to where and when they would occur," said one NVA platoon leader. "It normally arrived two hours prior to a strike." Soviet trawlers patrolling directly opposite the runway at Anderson AFB on Guam radioed Hanoi advance warning of any B-52 launch. North Vietnamese radar could pick up the bombers once they were 150 miles off the Vietnamese coast. The information would then be relayed south.

Studies by the Pentagon's Office of Systems Analysis brought into question the effectiveness of interdiction bombing in South Vietnam. An assistant secretary of defense, Alain Enthoven, noted that interdiction air strikes cost an estimated $2 billion and "probably killed fewer than 100 VC/NVA" in 1966 alone. His study also revealed that because many surplus Korean and World War II munitions were used, many bombs dropped were duds, providing the Vietcong with an invaluable source of high explosives. Guerrillas would recover the bombs and dismantle them, refashioning them into crude mines, grenades, and booby traps.

The southern Communists were employing the same strategy their northern comrades used in the war in North Vietnam's skies. Not aiming for an impossible quick victory over the sophisticated U.S. war machine, the Communist ground forces tried to inflict the highest casualties possible while denying the Americans victory, hoping they would eventually tire of the war.

*LZ X–Ray: Soldiers of the 1st Cavalry advance from behind the screen of a B–52 strike during the battle of the Ia Drang Valley on November 16, 1965.*

# Battle in the Skies

Hopes of a quick victory in the South were dashed by the American build-up, so Hanoi's leaders prepared for a long and costly struggle on two fronts. If they could neutralize U.S. bombing of the North, they felt certain that their guerrilla war in the South would wear down the Americans as it had the French.

From the first bombing raids in February 1965, the ruling Lao Dong (Communist) party began an intensive campaign to mobilize the country's population of 18.5 million in a "people's war against the air war of destruction." Once again Ho Chi Minh called his country to arms: "Each citizen is a soldier, each village, street, plant a fortress on the anti-American battlefront. . . . The war may last another five, ten, twenty years or longer, Hanoi and Haiphong may be destroyed, but the Vietnamese people will not be intimidated."

While Lyndon Johnson threatened North Vietnam with the jabs and thrusts of limited bombing, Hanoi weaved and bobbed, gaining time to

prepare for the body blows to come. Their strategy for survival employed classic guerrilla tactics. The key elements were to present the most elusive targets possible, denying the U.S. the advantage of overwhelming aerial superiority, while constantly increasing the air defense system to make America pay a heavy price for its air offensive. Hanoi's most pressing concern was to insure the flow of men and supplies south. Constant American air attacks had created "difficulties and confusion" within the transportation system, admitted the deputy chief of staff, Major General Nguyen Van Vinh. A British journalist, visiting the heavily bombed southern supply routes, reported a landscape "littered with broken bridges and pulverized roads."

To meet the challenge, Hanoi mobilized a vast army of workers armed with picks and shovels. Teen-age "Youth Shock Brigades" were formed as early as July and sent to embattled southern provinces to repair, camouflage, and construct roads. Mainly women, aged fifteen to twenty, these youths were given $1.30 a month plus food and clothing.

Before the dust even settled after an air attack, repair gangs would rush in to fill bomb craters and push aside disabled vehicles. When the U.S. began using delayed-action bombs, the youths would try to remove them with long wooden poles; others were trained to defuse them.

Hanoi claimed that during 1965, 42,000 kilometers of roads had been built or repaired. U.S. intelligence estimated that 97,000 Vietnamese worked full time on repair while another 370,000 to 500,000 devoted at least several days each month to the task. Using primitive tools and their bare hands, this vast army of workers could literally move mountains, as U.S. officials would soon learn. On April 12, 1966, B-52s made their first appearance over North Vietnam with orders to bomb a section of the thirty-five-kilometer-long Mu Gia Pass, which cut through the mountainous North Vietnamese-Laotian border region to the Ho Chi Minh Trail. Unleashing thousands of tons of high explosives, the thirty B-52s provoked a huge landslide, which, pilots reported, buried the narrow pass.

But twelve days later, Deputy Secretary of Defense Cyrus Vance was forced to admit to reporters that the strike, which cost $21 million, had failed to close the mountain roadway. Only two days after the mission, fighter-bombers had to be sent in to hit trucks traveling along the rapidly repaired route.

On the long journey south, drivers were solely responsible for their vehicles' safety and maintenance. Told by party officials to "love and care for their vehicles as if they were their own children," they carefully camouflaged their trucks with paint or bushes and palm fronds. Camouflaged way stations provided trucks and drivers shelter

during periods of intense American armed reconnaissance efforts. Even complete decoy truck parks were built to fool enemy airmen.

Truck convoys took advantage of American rules of engagement by establishing assembly points in areas known to be off-limits to the bombers. When attacked on the open road, they rushed to the nearest town or village where they knew they were safe from pilots who were under strict orders to avoid civilian casualties.

To avoid the relentless daytime air attacks, trucks began traveling in small groups of three or four under cover of darkness. Parking lights feebly illuminated the roads south to Thanh Hoa, and after that they were completely blacked out. Drivers felt their way along unmarked roads, lined sporadically with white stakes. Teen-age girls acted as traffic directors at key intersections. American pilots had to find these moving targets in total darkness.

Early in the war, twin-seated F-4 Phantoms, working in pairs, were considered the best aircraft for night armed recon missions. The lead plane was loaded with flares as well as rockets and bombs, while the second plane carried a full load of weapons. Once a target was spotted, the lead Phantom set off a flare overhead. As the trucks scurried for cover in the glow of high-intensity phosphorus, the team circled in for the kill. But the artificial flare light often played havoc with a pilot's sense of direction. As one navy commander described it, "the ground is black and the air is black, you get this flare going off and you don't know whether that flare is going down or sideways." An F-4 pilot had to rely on his back-seat navigator who kept his eyes glued to the illuminated instrument panel and called out altitude and directional readings. Eventually, sophisticated infrared scopes were employed to detect the heat of a truck's engine. But the North Vietnamese countered by setting decoy fires along roadsides to confuse the heat-sensitive equipment.

Bridges got special attention. North Vietnamese and North Korean engineers led specialized labor crews to maintain key bridges like the Dragon's Jaw at Thanh Hoa. Stockpiles of steel, iron, and bamboo, and even entire prefabricated bridge sections, were kept nearby. Repairs were conducted at a feverish pace throughout the night as the North Vietnamese knew the bombers would return at dawn.

As a back-up measure, secondary networks of bamboo bridges and ferry landings were constructed near existing structures to by-pass bombed-out bridges. Pontoon bridges—planks thrown across small skiffs or bundles of buoyant bamboo—were used at night, then cut loose and hidden in the thick jungle along the riverbank by day. All available craft were fitted as ferries. Sunken concrete bridges, built three or four inches below the water, were nearly impossible to detect from the air.

U.S. bombers just could not seem to stay ahead in the battle against the bridges. One pilot complained he was

*North Vietnamese rely on a hastily erected pontoon bridge outside Nam Dinh to transport supplies south after its predecessor was destroyed by U.S. bombs.*

dropping thousands of dollars worth of bombs against a "$13 bridge" made of "toothpicks." "It was discouraging," another said, "to go out on a mission at six in the morning, get over the target by seven, drop a bomb and destroy a bridge, fly over that target the next morning and it would be there!"

Railroad repairs were more difficult, and the North Vietnamese eventually abandoned the heavily bombed route south of Vinh. But other types of transport went into service to take up the slack. The country's 4,800-kilometer network of inland waterways was jammed with motor launches and sampans loaded with supplies. Carts drawn by water buffalo, wheelbarrows, and men on foot with carrying poles of bamboo balanced on their shoulders kept the arms and ammunition flowing southward. Bicycles streamed along the narrow roads and jungle paths. Traveling at night with a 150-pound load, a man could pedal forty kilometers before daylight.

Hounded by American aircraft during the entire journey south, workers were inspired by slogans emphasizing the importance of their job. "Each kilogram of goods arrived at destination," they were told by party cadres, "is a bullet shot in the head of the American pirates."

## A network of flame

Besides the weaponry needed for the struggle in the South, sophisticated air defense weapons from the Soviet Union and China soon crowded the docks at Haiphong and rail yards in Hanoi. When Rolling Thunder operations began, North Vietnam possessed fewer than 1,500 anti-aircraft guns, mainly 37MM and 57MM with optical sights and a maximum ceiling range of 18,000 feet. Within a year, the number of guns increased dramatically to over 5,000. Long-range 85MM and 100MM radar-directed guns now enabled the North Vietnamese to fire up to an altitude of 45,000 feet.

Highly mobile antiaircraft artillery—AAA—units were able to concentrate around significant targets or disperse into small ambush sites along routes frequently used by U.S. planes. Each gun battery would be carefully arranged to obtain maximum effect with a minimum of ammunition. Gunners were encouraged to study the tactics of American pilots, and villagers often filed detailed reports on local air raids.

Militiamen with small-caliber automatic weapons and even farmers with antiquated rifles would fire at low-fly-

*Ngo Thi Tuyen, a North Vietnamese militiawoman from Thanh Hoa Province, hauls AAA ammunition.*

*North Vietnamese gunners load a 100MM shell into a Russian-built gun with a range of up to 45,000 feet.*

*An American A-4 Skyhawk—brought down by North Vietnamese AAA fire—plunges earthward.*

ing aircraft. Although more of a morale-building exercise than anything else, the small-arms fire gave U.S. pilots a lot to think about before they ventured over a target at low altitude. They knew from experience that just one bullet, hitting a vital spot, could bring a multimillion dollar jet crashing to the ground.

A Chinese reporter, visiting North Vietnam in 1966, lavishly described the effect: "All over North Vietnam a network of flame stretches from coastline to sky, knit by AA guns and the rifles and machine guns of all the people. . . . Into it the American planes plunge like moths to a flame."

Conventional AAA and small-arms fire accounted for 80 percent of total combat losses during Rolling Thunder. Pilots generally started their attack runs at 12,000 feet and tried to pull out at 4,500 feet to reduce their exposure to the concentrated ground fire. But in those few moments, as they flew "straight and stable" toward the target to insure precision, they were extremely vulnerable to the streaming tracer bullets and bursting flak.

For Commander Jeremiah Denton, aboard the U.S.S. *Independence*, the tension began during preflight planning as he plotted his mission on maps dotted with colored pins marking AAA positions. "That's when you sort of get cold beads of sweat," he later said, "as you thought: Oh, my God, look at all those 57MMs, 37MMs, and I've got to roll in there and pull out there, and as soon as I do, there's no way we can avoid this whole batch of 37s over here." But that anxiety vanished once he was in the air. After earning the Distinguished Flying Cross, Denton was shot down near Thanh Hoa and captured on July 18, 1965.

Early on, F-100 Supersabres were sent in ahead of a strike force on "flak suppression" missions. Their job was to "soften up" North Vietnamese AAA defenses with napalm and antipersonnel bombs—including CBUs—designed to wipe out guns. Eventually, flak suppression was turned over to other planes within each strike group as the North Vietnamese merely abandoned their guns when they saw the Supersabres, remanning them again in time to fire at the trailing strike force. North Vietnamese gunners soon earned the grudging respect of American pilots as they remained at their guns despite the rain of bullets and bombs aimed at them.

## Guerrilla war in the air

Further challenging American air power were the Soviet- and Chinese-built Migs of North Vietnam's air force. Numbering only fifty-three Korean War vintage Mig-15s and 17s at the start of 1965, Hanoi's air arm appeared to be a pushover for sophisticated U.S. jets and their better trained pilots.

Most North Vietnamese pilots were novices who learned their skills in crash training programs in the Soviet Union or China. One admitted he had never even been in a car before he began flight training. With the help of their Soviet instructors and by sheer repetition, North Vietnamese pilots became very accomplished. They learned to put their smaller Migs' superior maneuverability to good use against the faster, yet heavier, American jets. The Communist pilots took to guerrilla tactics in the air, launching isolated hit-and-run attacks while avoiding large-scale battles.

Directed by a Soviet-style ground control radar network, the Migs shadowed an incoming strike force. They would harass the bombers with feints and close-in runs, often forcing American planes to jettison their heavy bomb loads in order to gain speed and take evasive action, thereby disrupting the mission. With their tighter turning radius, the Migs could elude any attempt at pursuit by the less agile U.S. planes.

After two F-105s were shot down on the second strike against the Dragon's Jaw in April, American commanders sent fighter escorts with each strike force. The F-4 Phantom, which had evolved into a multipurpose fighter-bomber, now returned to its original role as a fighter plane. Stripped of bombs and armed with air-to-air missiles, the F-4s flew Mig Combat Air Patrol (MIGCAP) be-

tween the bombers and North Vietnamese airfields. Once the F-4s appeared, the Migs retreated to their air bases around Hanoi and Haiphong, which were off-limits to U.S. pilots. It was not until two months later that U.S. fighters got a crack at the elusive Migs.

On June 17 two Phantoms from the U.S.S. *Midway* were flying MIGCAP for another strike against the Dragon's Jaw Bridge when the radar intercept officer in the lead F-4 picked up something on his radar screen. From the back seat Lieutenant John Smith alerted his pilot: "Four bogies heading southwest, thirty miles ahead." Commander Louis C. Page armed his Sparrow III radar-guided missiles and brought the two F-4s on an intercept course.

Accelerating to 850 knots, the Phantoms closed rapidly with the unidentified contacts, a mile every three and a half seconds. At ten miles from intercept, well within the range of their Sparrows, Page had the blips centered in the target circles on his radar scope. But air-to-air rules of engagement stipulated that positive visual identification had to be made before firing. Page waited, his finger poised above the firing button.

At five miles, Page spotted four aircraft strung out in a

*North Vietnamese fighter pilots stroll in front of their Mig-17s in late 1966.*

*Captain Larry Golberg sits in the cockpit of his F–4C Phantom in May 1966. The Phantom had a larger, comparatively more comfortable cockpit than other fighter-attack aircraft used in Vietnam.*

ragged single file heading straight toward him. But not until they closed within two miles could Page make out clearly the yawning nose intakes and bubble canopies of the Mig-17s as they began banking away from the on-rushing Phantoms.

Page squeezed off a Sparrow at the second plane in the formation; Lieutenant Jack E. Batson, his wingman, quickly sent another radar-guided missile at the third Mig. As they banked to the left, Page saw his missile burst right on the tail of the second Mig, blanketing the silver jet in a sheet of smoke and flame. The trailing Mig burst into a violent fireball, falling victim to a direct hit from Batson's Sparrow.

Cruising up through the clouds, the two Phantoms swung around sharply for a second pass. But when they broke back underneath the clouds, all they could see was a single parachute slowly drifting earthward.

Page, Batson, and their RIOs returned to the *Midway* later that afternoon to an enthusiastic welcome. Secretary of the Navy Paul Nitze, aboard on an official visit, was given the honor of announcing the first confirmed Mig kills of the war to the pilots and crew of the carrier. Three days later, *Midway* planes were to score another success in an unusual encounter.

When an air force Phantom went down during a mission forty miles southeast of Hanoi, four A-1 Skyraiders from the carrier were called in as rescue combat air patrol for the two crewmen who had bailed out. En route to the crash site aboard the lead Skyraider, Lieutenant Commander E.A. Greathouse received an urgent radio message. The U.S.S. *Strauss* in the Gulf of Tonkin reported that two aircraft were flying toward the Skyraiders at high speed. Greathouse pressed on despite continuing warning messages. Finally, Greathouse saw two Mig-17s running almost parallel to the Spads at 3,000 feet two miles away. As the supersonic, swept-wing jets streaked by, the navy commander continued on course, speculating that they had not spotted his low-flying formation.

Five miles ahead, the Migs swung around in a looping turn and bore down toward the plodding Spads. Just as each of the jets fired a rocket, Greathouse led his formation right into the oncoming Migs to throw off their aim. Jettisoning their 3,000 pounds each of bombs and rockets, the Spads dove to avoid the rockets, which fizzled out before reaching them.

While the Migs banked around for a second run, Greathouse led his flight into a valley between two lofty ridges to deny the jets maneuvering room. With the four Spads flying at 500 feet, the Migs could not attack from below and had no room to pull out of a high-speed attack run from above. The Migs held a 250-knot speed advantage over the prop-driven planes, but Greathouse countered with the Spad's tighter turning radius.

Splitting into teams of two, the Spads began flying in tight defensive "Luftbery" circles, a tactic developed in World War I. By maintaining a continuous turning orbit, each plane covered the other's tail, or "six o'clock position," the most vulnerable spot for a fighter because the pilot could not look directly behind from the cockpit. Each time the Migs skidded in on one plane in a shallow dive, the trailing Spad would open up with its .50-caliber machine guns on the exposed Mig's tail.

For five minutes the running gun battle raged over the Red River Delta. Two more rockets sputtered harmlessly underneath the lead pair of Spads. Using precise timing, the navy pilots finally broke the deadlock. With a Mig on their tail, Greathouse and his wingman scissored out of range leaving the startled Mig pilot heading into a hail of bullets fired by the second pair of Spads.

Trailing smoke, the Mig nosed down until one wing hit a small hill, cartwheeling the jet through the jungle in a sheet of flame. The second Mig disappeared into the northern sky and the navy planes continued on their mission. Lieutenant Clinton B. Johnson and Lieutenant (j.g.) Charles W. Hartmann were credited with "splashing" the third Mig of the war with the help of World War I tactics and World War II vintage airplanes.

## Setting a trap for the Migs

After these setbacks the North Vietnamese became more cautious. EC-121 early-warning radar planes with the code name Big Eye, which monitored Mig activity, picked up a change in tactics. As a strike force approached its target, Big Eye flashed a "Code Yellow" warning to the fighter-bombers indicating that Migs were airborne. The warning turned red when the Migs were ten minutes away, usually when the U.S. planes began their bombing runs as the Migs tried to disrupt the strike.

During missions after the downing of the Migs, the red warning would change back to yellow during the attack and flash red again after the last fighter had left the target area. The Migs obviously hoped to pounce on a crippled or straggling plane while its fighter escort was low on fuel and unable to engage them. Staff members of the 2d Air Division observed the new pattern and set a trap for the shadowing Migs.

On July 24 four F-4s from the 45th TFS at Ubon were assigned as fighter escort for a strike on an ammo depot at Yen Bai. Instead of flying in their usual position alongside the F-105 Thunderchiefs, they delayed their takeoff time by fifteen minutes. Maintaining strict radio silence, the Phantoms flew in the same formation and at the same speed and altitude as the preceding strike force. The F-4 pilots hoped to convince enemy radar operators that they were just another flight of bomb-laden F-105s.

Arriving over the target ten minutes after the Thunderchiefs had struck, Major Richard Hall's Phantoms established radar contact with two Migs. The ruse had worked. Igniting their afterburners, which injected fuel into the stream of hot exhaust from the main engines for added thrust, the F-4s quickly overtook the two Mig-17s. Major Hall and his wingman flew in high to watch for more Migs while Captains Kenneth Holcombe and Thomas Roberts, in the number three and four Phantoms, broke into the Migs. But the North Vietnamese pilots outmaneuvered them and came in from behind. Holcombe could see the muzzle flashes of the Mig's cannons in his rearview mirror as it fired at him. The two Phantoms split off in opposite directions with a Mig on each tail.

"Jinking" his plane in erratic weaving motions to throw off the North Vietnamese pilot's aim, Holcombe kept reversing his turn until the Mig chasing him finally shot by. But just as he was moving in for the kill, the Phantom's radar and communications systems went dead. Without them, Holcombe and his back-seat weapons systems officer could not lock their radar-guided missiles onto the Mig. While they tried to restore communications, the Mig recovered and, cannons blazing, streaked in across their nose. Ramming the throttle forward, Holcombe pushed the F-4 through the sound barrier at Mach 1.3 while executing a high-G barrel roll. The maneuver worked as the Mig once again overshot the gyrating Phantom. This time Holcombe punched off four heat-seeking Sidewinder missiles at the Mig ahead. Two of them hit, blowing the Mig apart.

Captain Roberts had also managed to shake the Mig-17 on his tail by climbing sharply. Unable to keep up with Robert's Phantom, the Mig fell away at 29,000 feet. Roberts quickly dropped out of the climb a few thousand feet behind the Mig and fired a Sidewinder. The missile detonated a few feet from the Mig's left wing, severely rocking the plane but failing to slow it down. Roberts fired two more Sidewinders, one of which flew right up the Mig's tail pipe, exploding in a brilliant flash of light.

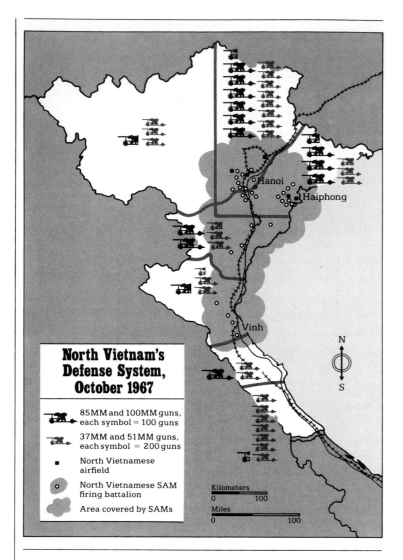

## North Vietnam's Defense System, October 1967

85MM and 100MM guns, each symbol = 100 guns

37MM and 51MM guns, each symbol = 200 guns

■ North Vietnamese airfield

◎ North Vietnamese SAM firing battalion

Area covered by SAMs

Hanoi

Haiphong

Vinh

Kilometers
0          100

Miles
0          100

Holcombe, Roberts, and their back seaters had chalked up the fourth and fifth Mig kills of the war and the first for the U.S. Air Force. With five of their Migs blasted out of the sky in less than two months, the North Vietnamese air force restricted itself to defensive patrols nearer the sanctuary of their air bases around Hanoi and Haiphong. Aerial dogfights became sporadic as the Migs challenged U.S. aircraft only when they ventured within the Red River Delta area. American planes appeared to have won mastery of the skies over North Vietnam.

But within two weeks of the air force victories, events in Vietnam would change the face of aerial combat. No longer would it be the realm of individual pilots pitting their skills and machines against each other, jousting in the dogfights of wars gone by. Technology had come of age in aerial warfare over Southeast Asia.

## A flying telephone pole

On July 24, four Phantoms were flying MIGCAP for a force of F–105s assigned to strike an explosives plant fifty-five miles northwest of Hanoi. With the recent Mig stand-down it looked as though the mission would be an easy one.

Three of the four air force pilots and their weapons systems officers were members of an advance party from the 47th TFS recently arrived in Thailand. Flying in the number two position was Captain Richard P. Keirn of the 47th TFS, a veteran of World War II.

"We were in the soup all the way," Keirn recalled, referring to the predictable dense clouds over North Vietnam. To keep in visual contact the Phantoms drew into a close "fingertip" formation and began their prearranged, high-altitude flight pattern forty miles west of Hanoi. Their radar screens revealed no airborne Migs in the area.

Suddenly, one of the pilots saw what he later said looked like a "flying telephone pole" rising through the clouds straight toward them. Seconds later, Keirn's plane was engulfed in a brilliant mustard-colored explosion. The other three F–4s veered off to avoid the shrapnel; two more blasts detonated harmlessly behind them.

Inside the cockpit of the stricken Phantom, Dick Keirn wrestled with the controls as the aircraft bucked and lurched through the air. He glanced into his rearview mirror to see "fire coming around my head." A sheet of flames raged through the rear cockpit where his back seater had once been.

Without a second thought, Keirn pulled the ejection handle between his legs and shot out of the burning Phantom. Seconds later the plane rolled over and disintegrated in a ball of fire. Bleeding from a piece of shrapnel stuck in his leg, Keirn felt a strange sense of déjà vu as he floated earthward.

Twenty-one years before, in another war on another continent, Keirn had been forced to bail out over enemy territory when his B–17 Flying Fortress was hit. He spent the last ten months of World War II in a German POW camp where his fellow inmates nicknamed the nineteen-year-old, "Junior." Finding himself drifting helplessly into hostile territory once more, Keirn thought to himself, "Oh shit, not again!"

Landing in thick forest, he unbuckled his parachute harness and tried to stand up, but the force of the ejection had dislocated his right shoulder and knee. For twelve hours Keirn crawled through the underbrush until his prophetic curse became reality. Surrounded by a dozen men and women armed with machine guns and machetes, he was quickly overpowered. This time Keirn would spend nearly seven years as a POW and earn a new nickname. His younger cell mates referred to the forty-year-old captain as "Pop."

Sitting in his tiny cell, Keirn had plenty of time to ponder the mysterious nature of his shoot-down. His suspicions were confirmed months later when newly captured pilots passed the word. The North Vietnamese were using Russian-made, SA–2 surface-to-air missiles.

American pilots had been aware of the presence of SAMs in North Vietnam since April 5, when a reconnaissance jet photographed a missile site under construction fifteen miles southeast of Hanoi. Within a month, two more sites were reported underway. Armed with 400 pounds of high explosives, the thirty-five-foot SA-2 had a lethal range of about twenty-five miles and a ceiling range of 60,000 feet. Guided by Soviet-made Fan Song radar equipment, the two-and-one-half ton missile could track a target at more than twice the speed of sound. The number of SAM sites encircling Hanoi and Haiphong was growing rapidly. Air commanders knew the effectiveness of Rolling Thunder operations would soon be in serious jeopardy.

As soon as the first sites were discovered, General Joseph Moore and Rear Admiral Edward C. Outlaw, commander of Task Force 77 at Yankee Station, had issued a joint appeal to destroy the SAM sites before they became armed and operational. The proposal went through the normal chain of command and, after what seemed to the two men an inordinate delay, was finally returned: disapproved. It was "beyond my comprehension," Admiral Outlaw later remarked.

American policymakers regarded the Soviet decision to deploy the SAMs as just another move in the complex game of bluff and counterbluff waged by the superpowers in Vietnam. "The clever theorists in Washington," wrote Gen. Westmoreland, "said it was all a matter of signals. We won't bomb the SAM sites which signals the North Vietnamese not to use them."

In fact the SAM sites, along with Mig airfields and Hanoi itself, were considered by Secretary McNamara as "flash points" to be carefully avoided. With Soviet technicians on hand to help build the sites and train North Vietnamese missile operators, any surprise attack might incur Russian casualties and trigger greater Soviet involvement in the war.

But when Keirn's Phantom was blasted out of the sky by a very real SA-2, military commanders demanded an immediate response. Realizing the SAMs could no longer be ignored, Washington agreed to a one-time only strike against the two sites suspected of firing at Keirn's F-4. It was left to the Pentagon planners and air commanders in the Pacific to devise an effective plan of attack.

SAMs were not new to the American military. They had learned of their destructive potential in 1960, when an air force U-2 piloted by Francis Gary Powers was shot down by an early prototype while on a secret, high-altitude reconnaissance mission over the Soviet Union. But this marked the first time American aircraft faced SAMs in a combat situation. None of the various tactics prescribed by the analysts to counter SAMs had ever been tested.

An unmanned drone was launched over North Vietnam to see if American planes could fly in above the SAMs' ceiling range. It disappeared from the radar screens while cruising at 60,000 feet, presumably shot down. That meant high-altitude operations would not be safe, so high-speed, low-level strikes seemed the best solution.

Since the SA-2 did not gain the speed and stability necessary to maneuver until it climbed above 2,000 feet, American planners called for strike planes to fly in against the sites below 1,000 feet.

## "The end of the world"

On July 26 USAF units in Thailand were briefed on the operational plan. Sixteen F-105s from the 12th Squadron at Korat were to split into two forces. One would hit SAM Site 6, forty miles west of Hanoi, while the rest launched a diversionary strike nearby. Simultaneously, another sixteen Thunderchiefs from the 563d Squadron at Takhli were targeted for SAM Site 7.

Assembling in the briefing room at Takhli that afternoon, pilots of the 563d Squadron were elated to hear they were finally going after SAMs. But when they listened to the strike plan they could not believe their ears. All four flights of four were to fly at a low level along the exact same path to the target. Captains Paul Craw, Kile Berg, Bill Sparks, and Marty Case, assigned as the last flight of four in the Takhli strike force, were unanimous in their opposition to low-level strikes against heavily defended targets, which would leave them exposed to even the smallest caliber ground fire. Sending all the planes above the same route only gave North Vietnamese gunners a further advantage. "Anytime you're running four flights of four one right after the other down the same old chute," reasoned one of the pilots, "they're going to have you pretty well fixed on altitude and direction."

When the strike, scheduled for the afternoon of the twenty-sixth, was postponed at the last minute because of bad weather, the four pilots together put in an unauthorized call to 2d Air Division headquarters in Saigon "to find out who the idiot was who did the planning." They were curtly informed that as captains their job was just to fly the missions.

Further doubts about the sanity of the planners crept into the minds of the pilots the next morning. As they underwent the seemingly endless series of prestrike briefings once more on July 27, changes in the types of weapons to be used kept coming in from Saigon. Sweating ground crews would finish loading 750-pound bombs onto the waiting F-105s when the order would suddenly be changed to rockets and napalm. It was obvious that the planners did not know what kind of weapons to use against the SAMs.

At Korat, the airfield was awash with confusion as ground crews frantically armed and rearmed the squadron's Thunderchiefs up to the last minute before launch. In the rush, two of the F-105s in Major Bill Hosmer's flight of eight were armed with only their 20MM Vulcan cannons. When Hosmer explained the situation to the control tower he was told to launch anyway.

Igniting their huge Pratt & Whitney jet engines, the

F-105 jockeys in both strike forces from Korat and Takhli wondered what lay ahead of them that afternoon. The newly activated SAMs were an untried adversary. One thing they knew was that the three days of inactivity following Keirn's downing had given the enemy time to prepare for a retaliatory strike. Just before taking off from Takhli, Case, standing on the ladder to the cockpit, exchanged some final words with the squadron chaplain. His old friend from cadet school, Kile Berg, told Case he had a premonition he would not be coming back.

Case, Berg, and the other pilots in the last flight in the strike force from Takhli, switched their radios over to the assigned frequency for the strike as they flew into North Vietnamese airspace to see how their squadron mates ahead were faring. They were stunned by the sounds crackling through their headphones. "Everybody was just screaming and yelling," recalled Case. Planes had already been shot down miles from the target.

Heading north across the Black River, Case could see the battle ahead. "It looked like the end of the world," he recalled. Black clouds of bursting flak, orange tracer bullets, flaming aircraft, and smoke swirled through the skies as far as the eye could see. The North Vietnamese were firing everything they had at the oncoming planes. "I've never seen a sky like that," Case said, "and I never want to see another one."

One of the squadron's lead Thunderchiefs was down. Case recognized the call sign as that of Walt Kosko. "He's landed in the river," came the report. Kosko had been forced to bail out over Laos just a few weeks before. He had landed alongside a road near the capital city of Vientiane. A surprised Kosko was quickly picked up by an American embassy staffer, on his way to work in a Detroit-built station wagon. This time Kosko ran into a different welcoming committee. As he swept past on his way to SAM Site 7, Case heard Kosko's squadron commander, Major Jack Brown, calling frantically for air cover as North Vietnamese soldiers swarmed toward Kosko's bright yellow life raft in the Black River.

Descending to 100 feet, the four Thunderchiefs of Case's flight roared up the Red River Valley. A few miles from the target, they ran into a virtual wall of antiaircraft fire. Case, last in the single file formation, could see the flak exploding dangerously close to the planes ahead. "We've got to get lower," he radioed his flight leader, "there's 37s going off right on top of us!" Kicking on their afterburners, the four F-105s plunged down to fifty feet. "We were doing about nine-nine on the deck," Case remembered, "going just as fast as we could."

In the lead plane, Paul Craw popped up to 200 feet over the radar vans in the center of the site and released his napalm. Following Craw, Kile Berg's F-105 was hit just seconds before he reached the target.

Flashing past Berg's floundering plane, all Case could see were the wings and tail, "everything else was flame."

He helplessly watched his friend's plane roll over and, in a matter of seconds, crash to the ground. Bill Sparks, in the number three position, anxiously called back to ask Case if he saw Berg get out in time. Case replied, "Nope, no way."

But Berg had survived. Case never saw his parachute through the smoke and flames because it was open for only seconds. A few hundred feet off the ground when he ejected, Berg swung once to the left and once to the right, then hit the dirt. Berg landed 150 feet from the burning wreckage of his Thunderchief and was quickly surrounded by a group of wide-eyed teen-agers toting "awfully big weapons." His premonition had proved true. Kile Berg did not return to Takhli that afternoon, nor did he leave North Vietnamese captivity for over seven years.

A few miles away, Bill Hosmer's flight from Korat continued the assault on SAM Site 6. Winding up the Black River, Hosmer was bringing the flight in on its attack run when he sighted a dust cloud coming from one of the launch pads. Thinking the North Vietnamese had fired a SAM, Hosmer warned his flight, "They've salvoed!"

But what Hosmer thought was a missile launch turned out to be the opening salvo of a barrage of AAA fire. The sky turned black around his flight as the pilots dove through the flak. As all the preceding flights from Korat had approached the site from the same direction and at the same altitude, the North Vietnamese gunners had blanketed the narrow corridor with antiaircraft fire.

Hosmer's wingman, Captain Frank Tullo, could actually see the muzzle flashes of the guns blazing away at him as he flew by at 200 feet. The next thing Tullo remembered seeing was the fire light on his instrument panel flashing its red warning. Glancing over at his young wingman, Hosmer saw a hundred-foot-sheet of flame pouring from the Thunderchief's engine.

With Tullo hit and two of his planes armed only with 20MM Vulcan cannons, Hosmer ordered his flight to abort its run. The flight leader sent the remaining six planes on ahead while he stayed behind to cover his wingman's crippled plane.

Tullo knew he would not make it back to Korat. His instruments became inoperative one by one as the fire ate through the plane's electrical wiring. When muffled explosions began ripping through the airplane Tullo ejected, landing in a field of elephant grass near the junction of the Red and Black rivers. Hosmer knew his wingman's position was critical. Downed only thirty miles southwest of Hanoi, Tullo's chances of rescue were slim. His F-105 low on fuel, Hosmer could do no more than call for a rescue team.

Not long after Hosmer headed homeward, two A-1 Skyraiders appeared from the south. Ignoring the heavy gunfire they drew, the Sandies slowly crisscrossed the valley, pinpointing Tullo's position without giving it away to the North Vietnamese who were also looking for the downed flier. They contacted Tullo on his emergency survival radio to tell him a chopper was on its way, then withdrew out of range of the persistent ground fire.

Two nerve-racking hours later, Tullo heard thrashing noises and spotted a group of armed militiamen crashing through the grass half a mile away. Sporadic gunfire echoed through the valley as the soldiers blasted away at any noises they heard. Tullo burrowed himself as deep as he could into the thick elephant grass as the search party inched its way closer.

Suddenly, Tullo heard the rumbling sound of approaching jet engines. The next thing he knew twenty to thirty U.S. fighter planes were swarming overhead. F-100s, F-105s, B-57s, and even a few navy fighters began strafing the militiamen as well as enemy automatic-weapons positions that had been lying in wait for any rescue attempt. Following the fighters were the two Sandies escorting a large, green aircraft that Tullo did not recognize. It was a CH-3 "Jolly Green Giant" cargo helicopter, recently arrived, which had been modified for air rescue.

Captain George Martin piloted the CH-3 right over Tullo, and the helicopter's crewmen lowered a cable with a horse collar attached. Slipping his head and arms through the collar, Tullo flashed "thumbs-up." He was hoisted five feet in the air when the winch jammed. With bullets whizzing past the hovering chopper, Martin revved

up his engines and sped out of the valley with Tullo dragging through the brush.

Unable to unjam the winch, Martin laid Tullo onto the ground and landed next to him. The minute Tullo saw the chopper's wheels touch down he sprinted toward the door, diving in head first just as a fusillade of automatic-weapons fire ripped into the helicopter. With his head ducked down into the well of the cockpit, Martin lifted the chopper up and out of the valley. A grateful Tullo scrambled up to the cockpit and hugged the burly chopper pilot. He knew he had been extremely lucky. No SAR mission had ever been flown that far north before.

Frank Tullo was the only pilot rescued that day. Walt Kosko, reported MIA, was never found and two other pilots died at the controls of their Thunderchiefs. Captain Bob Purcell was captured along with Kile Berg. After spending his first thirty-one days as a POW in solitary confinement, Berg was given a cell mate. Ironically it was Pop Keirn, the man whose supposed death he had been sent to avenge. Both pilots were presumed killed-in-action until early 1966, when they appeared in a Japanese television film of American fliers being paraded through Hanoi.

Despite the heavy losses, both SAM sites had been hit hard. But the Americans soon found out they had fallen victim to a clever trap. Poststrike reconnaissance photos

*Hours after his dramatic shoot-down and escape, Capt. Frank Tullo (in front with mustache) speaks with the SAR crew that pulled him out of North Vietnam. To Tullo's left is Capt. George Martin, pilot of the rescue helicopter.*

revealed both sites were decoys, filled with dummy cardboard missiles. The North Vietnamese had removed the real missiles and concentrated every available AAA gun in the area around the empty sites.

# Iron Hand

As the Americans soon found out, an entire SAM battery could be packed up in four hours, transported to a new site, and made operational again in another six hours. Local villagers were pressed into service to spread bamboo and straw along the uneven surfaces of narrow roads and jungle trails to protect the delicate equipment.

In an effort to locate the elusive missiles, Adm. Sharp ordered around-the-clock photo reconnaissance missions. The tactic paid off on August 8, when a low-flying RF-101 photographed an operational site. But by the time authorization was obtained to launch a strike the next day, the missiles had vanished.

A few days later, Washington declared open season on SAMs. On August 12, Adm. Sharp got the authority to launch anti-SAM search and destroy missions on his own initiative. They were code named Iron Hand. As usual there were certain restrictions. Photographic confirmation that the sites were operational still had to be obtained before they could be hit. Since the photos had to pass through a lengthy chain of command, the North Vietnamese had ample time to move the missiles elsewhere.

SA-2 installations within the restricted areas around Hanoi and Haiphong and in the Chinese border zone were off-limits. Not until late November were Iron Hand pilots allowed to hit SAM sites within these sanctuaries and even then only after they had launched a missile.

Pilots were baffled by the logic of the Washington-imposed restrictions. One navy flier recalled escorting a photo plane close to Hanoi where they sighted a rail convoy full of SAMs sitting dead on the tracks. When the photos were developed, they found the railroad cars were carrying 111 missiles. Admiral Outlaw, the commander of Task Force 77, immediately requested permission to hit the convoy before it was moved. But the plan was vetoed in Washington. "We had to fight all 111 of them one at a time," said the disgruntled navy pilot.

On the same day that Iron Hand missions were authorized, SAMs scored their second kill. While cruising fifty-five miles south of Hanoi on armed recon, a pair of navy A-4s reported "two spots of light-hunting" closing in on them. Twenty seconds later one of the Skyhawks plummeted earthward while the other, severely damaged, limped back to Yankee Station.

*A recon photo taken on May 26, 1966 by an RF-101 shows a North Vietnamese SAM site, including its radar vans.*

*Bombs from a USAF F–105F Wild Weasel, also carrying Shrike missiles, fall toward a SAM site in North Vietnam in 1967.*

Armed with the newly arrived Iron Hand orders, all available navy aircraft were launched in a "maximum effort" reaction strike. From late on the evening of Thursday, August 12, through the following Friday, Task Force 77's carriers catapulted 124 sorties in a massive SAM hunt. Without any definite plan, the navy planes zigzagged across the North Vietnamese countryside for thirty hours without locating a single operational site. Five aircraft and two pilots were lost to antiaircraft fire and seven other planes returned badly damaged. Seventh Fleet aviators soon dubbed the ill-planned, August 13 SAM hunt "Black Friday."

After the disastrous results of the hastily organized mass attempts to neutralize the SAMs, American planners tried another tactic, two- to four-plane formations known as "hunter-killer" teams. Flying well ahead of a second plane (or pair of planes), the lead "hunters" would try and spot a site pinpointed by reconnaissance aircraft or else lure an undetected site into firing a missile. Once the SAM site revealed itself, the hunters would streak in and drop napalm on the radar control van while the "killers" followed in with 750-pound bombs to deliver the coup de grâce.

Flying at low levels, hunter-killer teams were highly vulnerable to ground fire. Building fake sites and transmitting dummy SA-2 radar signals, the North Vietnamese would often lure American pilots into concentrations of heavy AAA fire, known as flak traps. According to one navy pilot, "the Iron Hand business was a good way to get blown away."

Lieutenant Colonel Robbie Risner, who had been the subject of a *Time* magazine cover story earlier in the year, soon found out how dangerous Iron Hand missions were. On September 16 he was leading a hunter-killer team in on a suspected SAM site near Thanh Hoa when he ran into a flak trap. Tracer bullets streamed up at the nose of his low-flying F-105. "They looked like they were coming in my intake," Risner recalled, "and sure enough they were because my engine exploded."

Risner spent the next seven-and-a-half years as a POW. Prison authorities, well aware of his reputation, made a special effort to "break" the senior American POW (see sidebar, page 160). "I would have much cause to regret that *Time* had ever heard of me," Risner observed.

More and more pilots flying Iron Hand missions were to suffer the same fate as Risner, and two frustrating months passed before Iron Hand chalked up its first SAM kill. On October 17 five navy planes from the U.S.S. *Independence* finally destroyed an operational site northwest of Haiphong near Kep Ha airfield.

## Wild Weasels

Except for this isolated success Iron Hand had nothing to show for its efforts to that point. One of the problems was the operation's reliance on photo recon overflights. The low-flying planes often tipped off North Vietnamese operators that they had been spotted and gave them time to move their missiles. They became even less effective as easily recognizable concrete installations, built by the

Russians, were gradually abandoned in favor of elaborately camouflaged makeshift sites. "Some looked like small villages, some like clumps of trees," remarked an F-105 pilot, "none even looked like a missile site." To regain the initiative the Americans dug into their bag of technological tricks.

Early in the Rolling Thunder campaign twin-engined EB-66Cs had been rescued from air force graveyards to fly electronic countermeasure (ECM) missions for the bombers. The EB-66s were crammed with electronic gear, operated by four technicians known as Ravens, and used to track Mig activity and jam North Vietnamese radar. The unarmed EB-66s were now given the additional task of monitoring the frequencies used by the radar-operated SA-2s.

Although their aging equipment lacked enough power to jam the high-powered Fan Song radar employed by SAM operators, the Ravens were capable of pinpointing a site but only when North Vietnamese radar operators switched on their sets. By then it was usually too late. It was obvious that something better was needed.

Since the Soviets had first introduced SAMs in the early sixties, American defense experts had been developing ECM devices specially designed to counteract the missiles. The Strategic Air Command, realizing the threat SAMs posed to their nuclear force, had already begun installing the new ECM gear in their B-52 bombers.

But Tactical Air Command thought the size and weight of the bulky equipment would jeopardize the performance of its smaller jets. Besides, a fighter pilot's creed had always been, "if you can see it you can evade it." Facing the SAMs for the first time in combat conditions in Vietnam, the pilots soon found they needed help to avoid the computerized missiles. "They could come out of nowhere and shoot you down and you'd never have a chance," one pilot said.

Navy technicians initiated Project Shoehorn in which they crammed as much ECM gear as they could into small "black boxes." Wedged into the nose cones of navy fighter-bombers, the devices monitored SAM radar frequencies and warned a pilot if he were being tracked. If a missile were launched, a loud gong-like tone would sound off in the pilot's headphones, giving him a few seconds to take evasive action.

A study by the navy's Bureau of Weapons had determined that an SA-2 needed five seconds to compute a course change. Pilots were told rapid, high-speed turns could leave a SAM sputtering in confusion. But the most effective maneuver was simply to dive for the deck. With the enormous thrust it needed to gain altitude and speed, the SA-2 could not easily reverse its upward course.

By the end of 1965, the air force came up with a specially equipped plane to search out and destroy SAM sites. Twin-seated F-100Fs and later F-105Fs were loaded with ECM equipment hung in pods underneath their wings and armed with Shrike air-to-ground missiles, capable of homing in on SAM radar frequencies. Flying in pairs, the so-called Wild Weasels accompanied each strike mission and were the first in and last out of the target area.

Once a SAM site switched on its radar, the Wild Weasels locked onto the signal. Sweeping in on the now-exposed site, the Weasels launched their missiles, which homed in on the site's radar beam. Marked by the smoke from the Shrikes, the site was then easy prey for a flight of two F-105s trailing the Weasels with full loads of bombs and CBUs.

But North Vietnamese missile operators eventually caught on. They began to recognize the distinctive maneuver the Weasels took before firing their Shrikes and learned to turn off their radar sets after they saw it, depriving the missile of a target. U.S. technology countered by adding a memory feature to the Shrike missile. The result was a deadly game of electronic "cat and mouse" in the skies over North Vietnam.

"There was a lot of dry faking in the Weasel game," wrote one pilot. "The SAM would look at the force with radar, the Weasel would see him and turn as if to fire a Shrike, and the SAM would shut off if he were smart. . . . And so it went, until the strike force got closer to the target. Then the SAMs got bolder and began firing missiles in spite of the danger of a Shrike."

Whichever way the game went, the Weasels stayed around a target site too long for comfort, offering themselves as live bait for the SAMs. Thrown into combat with little training and experimental equipment, a Wild Weasel pilot had a dangerously short life expectancy. An EB-66 pilot based at Takhli early in 1966 noted: "We had six Weasels on the flight line. Within six weeks they were all gone."

The newly developed ECM gear and weaponry—especially the Shrike missile—often could not be produced fast enough. By October 1965 there were only twelve Shrikes in the entire Pacific theater. By contrast, the number of Soviet-supplied SAMs was steadily rising. At the end of 1965 CINCPAC reported more than sixty sites stretching from Hanoi as far south as Thanh Hoa (see map, page 106). No fewer than 184 SAMs had been fired during the year, resulting in the loss of eleven U.S. aircraft, a 5.9 percent kill ratio. As American countermeasures were gradually improved, the ratio decreased dramatically to less than 1 percent by 1968.

But the effectiveness of SAMs could not be measured in statistics alone. Improved ECM equipment and changes in strike force tactics had only partially solved the problem. The SAMs had also forced a change in tactics that left the American pilots more vulnerable to conventional AAA fire and lessened their bombing accuracy.

At the beginning of Rolling Thunder, U.S. pilots had employed low-level bombing approaches to avoid being de-

*A flight of four F-105 Thunderchiefs en route to targets in North Vietnam prepare to refuel in flight from a USAF KC-135 Strato-tanker in January 1966.*

tected by radar. But as the bombing became more predictable and antiaircraft batteries blossomed across the country, approach altitudes were raised to between 15,000 and 20,000 feet, above the range of most North Vietnamese antiaircraft guns. Pilots employed a high-altitude, shallow attack dive, which gave them more time to line up their bombs before they reached the range of enemy ground fire.

With the introduction of SAMs, that high-altitude sanctuary disappeared. Pilots were forced to return to low-level tactics. "That put us right back down into that goddamned ground fire again," said a navy commander. Now pilots had to come in low, then pop up over their target and execute a steep bombing dive. This shortened the length of time they had to align their bomb sights and forced them back down into the range of AAA, increasing their margin for error.

The missiles could sometimes force a strike group to turn back before it even reached the target ahead. The mere call, "SAMs up!" would scatter an incoming attack force as pilots jettisoned their bomb loads prematurely in order to gain speed and outmaneuver the SAMs.

Forced to counteract the multiple threat of SAMs, Migs, and radar-directed AAA, the cost of Rolling Thunder missions rose dramatically. Each bombing mission now had to be accompanied by a flight of Wild Weasels, a fighter escort of Phantoms, orbiting electronic reconnaissance aircraft, and early warning radar planes, besides the usual array of support aircraft, such as KC-135 aerial refueling tankers, Search and Rescue (SAR) helicopters, and Rescue Combat Air Patrol (RESCAP) Skyraiders.

While North Vietnam's air defense umbrella denied American pilots superiority in the air, their more primitive methods of camouflage, labor gangs, and bicycle convoys kept the supplies moving southward in spite of the bombing. "If you place the damage on a dollar value basis, obviously this would probably be one of the most costly wars we have ever fought," reported Major General Gilbert P. Meyers, deputy commander of the 2d Air Division. "Ho Chi Minh can go on forever fighting the way he is because he is using limited resources." Although the military submitted plans for the invasion of North Vietnam and Laos, for the next two years the only alternative given serious consideration was more bombing.

113

# Upping the Ante

As North Vietnam dug in its heels, America brought more aerial might to bear. By the end of 1965, three aircraft carriers were stationed off the coast. The number of USAF squadrons, situated at air bases in Thailand, was expanded and they were deployed for longer tours of duty. Additional USAF and marine aircraft, based at a growing number of airfields in South Vietnam, were also available for Rolling Thunder missions. Among them were some of the most advanced products of U.S. aerospace technology.

When the U.S.S. *Independence* sailed into Yankee Station in June, she carried a squadron of unfamiliar jets alongside the Skyhawks and Phantoms on her flight deck. These aircraft, manned by a pilot and a bombardier/navigator (BN) seated side by side, represented the world's first all-weather tactical bomber. Equipped with a Digital Integrated Attack Navigational System, the A-6A Intruder was capable of locating and bombing a target at night and in bad weather.

Instead of the usual blips and shadows, radar readings appeared on a screen in the cockpit in the form of a visual representation of the terrain ahead. Once the appropriate coordinates were punched into the Intruder's computer system, the time and mileage to the selected target appeared at the bottom of the screen. A three-dimensional path then appeared on the screen, superimposed over the terrain image. The path, dubbed the "yellow brick road," guided the aircraft on the desired course. All the pilot had to do was make sure the plane was directly over the target at the right time: The system automatically released the bombs and provided a preplanned path out of the area.

While other aircraft were often grounded during the November–April northeast monsoon season in North Vietnam or obliged to operate at night by the artificial glow of flares, the Intruder could operate twenty-four hours a day in any type of weather. The twin-engine jet compensated for its subsonic speed with longer range and increased firepower. Each A-6 could carry more than seven tons of ordnance—more than the World War II B-29 could carry—to distant targets.

Although it took some time to perfect the new aircraft, by early 1966 the Intruder's destructive power became fully evident to the North Vietnamese. In April, when a power plant near Haiphong was leveled during a night raid, Radio Hanoi accused the U.S. of using B-52 bombers against its cities. In fact the raid was carried out by two A-6As from the U.S.S. *Kitty Hawk* with twenty-six 1,000-pound bombs.

Two new E-2A Hawkeye early warning aircraft arrived in the Gulf of Tonkin in November. Fitted with a revolving radar dome twenty-four feet in diameter atop its fuselage and a sophisticated computer system, the twin turbo-prop plane could direct strike aircraft to and from their targets and also could warn of any Mig threat. Able to stay aloft for up to seven hours, they were in effect orbiting communications centers, which relayed messages between strike forces and their carriers, directed airborne refueling, and aided in SAR operations.

Yet another symbol of American technological might appeared in early December, when the nuclear powered U.S.S. *Enterprise* sailed into Yankee Station. Carrying over ninety aircraft, the 90,000-ton carrier had a flight deck almost as long as four football fields. Combining with air wings aboard the *Kitty Hawk* and *Ticonderoga*, *Enterprise* planes flew the last Rolling Thunder strike of 1965.

Just before Christmas, President Johnson opened up the first targets inside the Red River Delta. Among them was the Uong Bi power plant, fifteen miles northeast of Haiphong, which produced 15 percent of North Vietnam's electrical output. This Russian-financed plant was struck

twice in mid-December, yet it remained in operation. On December 22, 110 planes were sent to finish the job.

Led by Skyhawks of the "Big E's" Air Wing 9, the jets turned inland north of Haiphong Harbor, staying low behind a stretch of ridges to mask their approach from the city's radar and AAA. But as they dove on the Uong Bi plant, enemy gunners quickly found their range, and the *Enterprise* suffered its first combat casualties. Two of the Skyhawks were hit in the first wave; one pilot was killed and the other captured. Three waves of planes, flying thirty minutes apart, pulverized the power plant, wiping out one-third of Haiphong's electrical supply and one-fourth of Hanoi's.

That same day, Intruders from the *Kitty Hawk* hit another previously off-limits target eighteen miles west of Haiphong. Using their radar bombing systems, the A-6s blasted the Hai Duong Bridge with thirteen tons of bombs. Ten direct hits demolished the center span of the bridge on the road to Hanoi. But an Intruder and an RA-5C photo jet were lost to SAMs.

## Johnson's "peace offensive"

On December 24, after the strikes at Uong Bi and Hai Duong, President Johnson ordered a thirty-hour Christmas cease-fire. Ground operations resumed on the twenty-sixth, but the bombing suspension was extended for twenty-four hours. The night before the bombing was to resume, the president unexpectedly phoned Washington from the LBJ ranch in Texas to order the pause extended indefinitely.

Pressure for another bombing pause had been steadily mounting during the year. More and more Americans had come to question the administration's Vietnam policy. Abroad, the escalated bombing fostered an image of a belligerent superpower relentlessly hammering a small, economically backward nation. Although Johnson had tried to keep civilian casualties low, the bombing presented Hanoi "with a near ideal mix of intended restraint and accidental gore," according to one Rand Corporation analyst, and the North exploited that to the fullest in the court of world public opinion.

At the end of the year, a number of foreign governments, anxious for negotiations, reported positive signs from Hanoi. In fact, since May the U.S. had maintained secret, unofficial contacts with North Vietnamese officials in Paris. In late November, Soviet Ambassador Anatoly Dobrynin informed McGeorge Bundy that a brief bombing pause would assure "intense diplomatic activity." A number of the president's own advisers, including Robert McNamara, urged him to consider the idea.

President Johnson was deeply skeptical. He had tried that door before in May only to have Hanoi slam it shut. But at the last minute he decided that a bombing pause might be beneficial if it were engineered the right way.

*Preceding page. Taking to the air again after the January 1966 bombing pause, F-105s unleash their loads against targets in the North.*

*Two A-6A Intruder jets from Attack Squadron 85 descend toward the U.S.S.* Kitty Hawk *in the South China Sea, their tail hooks extended to grab the carrier's arresting cable.*

In a top-secret cable to the newly appointed American ambassador in Saigon, Henry Cabot Lodge, Dean Rusk explained the president's objectives. "We do not, quite frankly, anticipate that Hanoi will respond in any significant way," he wrote. But with the Soviets pushing Hanoi for a political settlement and the Chinese adamantly opposed to the idea, perhaps the pause would widen the rift between the two Communist powers. Secondly, "the prospect of large-scale reinforcements in men and defense budget increases of some $20 billion," Rusk said, "requires solid preparation of the American public. A crucial element will be the clear demonstration that we have explored fully every alternative but that the aggressor has left us no choice."

On December 30, the president launched his highly publicized "peace offensive." Envoys were sent to foreign governments asking them to use their influence with Hanoi to arrange a meeting. Johnson's latest negotiating terms were announced at the White House and secretly passed on to the North Vietnamese by the U.S. ambassador in the Burmese capital of Rangoon. Drafted by Secretary Rusk, the fourteen-point U.S. initiative endorsed in principle most of Hanoi's Four Points. But it refused to accept participation of the Vietcong in a coalition government in Saigon as a precondition to negotiations.

Hanoi responded as Rusk had predicted. A foreign ministry spokesman condemned the initiative, saying its purpose was "to force on the Vietnamese people acceptance of U.S. terms." The final straw came in a public letter issued by Ho Chi Minh on January 28 in which the Communist leader denounced Johnson's offer as "deceitful." After the pause's thirty-seventh day, with no sign of give on Hanoi's part, on January 31 the president ordered the bombing resumed.

## A return to gradual escalation

Hanoi's rejection of Johnson's peace initiative brought intense debate in Washington over the future course of Rolling Thunder. The military continued to press for intensified bombing, marshaling an array of statistics to emphasize the destructive potential of U.S. air power. They flashed color-coded charts at briefings to show the rising number of attack sorties, which had delivered an average of 1,600 tons of bombs per month during the last quarter of 1965. Rolling Thunder had claimed 15,000 waterborne craft, 800 trucks, and 650 pieces of railroad rolling stock. Twenty-seven percent of North Vietnam's electrical capacity had been wiped out in 1965, the statistics said, and the bombing had caused roughly $63 million in damage.

*President Johnson turns to McGeorge Bundy moments after announcing the resumption of the bombing on January 31, 1966.*

The generals believed the bombing had "substantially" reduced Hanoi's ability to support the war in the South, but they thought it had been carried out too timidly to destroy the enemy's will to do so. Despite the fact that the geographic scope of the bombing had been enlarged to include the northwest sector of North Vietnam by the end of 1965, only two or three new targets were being approved for each biweekly Rolling Thunder period. Military leaders complained that this denied them flexibility and the element of surprise necessary for effective air operations. The North Vietnamese were able to concentrate their air defenses as U.S. planes were sent in day after day against the same targets or on armed reconnaissance along the same narrowly defined routes.

Political restrictions limiting the bombing to transportation targets in southern North Vietnam merely provided Hanoi with a military staging area immune from attack, according to the Joint Chiefs. In the Red River Delta sanctuaries, Hanoi's war-supporting industries and military stockpiles remained unscathed. Supplementing this untouched economic and military resource base was a growing influx of Soviet and Chinese supplies.

In January, CINCPAC Adm. Sharp outlined a bombing campaign that he believed would bring Hanoi to its knees.

The plan involved denying North Vietnam its external support by mining Haiphong Harbor and cutting the rail line to China; destroying all war-making resources within the country, including military facilities, power plants, petroleum, oil, and lubricants (POL) stockpiles; and increasing pressure on transportation targets. The JCS endorsed Sharp's plan and passed it on to the secretary of defense.

McNamara adjudged Sharp's "fast track" bombing scheme as too risky. Mining Haiphong Harbor and cutting the railroad to China might bring the U.S. into direct confrontation with the Soviets and the Chinese. North Vietnam's defiant stance during the bombing suspension had also reinforced his belief that bombing alone could not force Hanoi to negotiate. North Vietnamese leaders appeared willing to endure any level of bombing as long as they saw the possibility of a victory on the ground in the South.

Instead, McNamara recommended to the president that he continue to center the bombing on southern supply routes to reduce the level of infiltration into South Vietnam. He did endorse, however, an increase in the number of attack sorties from 3,000 to 4,000 per month. He thought the modest increase would make things more difficult for Hanoi and help "maintain the morale of our South Vietnamese allies."

But President Johnson rejected both the JCS' and McNamara's proposals. "I was always convinced," Johnson wrote in his memoirs, "that the bombing was less important to a successful outcome in Vietnam than what was done militarily on the ground in the South." Some of his advisers had also warned that a too sharp resumption of the bombing might add credence to claims that the pause had been a ploy to justify further escalation when Hanoi turned down the U.S. offer.

Rolling Thunder resumed in February at an even slower pace than the previous year, much to the dismay of the generals. Total attack sorties for the month reached only 2,809. The president refused to approve any long-range plans and continued to control the targets, doling them out one by one in each new biweekly package. Although more targets were opened up in the northwest sector and some in the Red River Delta would be authorized in 1966, the bulk of effort continued to be aimed at transportation targets south of the twentieth parallel.

## From Cold War to limited war

Despite the generals' "can do" attitude, American air power was struggling to adjust to a role it was woefully unprepared for, trying to adapt an air arm designed for strategic nuclear warfare to a limited political conflict. Through most of the cold war period of the 1950s, the theory of massive retaliation had dominated American military thinking, with emphasis on the development of strategic nuclear forces at the expense of tactical aircraft procurement and training in conventional tactics.

Many tactical fighter–bombers approved for production were built to carry nuclear weapons. Because of the vast power of a nuclear device, pinpoint accuracy was not essential. Even if a pilot missed by 1,000 feet, he could be certain of obliterating his target.

American pilots, trained in tactics and aircraft geared primarily toward strategic offensives against other industrialized nations, found themselves unprepared for the Vietnam War. They had to relearn the fundamentals of dropping conventional "iron bombs" accurately on small, mobile targets. "It's ridiculous!" exclaimed General Gilbert Meyers. "We haven't improved that capability one iota since World War II."

To become qualified in dive bombing, a pilot had to place a string of bombs inside a circle 280 feet in diameter. This was not good enough in Vietnam, where the target was often a moving truck or a small bridge. That kind

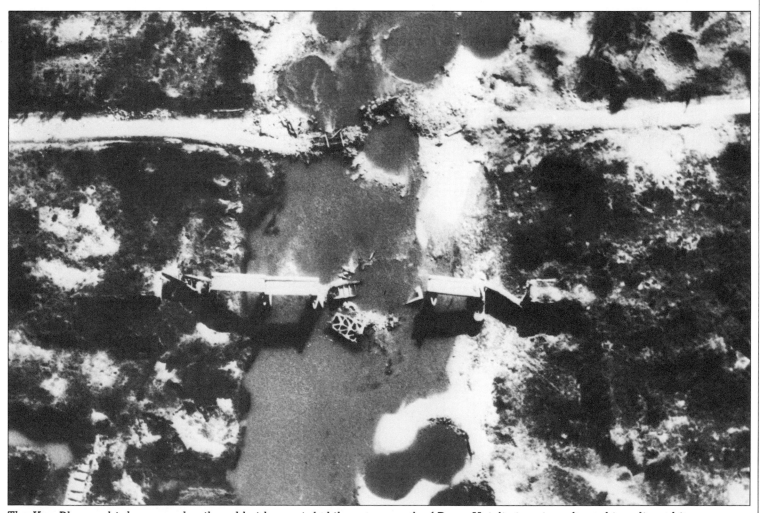

*The Xon Phuong highway and railroad bridges, eight kilometers north of Dong Hoi, lie in ruins after taking direct hits.*

of precise bombing would be difficult on a controlled training range under ideal conditions, but in Vietnam it had to be done in varying weather against targets ringed by AAA batteries while threatened by SAMs from below and Migs from above.

Many of the officers who determined tactics and decided how many and which types of aircraft would be assigned to each target had little firsthand knowledge of the capabilities of the planes in use over Vietnam. Those who had risen through the ranks in the 1950s, when the emphasis was on strategic bombing, found their theories of low-level navigation and nuclear weapons delivery totally inappropriate. Older staff officers tried to apply the lessons of World War II but soon found that the increased size, weight, and turning radius of a modern fighter-bomber had outmoded earlier tactics.

Most American fighter-bomber aircraft were ill-equipped for their new role. The workhorse of Rolling Thunder operations was the air force's F-105 Thunderchief, which flew approximately 75 percent of the missions against the North. Billed as the world's largest and fastest single-seat fighter-bomber, the Thunderchief weighed over twenty-five tons fully armed and could reach a maximum speed of Mach 2.2. Plagued by early design and production problems, it was referred to as the "Ultra Hog" or "Lead Sled" by skeptical pilots. Even when the bugs were finally worked out, fighter pilots called it the "Thud."

Fitted with an internal bomb bay that could carry up to four tons of nuclear weapons, the F-105 was originally designed for high-speed strikes against strategic targets. Its non-self-sealing fuel tanks made the plane highly vulnerable during low-level runs in heavy ground fire. A vast array of switches and arming procedures complicated the pilot's job inside the cockpit.

Still, the F-105's speed and ability to carry a large weapons load made it the logical choice for Rolling Thunder missions. The addition of four wing pylons and attachments under the bomb bay increased its weapons load to over six tons. A 360-gallon fuel tank added inside the bomb bay increased its range. A Vulcan cannon in the nose cone could fire at the rate of 6,000 rounds of 20MM shells per minute. But all this firepower was useless unless a pilot could deliver it on target.

Beyond the problems of refining and learning new tactics, the many rules and regulations dictated by the U.S. high command further complicated a pilot's task. In keeping with the president's wishes to avoid civilian casualties, pilots were prohibited from flying missions within a ten-

*On the outskirts of Hanoi, a North Vietnamese antiaircraft company goes to work in October 1967. Seen here are the widely used Russian-built KS-18 85MM guns, capable of reaching altitudes of 30,000 feet.*

*A Thunderchief pilot dives toward his target in North Vietnam, firing a volley of 2.75-inch rockets, on April 8, 1966. Shortages of heavy bombs in late 1965 and early 1966 hampered Rolling Thunder.*

mile radius of Hanoi and a four-mile radius of Haiphong. Outside these "prohibited zones" but within thirty miles of Hanoi and ten miles of Haiphong were other "restricted zones," in which American pilots could fire on AAA batteries and SAM sites only in self-defense and then only if they were not located in populated areas. U.S. planes also were not allowed to enter a zone thirty miles south of the Chinese border in order to avoid the possibility of clashes with Chinese Migs.

The restricted and prohibited zones were only part of a large set of U.S. rules of engagement. When air force Colonel Jack Broughton arrived in Southeast Asia he was amazed by their number and complexity:

If you were standing still and examining the rules under classroom conditions, they were not easy to comprehend and the pilot was hard pressed to catalog all the do's and don'ts and correlate them into the job we laid on him. When you have this same problem moving at 600 [knots], under lousy weather and navigation conditions, and admitted that a lot of people were desperately trying to kill you, you had a problem that was difficult for the best to solve.

Pilots also endured equipment shortages of every kind. The most critical shortage was sufficient quantities of 750-pound bombs and large rockets. "All the emphasis had been on strategic weapons for so long that everybody had forgotten that we might need tactical weapons again," confessed Lieutenant General Albert Clark, vice commander of TAC. "We started down there with what was left over from World War II."

Production of conventional "iron bombs" had virtually ceased as the military began developing more advanced types of tactical weapons, such as CBUs and missiles like the Shrike. Meanwhile, as the bombing intensified, the stockpiles of World War II and Korean surplus bombs dwindled rapidly. "We are very low on bombs," one F-105 pilot recorded in his diary. "[We] have no rocket fuses. We are carrying two 750-pound bombs into areas and getting shot at while delivering this load which we know is inadequate to do the job."

Although the American public was unaware of the situation, the shortage was well known to the enemy. While on R & R in Hong Kong during the Christmas 1965 bombing pause, Captain James P. Coyne, a 2d Air Division staff officer, met the Polish ambassador to Peking while on a sightseeing tour. The talk turned to the war and the Pole commented: "Ah, now you've stopped the bombing."

"Yes," Coyne replied, "the President is giving them a chance to assess the damage and realize we're going to

*The "bomb gap." Secretary of Defense McNamara's claims that the reported bomb shortage in Vietnam was a lot of "baloney" left many unconvinced.*

**"WILL THAT BE ALL, MR. McNAMARA?"**

really hit them if they don't come to the negotiating table." "No," the diplomat countered, "you have stopped the bombing because you are out of bombs." Coyne was stunned. Later he would discover the Polish ambassador was partially right. Although the JCS had opposed the extended pause, they welcomed a short halt as an opportunity to refill the supply stockpiles.

When the bombing resumed in February and shortages remained acute, intimations of the problem began circulating in the press. Later that month, McNamara said in response to questions about the shortage, "All this baloney about lack of bomb production is completely misleading." According to his systems analysts there were more than adequate supplies. Pilots were unconvinced. "If McNamara can't send us bombs," said one aviator, "he ought to send us some of his baloney. We have to drop something."

In February, newspapers reported that the Defense Department had repurchased for $21.00 apiece more than 5,000 bombs that had been sold to West Germany for scrap at $1.70 each. Later, the Pentagon admitted that for the Vietnam War the U.S. had "reacquired" 18,000 bombs sold to Allied nations.

The problem was not only in numbers. Bombs were shipped to Vietnam in their component parts—casings, tail fin assemblies, and fuses. Each of these parts came in many types, each designed to suit different circumstances. Casings, which contained high explosives and shrapnel in varying ratios that determined the bomb's blast and fragmentation effect, came in a variety of shapes and sizes. Older, World War II–style "fat bombs" were better suited to aircraft with an internal bomb bay, like the B-57. On

smaller fighter-bombers, like the F-4, which carried its bombs slung on pylons underneath its wings, slimmer bomb casings were preferred to reduce wind resistance.

Fuses, which screwed into the noses of the bomb casings, came in two basic types. The most common fuse was armed by a propeller that began to spin once the bomb was dropped. This delayed arming device enabled the aircraft to be well clear of the bomb before it was armed. Another design, used for delayed detonation, contained a vial of acetone separated from the fuse by a glassine or mica disc. Once the bomb hit, the vial would break, releasing the acetone, which ate through the disc and activated the fuse. The thickness of the disc determined when the bomb would explode.

Tail fins also varied between "low-drag" models, which had little wind resistance, and the "high-drag" types, which had fins that popped open upon release to retard the bomb's descent. Low-drag fins were fine for high-altitude bombing attacks, but if a pilot needed to drop his bombs at a lower altitude, the high-drag fins extended the bomb's "free fall" time by several seconds, allowing the aircraft to clear the target before its bombs exploded.

Component parts had to be selected to suit varying situations. Against a strong bridge, for example, a small number of large bombs was preferable to many smaller ones. By the same token, heavy bombs with delayed-action fuses might pass right through a bridge and explode in the water, leaving nothing more than a small hole in the bridge's surface. Mistakes in orders and planning, compounded by the lengthy supply line, often resulted in the mismatching of ordnance and targets, leaving a squadron without the means to accomplish its assigned missions.

"Sometimes," said an air force officer, "the bomb bodies arrive by ship at Saigon and the fins were over in Bangkok and the fuses were up at Da Nang. You might have all the parts and no single bomb. I know of one occasion when we had C-130s flying bomb parts from one place to another to put a strike together."

Rumors of shortages in aircraft, particularly the versatile F-4 Phantoms used by both the air force and the navy, and even a shortage of pilots, surfaced in the newspapers early in 1966. Navy Department figures revealed that attack pilots were flying an unusually high average of nineteen missions per month over North Vietnam, while some even flew twenty-eight. Air force pilots were similarly overextended.

Originally, various fighter squadrons were rotated through Southeast Asia for three-month tours of temporary duty. But as the air war escalated the 2d Air Division was upgraded in stature (and renamed the 7th Air Force), and its F-105 pilots based in Thailand found their tours extended indefinitely. The number of missions increased and so did the stress on a pilot who faced longer exposure time to enemy fire. Many flew 2 missions a day over North Vietnam. Eventually a ceiling of 100 combat missions was set, after which a pilot would be rotated home.

This required a fresh supply of pilots, so the Defense Department stepped up pilot training programs, an expensive and lengthy process. The average cost of basic flight training for an air force pilot was over $75,000 plus $2,000 per hour for advanced training. Eighteen months and more than $100,000 were needed to train a navy pilot.

To solve the immediate problem, the services plucked qualified aviators from desk jobs and shore duty. Many were older officers with little experience in the newer aircraft they were assigned to fly. After abbreviated refresher courses, they went into combat. Even under these risky circumstances, many volunteered in order to gain the combat experience necessary for career advancement.

Whether the new fliers were seeded among existing squadrons, as in the air force, or formed into new units with a sprinkling of combat veterans as the navy preferred to do, the infusion of untested pilots led to an overall decline in squadron efficiency. Each unit's fighting capabilities fluctuated dramatically as the experienced pilots were forced to spend more of their time training newcomers under combat conditions.

## "A bean-counting kind of war"

President Johnson did not want the war to cut into his cherished "Great Society" programs at home, so to a certain degree, the shortages in pilots, planes, and munitions were a product of his hope to fight the war in Vietnam on the cheap. No one was better qualified to attempt to make the "guns and butter" policy work than Robert McNamara. McNamara's ability to reel off complicated statistics on any relevant subject amazed many subordinates and left stenographers struggling to keep pace. Surrounded with bright, young analysts, often referred to as the "whiz kids," the secretary kept close tabs on almost every facet of the sprawling bureaucracy in the Pentagon.

Civilians in his own Systems and Analysis Division and in Assistant Secretary of Defense John McNaughton's International Security Agency provided him with up-to-date estimates of the costs and results of various programs, especially Rolling Thunder. The secretary took a personal interest in even the smallest details. After a strike against a major bridge in Laos, the bomb damage assessment photos, along with the pilot who took them, were immediately whisked to Washington. The bewildered pilot "ended up on his hands and knees with Secretary McNamara on the floor of his office," an air force general recalled, "while McNamara was busily engaged in discussing various entry points towards the target area, the initial points, pull-out tactics, and things of this sort."

Predictably, civilian involvement in tactical aspects of the air war created resentment among professional soldiers. Military men bitterly assailed the "armchair generals" with their "accountant mentalities" who evaluated the effectiveness of the bombing by employing a balance sheet of costs versus gains. But the generals proved willing and adept at playing the numbers game themselves. McNamara tended to rely on the number of sorties flown to measure Rolling Thunder operations. Therefore, to support their arguments that not enough was being done, the generals put pressure on area air commanders to fly all the missions allotted to them during each biweekly period. "Obviously, if you do not fly them," said General Gilbert Meyers, the deputy director of the 2d Air Division, "[the civilian analysts] can make a case that you really don't need them anyway."

This often resulted in pilots being sent up in marginal weather or directed against targets they had already destroyed. When a set of previously off-limit targets was released, there would be a mad dash to strike them before Washington had a chance to reconsider. USAF Colonel Jack Broughton felt that the hastily organized missions defied military logic, exposing pilots and planes to unnecessary risks. "We had waited a long time for these targets," he noted, "and could afford to wait a few more minutes to do the job right."

The obsession with high sortie rates continued even during the severest moments of the bomb shortage, which resulted in a policy of sending a fixed number of planes with fewer bombs on some missions rather than loading all available bombs on fewer planes. The practice unnecessarily exposed some pilots to enemy defenses.

A letter to the editor of *Aviation Week* magazine sent by

123

# A "Thud" Mission

A typical Rolling Thunder mission began the day before a planned strike when the orders were issued from Saigon to the combat operations centers of USAF fighter wings based in Thailand. Staff officers then broke down the lengthy messages into the particular portions that dealt with each air wing and translated them into specific instructions for the three squadrons in each wing. Known as fragmentary orders, or "frags," these specifics included the scheduled times, number of aircraft, types of weapons, and navigational details for a primary target and two alternates.

The pilots selected for the mission received maps, navigational cards, and intelligence reports on each of the three targets. Sometime during the night, the mission commander received word from headquarters finalizing the primary target. A typical F-105 "Thud jockey" then went through the following routine:

After a few hours' sleep, the pilot is awakened for the preflight briefing. Forgoing any deodorant or after-shave lotion, the scents of which would make a North Vietnamese search party's job easier if he were forced to bail out into the jungles of North Vietnam, the pilot slips into his flight suit.

Pilots then assemble in the squadron briefing room where they are updated on weather conditions and probable enemy defenses en route to and within the target area. Each flight of four planes is assigned a radio call sign. After rechecking last-minute details with the other pilots in his flight, the pilot heads to the personal equipment shack to don his gear.

First, he wriggles into the tight, waist-high G-suit that automatically inflates during high-speed maneuvers to keep the increased force of gravity from draining the blood from his head, which could cause him to black out. Then he puts on his multipocketed, mesh survival vest, which contains a two-way radio, flares, a miniature first aid kit, a .38 revolver, and a dozen other pieces of survival gear. After strapping a fifty-pound parachute onto his back, the pilot, now wearing over eighty pounds of equipment, picks up his helmet and heads out to the flight line.

Climbing into the cockpit of an F-105 Thunderchief, the pilot starts the engine with the ground crew; all systems are then checked with the crew chief. The pilot then taxis the plane to a point near the end of the runway where the arming crew pulls the red safety clips off the bombs and rockets slung under the plane. Armed and ready, he takes off, rendezvous with the three other planes in his flight, and heads toward North Vietnam.

Somewhere over Thailand, the pilot receives coordinates for a meeting with an orbiting KC-135 refueling tanker. Maneuvering the plane behind the giant flying gas station, the pilot holds a stable speed and heading to enable the tanker crew to lower a boom into the fuel receptacle atop the Thud's nose cone. The trauma of metal-to-metal contact in the air lasts approximately six minutes. But the Thud will need every ounce of fuel if it is to be pushed through maximum performance maneuvers.

Crossing into North Vietnamese airspace, the pilot switches radio channels to a predetermined strike frequency. The flight leader's voice breaks in over the headset, reminding the pilot to activate the nine separate switches controlling the bomb release mechanisms and to turn on the electronic countermeasures gear. Alone in the tiny cockpit, the pilot hears only the sounds of his own breathing over the muffled whine of the jet engine.

While flashing over the North Vietnamese countryside at 600 miles per hour, the pilot scans ahead for prominent landmarks, such as roads, rivers, or towns, that are marked on the map. If the cloud cover has made visual sightings impossible, he has to rely solely on instruments, the most important being the Doppler navigation system. Once fed with the precise geographical coordinates of the point the aircraft is flying over and the target desired, the Doppler computes the relevant course bearings as well as the time and distance to get there. Navigation has to be precise or a pilot could end up searching for the target and become a sitting duck for enemy gunners.

Miles from the target the pilot's headset comes to life, emitting eerie electronic noises that warn that Mig and SAM radar has begun stalking his aircraft. Keeping watch on the ground for the flash of swirling light that means a SAM has been launched, he also follows the dotted lines appearing on the radar scope, which indicate shadowing Migs. If a pilot confirms that a SAM has been launched, he immediately warns the rest of his flight, and the pilots dive to avoid the missile. If a pilot manages to run this gauntlet without having to jettison his bombs to pick up speed and avoid the Migs and SAMs, and if he is able to pick his way through the usual AAA fire, the hardest part still lies ahead.

Picking up air speed and altitude, the pilot takes a quick but detailed look at the target and rechecks the armament settings. At a predetermined altitude, he rolls the plane into a forty-five-degree dive. He now has six to nine seconds before he has to pull out of the dive to line up the target in the optical aiming device. Coaxing the rudder pedals, throttle, and control stick simultaneously, the pilot constantly makes adjustments to maintain the exact air speed and dive angle.

Nothing can be done to avoid the ground fire while the pilot is in his attack dive. He knows that if his bombs are not exactly on target, he will only have to return to the target. But once he presses the "pickle" button releasing the bombs, the pilot's instinct for survival takes over.

Pulling back on the control stick, the pilot lights up the afterburner, fighting off the G-pressure of the pullout as the Thud surges skyward. Now, with his back turned toward the ground fire, a pilot flies by instinct, "jinking" in rapid rolling and twisting maneuvers, trying to offer the worst possible target to enemy gunners.

Heading for home, he passes through the same gauntlet of Migs and SAMs. To make sure he has enough fuel to make it home, he hooks up again with the refueling tankers. Finally, the pilot lands back at base. Out of a total mission time of two hours, the pilot was over the target area for perhaps only ten minutes and the target itself for only seconds. But his flight suit is soaked with sweat. After debriefing with the operations officer, there would be another mission, perhaps even that afternoon.

an anonymous air force F–4 pilot in September 1966, illustrated the frustrations felt by many combat pilots.

The war here in Vietnam has become a political football, an exercise in glowing reports, outstanding new records and promises of "turning the tide" . . . it is time that the facts be given. . . . There is nothing more demoralizing than the sight of an F–4 taxiing out with nothing but a pair of bombs nestled among its ejector racks. However, it looks much better for the commander and the service concerned to show 200 sorties on paper, even when 40 or 50 would do the same job.

The numbers game also exacerbated the traditional rivalry between the air force and the navy, each constantly competing for Defense Department funds. The navy did not want the air force flying more missions than the navy did and vice versa. "It was a silly kind of bean-counting," recalled one navy commander, "but it was a bean-counting kind of war."

During the early stages of Rolling Thunder, navy and air force commands squabbled constantly over which should attack the relatively few targets authorized by the Pentagon. Overlapping command structures and poor communications between navy carriers and air force headquarters in Saigon often resulted in confusion and duplication. For example, an air force strike force might arrive over a target only to find that the navy had been there already. To improve coordination, the two services eventually agreed upon a plan dividing each day into six- and three-hour segments, each segment to be controlled by each service on a rotating basis. This arrangement soon proved ludicrous. If the weather was bad over the gulf and navy aircraft were launched late, or the same happened with air force planes in Thailand, aircraft flying missions in the next rotation could overlap the delayed strike forces.

By the end of 1965, an interservice committee divided North Vietnam into six separate "route packages," splitting responsibility for the areas between the two services (see map, this page). There was one exception: Ultimately Gen. Westmoreland was given control of air operations in

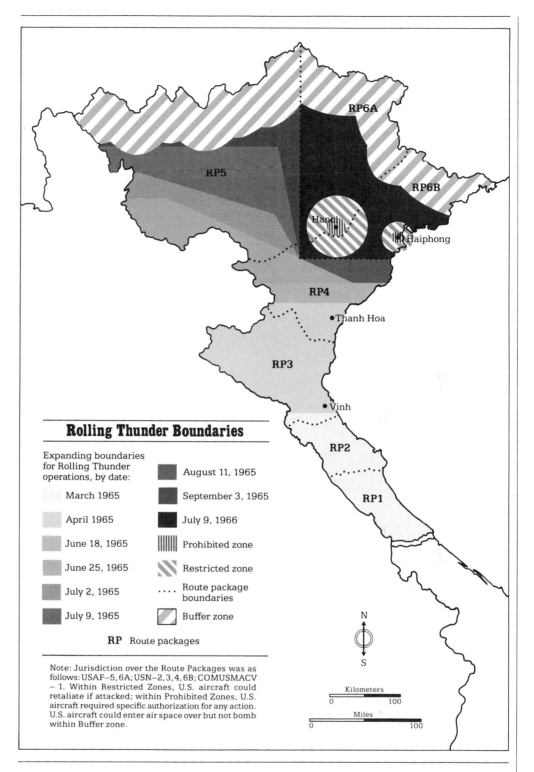

**Rolling Thunder Boundaries**

Expanding boundaries for Rolling Thunder operations, by date:

March 1965

April 1965

June 18, 1965

June 25, 1965

July 2, 1965

July 9, 1965

August 11, 1965

September 3, 1965

July 9, 1966

Prohibited zone

Restricted zone

Route package boundaries

Buffer zone

**RP** Route packages

Note: Jurisdiction over the Route Packages was as follows: USAF–5, 6A; USN–2, 3, 4, 6B; COMUSMACV – 1. Within Restricted Zones, U.S. aircraft could retaliate if attacked; within Prohibited Zones, U.S. aircraft required specific authorization for any action. U.S. aircraft could enter air space over but not bomb within Buffer zone.

Kilometers
0      100

Miles
0      100

Route Package 1, the zone closest to South Vietnam. He was empowered to call upon air force, navy, marine, or army aircraft to strike targets in that "extended battlefield" area. Route Package 6, encompassing Hanoi and Haiphong, was divided between the air force and the navy. The air force was assigned the area northwest of Hanoi while the navy took the region between the capital and the coast, including Haiphong. The "barrel," or "corner," as pilots came to call Pack 6, soon was fortified by the North Vietnamese into one of the most heavily defended areas in the history of aerial warfare.

125

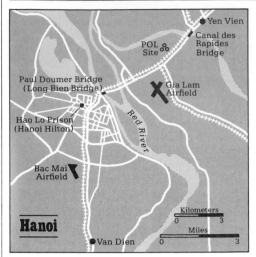

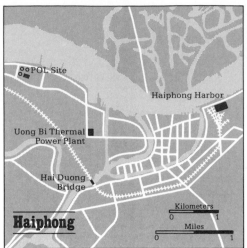

# "You may not wake up tomorrow"

In March, the Joint Chiefs once again pressured McNamara to escalate the bombing. But this time they modified their plan from an all-out assault to a concentrated campaign against a single target system—North Vietnamese POL facilities: The Chiefs claimed that their destruction would drastically reduce Hanoi's ability to move men and supplies south.

Since rail lines in southern North Vietnam had been virtually destroyed, Hanoi relied heavily on trucks and motorized boats to move supplies. As a result the North's dependence on imported petroleum products had increased dramatically. During 1965, Hanoi imported 170,000 metric tons, stored in large receiving areas in Haiphong Harbor and at tank farms in Hanoi. In early 1966 the rate increased by at least 50 percent. Ninety-seven percent of North Vietnam's total POL supplies were stored in only thirteen sites, offering a highly concentrated target. Without petroleum and oil for its trucks and motorized watercraft, Hanoi would have to resort to less efficient transportation, such as bicycles, porters, and sampans. The Joint Chiefs' proposals were supported by a CIA study, which found that attacks on POL facilities could be a more effective anti-infiltration measure than tracking down individual trucks and motor boats and attacking them.

U.S. pilots agreed. "Many times as we come in over Haiphong we'll see a Russian tanker standing in or tied up at a pier," recalled a navy pilot. "Its crew will wave at us and we'll wave back. But then for the next six weeks we chase individual oil trucks down camouflaged roads."

The POL campaign proposal underwent intense scrutiny in Washington during the next few months. At the Pentagon, some questioned whether the attacks could achieve the results the JCS predicted in light of Hanoi's resourcefulness in counteracting the effects of U.S. bombing efforts. The nine POL sites recommended by the JCS were inside the Hanoi and Haiphong restricted zones, and many civilians were apprehensive about striking so close

to major population centers. Others thought the raids would be seen as a major escalation and only invite the Communists to further increase the pressure on the South. On April 1, McNamara gave the plan his tacit approval, telling the president he thought the strikes would "create a substantial and added burden on North Vietnam."

Continuing political problems in South Vietnam caused President Johnson to defer for over two months a decision on McNamara's recommendation. When authorization came on June 22, the extremely cautionary tone of CINCPAC's message to air commanders reflected the president's apprehension.

Every precaution was to be taken to avoid unnecessary civilian casualties. Only the most experienced pilots were to be used, and planners were told to select the best axis of attack to avoid population areas. The strikes would not take place unless the weather permitted visual identification of the target in order to insure strike accuracy. To limit pilot distraction, pilots were ordered to make maximum use of ECM to hamper SAM and AAA fire, but they could launch suppression strikes against SAM and AAA installations only at sites outside population areas. Navy pilots assigned to hit POL sites in Haiphong were warned against damaging foreign—and especially Soviet—ships in the harbor. No ship was to be fired upon unless it fired on U.S. aircraft, and then only if the vessels were clearly of North Vietnamese registry.

For an entire week, McNamara received hourly reports on the weather in the Hanoi-Haiphong area. On June 28, General Wheeler got final authorization to launch the strikes the following day. As the orders flashed to air force and navy commands in Southeast Asia, President Johnson pondered the possible repercussions of his decision. "In the dark of night," he later recounted, "I would lay awake picturing my boys flying around North Vietnam asking myself an endless series of questions.... Suppose one of my boys misses his mark when he's flying around Haiphong? Suppose one of his bombs falls on one of those ships in the harbor? What happens then?"

That night, as American jets streaked toward their targets, Johnson showed his concern to his daughter Luci. When she asked what was troubling him, the president told her of the raids and explained that in a nuclear age one mistake could mean the end of the world. "Your daddy may go down in history as having started World War III," he told Luci. "You may not wake up tomorrow."

A recent convert to Catholicism, Luci told her father that when she was troubled she went to pray at St. Domenic's Cathedral in southwest Washington. A little after ten, Johnson ordered a limousine and drove to the church through a driving rainstorm with Ladybird, Luci, and her fiancé. After a few minutes of prayer, the presidential party returned to the White House where Johnson lay awake until first news of the strikes arrived late in the morning.

In Thailand the night before the attack, air force pilots stayed up until midnight checking and double-checking every detail. Mission commanders passed on the navigational coordinates and a plan of attack to pilots who then marked their maps with the times and distances to various checkpoints. The maps were then cut, taped, and folded in accordion fashion to make them easy to handle in the cramped cockpits. Although Hanoi had been photographed extensively by recon jets, this would be the first time American pilots tested Hanoi's air defense system.

## The POL strikes

The operations officer of the 354th Squadron, Major James H. Kasler, was scheduled to lead the four flights from the 355th TFW. Kasler had seen duty as a tail gunner in World War II and had shot down six Migs in the Korean War. During his five-month tour with the 354th at Takhli, he had built an impressive record as a flight commander. One of his wing mates called him a "one man air force."

Eight Thunderchiefs from the 388th TFW at Korat led by Lieutenant Colonel James R. Hopkins were to strike first, approaching Hanoi from the south and using a string of low mountains southwest of the capital as a screen against early detection.

Kasler's four flights from Takhli were to fly in from the

*No room for error. Major James H. Kasler (center) discusses last-minute details with pilots of the 355th Tactical Fighter Wing before leading the attack on Hanoi's POL complex on June 29, 1966.*

North. Although the POL tanks were in Hanoi's northern outskirts, the mission planners required all strike aircraft to start their bombing runs from the south so that any plane overshooting the target or suffering from a bomb ejector malfunction would not drop a bomb into the city. This meant that Kasler's F–105s would have to overfly the target and execute a difficult 180–degree pop–up turn over the city in order to achieve the necessary attack altitude on the required northerly attack heading.

The morning of the twenty–ninth, Kasler's sixteen Thunderchiefs began their long ground roll down the runway at Takhli. Loaded with eight 750–pound bombs apiece, they strained to reach the necessary air speed of 205 knots that would send them airborne. Assembling in formation, the F–105s topped off their fuel tanks from orbiting KC–135 refueling tankers, then sped across the border to their first checkpoint along the Red River just north of Yen Bai. Kasler descended to 300 feet atop a layer of dense fog and turned southeast along the far side of a mountain range 1,700 meters high that led to Hanoi, which U.S. pilots had christened "Thud Ridge." Since the North Vietnamese were unable to mount any guns along its steep, craggy peaks, Thud Ridge provided F–105 pilots with an open path to the Red River Delta.

Over his radio, Kasler could make out Hopkins's voice as he led planes of the strike force from Korat out of the target area after their attack. Kasler inquired by radio whether the fog extended over the target. Hopkins reported the skies over Hanoi were clear but warned, "There are Migs airborne." Turning south at the end of Thud Ridge, Kasler emerged from the fog to see two black funnels of smoke over the POL fields.

At that instant, enemy artillery began blinking its deadly message at Kasler's F–105s. Within seconds the sky was dotted with hundreds of white, gray, and black puffs. Kasler pulled the Thunderchiefs through the flak in a climbing 180–degree turn. At 11,000 feet he cut his afterburner and rolled his plane into its attack dive. Kasler noticed that the Korat force had hit the tanks on both ends of the POL complex, so he aimed his dive in between the two columns of smoke. Soon he saw a tantalizing sight. "I could hardly believe my eyes," he said. "My entire view was filled with big, fat, fuel tanks!"

Releasing his bombs, Kasler made a rolling pullout to the right. He circled the target as the rest of his planes followed in on the burning oil tanks. Kasler saw the two columns of smoke merge "into one huge boiling red and black pillar." Secondary explosions transformed the POL site into an inferno. "As I climbed back to about 5,000 feet," Kasler noted, "I could see flames leaping out of the smoke thousands of feet above me."

At the same time, to the east, twenty–eight navy A–4s from the U.S.S. *Ranger*, led by Commander Frederick F. Palmer, were pounding POL facilities at Haiphong. A second navy strike force, from the *Constellation*, hit the Do Son POL site located at the tip of the peninsula forming the southeast arm of the harbor at Haiphong. Navy patrol vessels offshore could see clouds of smoke rising to 20,000 feet.

All told, 116 navy and air force aircraft struck at the three POL sites in the heart of North Vietnam. Surprisingly, only one aircraft was lost. Captain Murphy Neal Jones was captured after he bailed out of his damaged F–105. The only other air casualty was one North Vietnamese Mig–17 pilot, shot down by an Iron Hand F–105D flying anti–SAM support, which made Major Fred L. Tracy the first F–105 pilot to be credited with a Mig kill.

## Strangling the POL system

American officials found initial reports of the raids to be extremely encouraging. Eighty percent of the thirty–two tank POL farms at Hanoi and 95 percent of the facilities in Haiphong had been destroyed, perhaps 60 percent of North Vietnam's entire supply. Gen. Meyers called the coordinated attack on the POL sites, "the most important strike of the war to date."

Secretary McNamara explained the strikes at a Pentagon news conference the next day. He told reporters that the decision to attack the sites was based on North Vietnam's increased use of trucks and motorized junks to infiltrate supplies. He said the raids were designed to prevent Hanoi's transforming the war "from a small–arms guerrilla action against South Vietnam to a quasiconventional military operation involving major supplies, weapons, and heavier equipment."

Although the strikes had been the first launched against targets near Hanoi and Haiphong, the secretary emphasized that they did not represent a departure from the administration's policy against bombing population centers. He stressed the precautions that had been taken to avoid civilian casualties. The raids were merely an extension of the bombing campaign against North Vietnamese infiltration targets, McNamara said, not an attempt to widen the war.

Nevertheless, the raids provided spectacular headlines around the world. Radio Hanoi predictably denounced them as a "new and serious step," claiming U.S. planes had indiscriminately strafed residential areas and killed civilians. Of greater concern to U.S. officials were the reactions of China and the Soviet Union. Moscow labeled the action a step toward further escalation of the war but stopped short of any threats of retaliation. Peking took a more strident tone, claiming the U.S. had "pushed back the boundaries of war" and warned of "due punishment." But reading between the lines, Washington deduced that Hanoi's allies were unwilling to do more than to promise more aid.

Peking's and Moscow's relatively mild reactions, coupled with initially positive damage reports and low

*Smoke from burning fuel rises 35,000 feet into the air after Hanoi POL site was hit on June 29.*

*While Hanoi's fuel tanks burn, jets from the U.S.S.* Ranger *blast Haiphong's oil depot on June 29, 1966.*

casualties, induced a decision to continue the anti-POL campaign. On July 8 McNamara cabled Adm. Sharp that President Johnson wanted to give "strangulation of North Vietnam's POL system first priority." Strikes against the remaining fixed POL sites, as well as follow-up strikes against the tank farms at Hanoi and Haiphong, were authorized. The limits on armed recon missions were lifted in order to destroy smaller sites dispersed in the countryside and to cut off any shipments of POL supplies by rail from China. Pilots were elated to be able to attack these targets instead of chasing trucks through the jungle. "Now you know you're really hitting instead of just slapping them on the hand," said one naval aviator.

Hanoi had been caught by surprise on the twenty-ninth, because its air defense command was going through a shakeup. But for the follow-up strikes into the heart of their country, the North Vietnamese quickly closed ranks. Prepositioned antiaircraft batteries took a heavy toll in pilots and planes. The North Vietnamese began firing SAMs in volleys despite the danger from Iron Hand and Wild Weasel aircraft. North Vietnamese pilots became more aggressive, constantly challenging American bombers as they attacked targets within striking distance of their Mig airfields. The U.S. lost forty-three U.S. aircraft

in July alone, the highest monthly rate since Rolling Thunder began in March 1965.

On August 8, a little over a month after leading the first POL raid, Maj. James Kasler also fell prey to North Vietnamese ground fire. He was captured by hill tribesmen waving machetes and four days later found himself in cell #18 at Hao Lo Prison in Hanoi. Running a high fever and nearly delirious from the pain of a severely broken leg suffered during ejection, Kasler was told by his captors, "If you want to live you will cooperate with us." But he refused to sign a confession of his "crimes" against the Vietnamese people. Eventually he was taken to a hospital where his leg was set and placed in a cast and then he was shifted to another POW camp southwest of Hanoi, nicknamed the "Zoo" by American POWs.

## A strategic failure

Secretary McNamara carefully monitored the POL campaign. By the end of July, the Defense Intelligence Agency estimated that 70 percent of North Vietnam's fixed POL facilities had been destroyed. Storage capacity had been reduced from 185,000 metric tons to 75,000 tons. Soviet tankers vanished from Haiphong Harbor during July.

When they returned in August, they were forced to off-load their cargo in drums since the port's pumping equipment had been demolished.

Many Soviet-bloc tankers by-passed Haiphong altogether, either by unloading their cargo in Chinese ports for rail shipment to Hanoi or anchoring well off the coast where their oil could be pumped into shallow draft barges. During the day the North Vietnamese barges sheltered themselves from air attack by lying close alongside the neutral tankers. At night they dashed for the safety of camouflaged off-loading points on the coast, while U.S. Navy A-6s and A-4s patrolled overhead.

By late August the POL raids had reached their peak. Nearly all the North's centralized POL storage tanks had been wiped out. But Hanoi had been preparing for this eventuality for over a year. From the first bombing raids in February of 1965, North Vietnam had begun a crash program to decentralize the nation's meager industrial resources from the Red River Delta to reduce their vulnerability to air attacks. Precious POL stores were at the top of the list.

Construction of underground tanks near key transportation routes began as early as the summer of 1965. Fifty-five gallon drums of fuel oil were stockpiled in villages and towns where they would be safe from American bombers. The size of the effort was apparent to a visiting journalist who reported seeing "oil barrels strewn all over the North Vietnamese landscape."

As a result, the loss of its large POL storage facilities created only minor, short-term inconveniences for Hanoi. American aircraft had been able to locate and destroy little more than 7 percent of Hanoi's dispersed stores; air strikes against such small, hard-to find sites were prohibitively costly in terms of munitions, aircraft, and pilot losses. Having reached the point of diminishing returns, the POL campaign was halted on September 4.

Eight days later a joint CIA-DIA appraisal ruefully reported to McNamara that the campaign had been a strategic failure. "There is no evidence yet of any shortages of POL in North Vietnam," their report read, "and stocks on hand, with recent imports, have been adequate to sustain necessary operations." Ho Chi Minh had deftly used the strikes as a political lever to extract further pledges of aid from Moscow and Peking to offset his losses. The joint report also concluded that, despite increased efforts against transportation routes and equipment, "Hanoi retains the capability to continue support of activities in South Vietnam at even increased combat levels."

*A rescue crew picks through the rubble of a village near Hanoi bombed by U.S. aircraft on December 2, 1966.*

A few months later, Secretary McNamara would testify before a Senate committee that "the bombing of the POL system was carried out with as much skill, effort, and attention as we could devote to it and we still haven't been able to dry up those supplies." The failure of the POL strikes marked the beginning of McNamara's disillusionment with the Rolling Thunder campaign and with the Joint Chiefs' claims of what it could accomplish. A report he had commissioned by an independent panel of top civilian scientists, submitted on August 29, reinforced his opinion and offered an alternative.

Known as the Jason summer study group, the blue-ribbon panel concluded that Rolling Thunder had "had no measurable direct effect" on Hanoi's ability to support the war "nor shaken her resolve to do so." As an alternative means of halting infiltration, the group proposed an anti-infiltration barrier—an "electronic fence" of acoustic and seismic sensors—across the DMZ, extending west into Laos across the Ho Chi Minh Trail.

Later in the year McNamara incorporated the barrier concept into a plan of action he drafted for the president. He told Johnson that Hanoi had shifted its strategy to one of "keeping us busy and waiting us out." With the inability of ground forces to land a knockout blow against the VC and the apparent ineffectiveness of the bombing, McNamara saw "no reasonable way to bring the war to an end soon." He suggested consolidating the U.S. effort into a solid military posture that would discourage Hanoi's strategy. The plan called for stabilizing ground force levels, increased pacification efforts in South Vietnam, leveling off the air war and gradually replacing it with the anti-infiltration barrier, and a serious attempt at negotiations.

## Bombing and negotiating

Prospects for a negotiated settlement, negligible since Hanoi's rejection of Johnson's last attempt in January, appeared to brighten in November. On the thirtieth, after nearly six months of secret negotiations between Polish and American diplomats, code named Project Marigold, Washington was informed of Hanoi's tentative agreement to "direct" conversations in Warsaw. According to the Poles, Hanoi had dropped its demand for NLF participation in Saigon's government as a precondition to negotiations. But the U.S. would have to agree to at least a suspension of the bombing and propose a "reasonable calendar" for the withdrawal of U.S. troops from South Vietnam. On December 1, Washington agreed to the meeting in Warsaw but warned that the bombing would stop only after an agreement had been reached on mutual steps to de-escalate the war.

The next day, December 2, twenty navy planes struck a truck depot and army barracks at Van Dien, five miles south of the center of Hanoi. Air force jets also hit the Ha Gia oil facility fourteen miles north of the city. The raids,

authorized on November 10 but delayed because of bad weather, were the first strikes against targets in the Hanoi area since the POL campaign had been halted in September. Eight U.S. aircraft were lost that day, the most in a single day to date. Radio Hanoi accused the U.S. of deliberately attacking populated areas and killing scores of civilians. Defense Department spokesmen denied the accusation and suggested the damage could have been the result of debris from spent antiaircraft shells or stray SAMs.

On December 4, while U.S. Ambassador John A. Grenouski was preparing to meet the Polish foreign minister in Warsaw to iron out the details of the forthcoming meeting with North Vietnamese representatives, U.S. warplanes continued their assault, striking the Ha Gia POL site along with a railroad switching yard at Yen Vien, four and a half miles from the center of Hanoi.

At 11:30 A.M. the following day, Grenouski was summoned by the Polish foreign minister and told that the recent bombings put the meetings in doubt. For the next ten days Grenouski shuttled between the U.S. Embassy and the foreign ministry building, trying to pin down the Poles on a meeting date. All he received were reproaches for the Hanoi raids and vague assurances that the meeting would take place soon.

Within days the diplomatic fencing became academic. On December 13 and 14, American bombers restruck Van Dien and the railroad yards at Yen Vien. Hanoi once again charged that bombs had fallen in the city, killing more than 100 people. Although U.S. officials again denied the claims, it was later acknowledged that at least two air force pilots had missed their targets.

Low cloud cover hampered visibility over the city, causing the two pilots to mistakenly hit a railroad switching yard two miles from the center of Hanoi. Some of the rockets went wide of the target and landed near the Red River in a section of slum dwellings that went up in flames. Another stray rocket landed in the diplomatic quarter, damaging the Rumanian, Chinese, and, ironically, Polish embassies.

On the fifteenth, Grenouski met with an unsmiling Polish foreign minister. Referring to the "brutal raid" on a residential area of Hanoi as "the last drop that spilled over the cup," he told the American that the North Vietnamese had instructed him to "terminate all conversations." Although Johnson tried to salvage the situation by creating a ten-mile strike-free circle around Hanoi, the Marigold channel had been closed.

Those who knew of the secret discussions were puzzled by the apparent failure of Washington to coordinate military and diplomatic efforts. Some suggested that the president, recovering from an operation in Texas, must not have been fully informed of the timing of the strikes and the progress of Marigold negotiations. Soviet Ambassador Dobrynin asked a State Department official if U.S. military

*Nguyen Thiep Street in Hanoi was hit on December 14, probably by bombs meant for a railroad overpass nearby.*

leaders were "deliberately trying to frustrate" any negotiated settlement.

But President Johnson had gone through the entire process with full knowledge of the situation. Frustrated by the failure of past negotiating efforts, he had approved the Hanoi targets in early November. After the uproar caused by the December raids, a number of mid–level State Department officials lobbied for an end to further strikes around Hanoi. They argued the raids were crippling the Poles' efforts while merely handing Hanoi an enormous public relations advantage.

But Dean Rusk and Walt W. Rostow, who had replaced McGeorge Bundy as the president's national security adviser earlier in the year, both counseled Johnson against any change in Rolling Thunder. Hanoi had been adequately warned that the bombing would continue until a settlement was reached. Said one official: "When Uncle Ho really decides it's in his interest to talk, the fact that we bomb here or there is not going to stop him." After the meeting with the North Vietnamese in Warsaw failed to take place, President Johnson suspected the Marigold channel was a "dry creek." He agreed that if the Poles had accurately reported his position that the bombing

would not stop before talks were begun, Hanoi could hardly use the raids as an excuse for backing out.

Whatever the reason for Hanoi's decision to abandon Marigold, the episode revealed that neither side considered negotiations to be in its best interest at that time. It also exposed a number of inherent weaknesses in the administration's rationale for the bombing. Civilian theorists found their subtle blend of diplomatic incentives and military signals had backfired. Washington's insistence that the bombing would not be halted until reciprocal concessions were forthcoming from Hanoi proved a huge stumbling block in the path of a political settlement. Meanwhile, the generals' assurances of surgically precise bombing that could hurt North Vietnam without inflicting substantial civilian casualties were exposed as unrealistic.

As a result, by early 1967 the debate in Washington over the bombing policy had polarized even further between those who wished to de–escalate the bombing in order to promote a negotiated settlement and those who believed unrestricted bombing could bring a successful military solution to the war. Caught in the middle, President Johnson saw his options dwindling rapidly.

# The Struggle to Survive

The people of North Vietnam answered Operation Rolling Thunder with an almost uncanny ability to offset the effects of America's aerial might. No sooner were roads, bridges, power plants, and factories struck than they were repaired again. But North Vietnam's dogged determination to maintain the war effort at any cost demanded sacrifices and hard work from the people and put a severe strain on the country's already poor economy.

Food shortages became widespread, especially in urban areas, as farm work-

*Employees of a bicycle factory in Hanoi scramble out of ground shelters to man defensive positions during an airraid drill. Part of the factory was destroyed by U.S. bombers on December 14, 1966.*

ers were pressed into service repairing damage inflicted by the bombing. Rationing was in effect throughout most of the country. Long lines could be seen in front of government stores, and collective street kitchens began springing up in downtown Hanoi. Signs of malnutrition, especially among children, were noticed by foreign observers.

*Left. Hundreds of workers repair a bombed-out dike in Ha Tinh Province in southern North Vietnam.*

*Above. In a factory hidden from American aircraft in a cave near Thanh Hoa, workers use Russian and Chinese machines to manufacture spare motor parts.*

In Hanoi there was a notable "grimness" according to British Consul John Colvin. On June 29, 1966, fearing the Americans would eventually resort to terror bombings of the city itself, Hanoi's leaders ordered the evacuation of everyone except those "truly indispensable to the life of the capital." The same day, U.S. warplanes began bombing petroleum and oil storage areas in Hanoi and Haiphong. By 1967 Hanoi's population had been reduced in half. Children and entire schools were transferred to the relative safety of rural areas, which placed a strain on many Vietnamese families, which were traditionally tightly knit.

As Rolling Thunder bombings intensified and reached closer to the heart of North Vietnam, the country's leaders clung tenaciously to their goal of reunifying Vietnam under their rule. "Hanoi and Haiphong and a number of cities and industries may be destroyed," President Ho Chi Minh said in July 1966. "But ... our people and combatants are united and of the same mind, fearing no sacrifices or hardships, and determined to fight until complete victory."

The war effort dominated daily life. Films, songs, and poems, idolizing the heroes of ancient wars, carried inspiring patriotic messages to the people. Party slogans, exhorting the need for a strong, united home front, were visible on city streets and on factory shop walls.

North Vietnam's economy was decentralized to better enable the country to absorb the shock of continual bombing.

Left. Workers labor beneath posters bearing patriotic slogans at a plant that produced 50,000 bicycles in 1967. The poster farthest to the right reads: "March forth! Total victory will be ours."

Above. A teacher conducts a reading lesson at a school evacuated to the countryside. Behind her is the camouflaged entrance to an airraid shelter.

Prized plans to build up a heavy industry sector were reluctantly scrapped as large factories, mainly located in the heavily populated Red River Delta region, were broken up and scattered in caves and small villages throughout the countryside in order to present a less concentrated target for U.S. planes.

In the more heavily bombed southern regions, entire villages moved underground. Miles of trenches were dug to enable farmers to work their fields in spite of the frequent air attacks. By the end of 1968, Hanoi claimed to have dug 30,000 miles of trenches and 21 million bomb shelters throughout the country.

Women took over many of the jobs traditionally performed by their husbands, many of whom were at war in the South or in local militia. They worked in factories, repaired roads and bridges, and could even be seen manning antiaircraft guns. In the cities, although usually separated from their children who had been evacuated to the country, they worked clearing rubble or acting as aircraft spotters on rooftops in addition to their normal household duties.

War had become "a way of life for Hanoi," according to veteran American correspondent, David Schoenbrun, who had been with the French at Dien Bien Phu. Arriving in North Vietnam on August 22, 1967, just eleven days after U.S. warplanes destroyed the Paul Doumer Bridge, the only major bridge across the Red River within one hundred miles of Hanoi, Schoenbrun witnessed the extent of North Vietnamese determination.

Driven to the edge of the Red River, he was led down into the ankle-deep mud of the riverbank to board a flat-bottomed barge tied to a tiny, antiquated tug boat. "This is the Red River ferry," his escort proudly told the reporter. "We have three operating constantly and we are getting through despite the bombing of the bridge."

Schoenbrun had heard the stories of the famed "bicycle supply-trains" but never believed them. Now he saw one with his own eyes.

They have devised a bicycle with a plank soldered above the back wheel, to each end of which is attached a huge straw basket, about three feet in diameter, capable of holding fifty pounds each. That makes a hundred pounds per bicycle, or one ton per every twenty bicycles. And they have literally thousands of bicycles available night and day.

During his two-week stay, Schoenbrun would see and hear the same thing wherever he went. " 'We are getting through!' It was a chant, a litany, a prayer, and a boast," said Schoenbrun. "Sacrifice was accepted as a challenge and almost a privilege to their cause. What mattered most was 'to get through.' "

Left. Women atop an observation tower scan the skies for signs of incoming planes. Once a formation of bombers was spotted, the alert was spread by radio, telephone, and, in rural areas, by drums and gongs.

Right. No escape from war. A young couple dawdles on a bench next to the entrance to a bomb shelter in a park in Hanoi.

Below. Shoppers in Hanoi rush to buy goods in a department store during a brief bombing pause during Tet in February 1967. Consumer goods were at times in short supply in the North.

# Year of Strategic Persuasion

By the end of 1966 North Vietnamese Migs had become an increasing problem for Rolling Thunder pilots. Although the Migs had downed only ten U.S. aircraft, American air strategists were alarmed at the rising number of instances in which U.S. bombers were forced to jettison their bombs before reaching their target to gain enough speed and agility to evade the aggressive Migs. During the last four months of the year, 192 USAF planes were intercepted by Migs. Of these, 107—56 percent—were forced to release their bombs prematurely.

Partly responsible for the Migs' success was the introduction of Soviet-built Mig-21s. With a maximum speed of 1,385MPH—Mach 2.1—at high altitudes, the Mig-21 could more than equal the speed of USAF F-4 Phantoms and navy F-8 Crusaders. Whereas the armament of the older Mig-15s and 17s consisted of only 23MM and 37MM cannons, the Mig-21 also packed four Atoll heat-seeking missiles, allowing it to attack from

longer range with less risk. The North now possessed a jet fighter that could match the best the U.S. had to offer.

Mig pilots were also growing more aggressive. Their flying skills and tactics had improved considerably, thanks to the work of Soviet and North Korean instructors. Operating at high altitudes, Mig-21s were guided behind U.S. strike forces by ground control intercept radar. Swooping down in high-speed attack runs, they launched their missiles and zoomed above and away before the U.S. planes could react. The slower Mig-17s flew defensive screens at lower altitudes.

Even stripped down, F-105s were too heavy to outduel the more agile Migs and had to rely on their superior speed when attacked. To respond to the new threat, F-4 Phantoms were withdrawn from the strike force to act solely as fighter interceptors. This meant that fewer bombs were being delivered on each target at the same expense as before.

## Operation Bolo

Gen. William "Spike" Momyer, who had replaced Gen. Moore as commander of the 7th Air Force in July 1966, had repeatedly requested authority to strike all five Mig bases in North Vietnam. Washington had denied his requests fearing that destruction of the airfields would only give Hanoi the opportunity to use bases in southern China, which might spark clashes between U.S. planes and Chinese Migs. Since Mig airfields were off-limits to American bombers, Momyer knew that a large air battle was the only way to reduce the Mig threat. From past experience, Momyer knew North Vietnamese planes would put up a big effort after the upcoming Christmas and New Years' stand-downs, during which they would have time to train and refine their tactics. He and his staff prepared a surprise for them in 1967.

Momyer's plan, code named Operation Bolo, called for a force of fifty-six Phantoms divided into two groups. The main force, consisting of F-4s from the 8th Tactical Fighter Wing would sweep in from the west over the airfields at Phuc Yen and Gia Lam around Hanoi. Phantoms from the 366th TFW would approach from the east to cover the air bases at Kep Ha and Cat Bi to the north and east, creating a pincer and blocking off any possible escape routes to the safety of the Chinese border. Twenty-four F-105F Wild Weasels would provide anti-SAM support for both fighter groups.

The trick was to entice the Migs into battle by making the F-4s of the 8th TFW look like "just another daily strike force" of unescorted F-105s, recalled Momyer. Normal F-105 refueling rendezvous tracks, approach routes, alti-

tudes, and air speeds were assigned to the Phantoms to deceive enemy radar operators. Call signs named after automobiles, traditionally used by the Thunderchief pilots based at Korat, were to be employed in case the North Vietnamese were monitoring their communications.

Because of the size of the operation and the new procedures involved, pilots of the 8th TFW underwent three days of intensive briefings at their base in Ubon, Thailand. Basic air-to-air tactics, given little emphasis during the early Rolling Thunder period, were reviewed and refined. Air crews were warned not to try and outturn the more agile Migs.

Colonel Robin Olds, commander of the 8th TFW, was assigned as mission leader. A plain-talking commander, the World War II ace was greatly admired by the men who served under him. But Olds's maverick style won him no popularity contests with the brass at the Pentagon. Rumor holds that he never saw action in Korea, where fighter pilots made their careers, because of bureaucratic infighting. But in Vietnam, Olds had another chance.

On January 2, 1967, the F-4s of the 8th TFW took to the air with Olds in the lead. His flight had ironically been assigned the call sign "Olds." Following five minutes behind was "Ford" flight, led by Colonel Daniel "Chappie" James, the wing's deputy commander for operations. The black aviator took a lot of joshing about his size. When asked by a ground crewman how he squeezed his six-foot-four, 220-pound frame into the cockpit, James replied, "Son, I don't get into it. I put it on."

A heavy overcast hampered visibility as Olds's decoy Phantoms cruised toward Hanoi. Olds and his team did not know it then, but the Phantoms assigned to the eastern section of the trap were unable to make it through the clouds over their objectives. Olds's flight entered the airspace over Phuc Yen on schedule, but there were no Migs in sight. Not expecting a strike force under such poor weather conditions, the North Vietnamese were slow to react. By the time they scrambled their Migs, Olds's flight had already overflown the airfield twice. As Olds led his Phantoms in a third pass over the airfield, James entered the target area with Ford flight. The relative quiet was broken when a pilot in Ford flight broke in on the radio with an urgent warning: "Olds, you have Migs at your six o'clock!"

Mig-21s popped out of the clouds from every direction. Olds broke away in a sharp left turn and could see in his rearview mirror the pitch-black cavity of a pursuing Mig's nose scoop. But the World War II ace knew that his tight, angling turn had thrown off the Mig pilot's aim. Another Mig popped out of the clouds in a wide turn right in front of Olds. He immediately went after him, counting on his number three and four men to slice in on the Mig still trailing behind. Aiming his targeting pipper on the banking Mig, Olds radioed his back-seater to "lock on" with their radar-guided Sparrow missiles.

A high-pitched clanging came over his headphones telling Olds that the missile had sniffed out its prey. Pressing down on the stick-mounted trigger, he sent a pair of the Sparrows hurtling toward the Mig. But in midflight, the radar lock broke and the two missiles strayed off course. As the Mig dove, Olds hurriedly aimed and fired two heat-seeking Sidewinders, but they too fell away behind the disappearing Mig.

Another Mig-21 emerged from the clouds to his right, making a looping turn to the left. Igniting his afterburners, Olds's Phantom leaped into a breathtaking, high-speed forty-five-degree climb behind the banking Mig. "I got on top of him and, half upside down, hung there," he later recalled. Waiting for the unsuspecting North Vietnamese pilot to finish his turn, Olds followed behind, completing his well-timed roll so that he was 3,500 feet behind the Mig at a slight angle. Olds aimed his cross hairs on the Mig's tail pipe. Pumping the trigger twice, Olds unleashed two Sidewinders. The first one hit home, erupting in a brilliant red flash on the fleeing plane's right wing. Olds later wrote: "The whole wing is torn completely off at the roots and the rest of the Mig tumbles forward, end over end, then falls lurching and spinning into the clouds below."

Olds then scanned the sky to try and determine how the battle was progressing. Unable to see through the broken clouds, Olds relied on the sounds coming over his headset. He later reconstructed what he heard that day in an article for *Air Force* magazine:

"Look out, Walt, he's at your seven and firing!"

"Get him off!"

"I got one! I got one!"

"Lead, there is one more closing at five—fast—break right now!"

"Razz, he overshot—get him—ah, beautiful, tremendous."

"Rambler lead, there they are—two o'clock—two of 'em—slightly low."

"OK, attacking."

Colonel Robin Olds, commander of the 8th Tactical Fighter Wing, is swept up by his pilots after flying his one hundredth, and final, combat mission over the North on September 23, 1967.

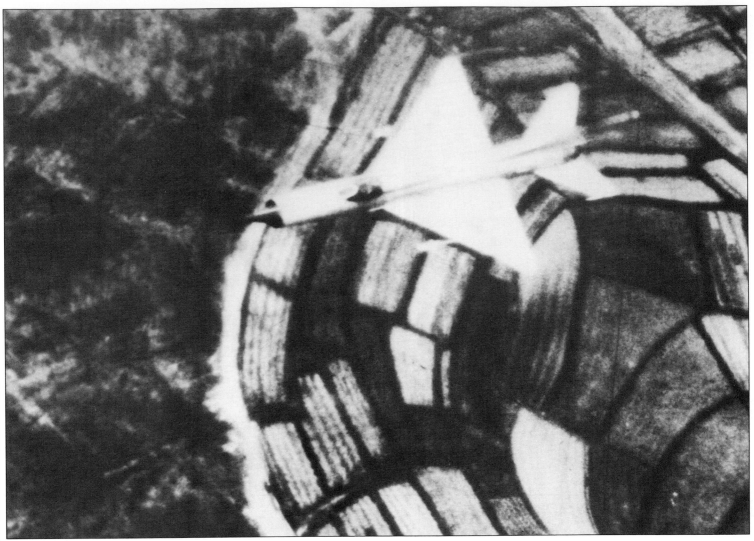

*A Mig-21 Fishbed flies over North Vietnam on January 4, 1967.*

"Rambler, look out, one coming in from three o'clock—break, break!"

"Rambler Three here—I've got two Migs, three miles at twelve. Engaging. Four, take the one on the right."

"Look at that! Look at that! He's ejecting!"

"Olds, this is Ford. Four SAMs coming up at your six o'clock. Don't break, they're not guiding."

"Olds lead, this is Ford. I'm right behind you, Chief. Don't worry. I'm covering your tail!"

In all, the furious dogfight lasted for fifteen minutes before the last Mig broke contact. All twenty-eight F-4s made it back to Ubon, where the excited Phantom jockeys, their adrenalin still flowing, recounted their individual duels. They knew the battle had been a success, but they did not know how successful until their postflight debriefing revealed that they had shot down seven Migs. Colonel Olds reported the results to a smiling General Momyer in Saigon. Although nothing like the huge aerial dogfights of World War II and Korea, Operation Bolo gave the U.S. its first major aerial victory of the war. Nearly half of North Vietnam's inventory of sixteen Mig-21s had been wiped out in a single blow.

## Worth the price?

Although Operation Bolo gave U.S. pilots cause to celebrate, a growing chorus of doubts about the bombing was surfacing back home. In early 1967, the *New York Times* published a series of articles by assistant managing editor Harrison Salisbury, who visited Hanoi over New Year's, 1967. The reports of the first American journalist allowed into North Vietnam included vivid descriptions of bombed-out city streets and small villages, leaving the impression that U.S. planes were bombing targets of doubtful military value and killing large numbers of civilians. Specifically, he pointed to the "deliberate U.S. attacks on human lives" in the city of Nam Dinh, which he labeled "a cotton and silk textile town containing nothing of military significance." But as one Western diplomat, who met Salisbury during his visit, noted: "The city in fact contained POL storage, a power plant, and a railroad yard and was surrounded by antiaircraft and missiles."

Administration officials were appalled by Salisbury's reports, and they pointed out that many of his allegations could be traced almost verbatim to English language versions of official North Vietnamese communiqués. Whatever the source of Salisbury's reports, their appearance in the *New York Times* brought home to the American public for the first time the effects of the bombing, and many did not like what they read. They had been reassured that the bombing was being carried out with surgical precision against only military targets. Salisbury's reports now forced the administration to admit that no matter how hard they tried, there would always be damage to private property and civilian casualties. The revelation only served to widen the administration's "credibility gap."

Criticisms of the bombing on purely strategic and economic rationales were also increasing. *Newsweek* magazine estimated that the U.S. had by then lost $2.5 billion worth of aircraft over North Vietnam and showered approximately $1.5 billion worth of bombs on North Vietnam, yet Hanoi seemed even less willing to negotiate now than before the bombing had begun. Even conservative *U.S. News & World Report* began asking whether the air war was "worth the price."

In Washington a growing number of civilian officials within the administration were asking the same question. A CIA study found that the direct operational cost of running the air war had nearly tripled, from $460 million in 1965 to $1.2 billion in 1966. Although the CIA estimated that the level of damage inflicted upon North Vietnam had also risen from $70 million to $130 million, it now cost $9.60 to inflict each dollar's worth of damage in 1966 compared to $6.60 in 1965. Even then, damage estimates were not very reliable as the military often exaggerated its claims. "There is incredible overestimation on the damage we do," said a navy pilot aboard the U.S.S. *Oriskany*. "We tell about the bridges, trucks, barges, and POL storage areas which we've blown to hell every day, and . . . if you took the combined estimated BDA [bomb damage assessment] reports from just the time we've been here, a total like that would cripple the little nation."

That obviously had not happened. An increasing number of studies reported that the bombing had failed to achieve its primary objectives. A year-end CIA assessment issued early in 1967 noted: "The evidence available does not suggest that Rolling Thunder to date has contributed materially to the . . . reduction of the flow of supplies to the VC/NVA forces in the South or weakening the will of North Vietnam. . . ."

Despite these negative verdicts, the bombing campaign was stepped up in early 1967, albeit slightly. No new targets were approved for Rolling Thunder strikes in the first few weeks of the year. In fact, President Johnson ordered a bombing halt beginning on February 8, during the Vietnamese Tet holiday, in response to another signal that the Communists might be willing to negotiate. However, when efforts at contact between Washington and Hanoi descended to acrimony yet again, the bombing was resumed six days later. Hanoi took advantage of the six-day lull to move an estimated 25,000 tons of supplies south down the Ho Chi Minh Trail to South Vietnam.

A frustrated Lyndon Johnson had had enough. "We've done all this diplomacy . . . now let's do the job!" he told his aides. Johnson decided to turn up the pressure. The only question was how much.

The president pondered the available options. Earlier that year, the Joint Chiefs had passed on to him the recommendations of Admiral Sharp. The JCS, arguing that the discouraging results of Rolling Thunder were the fault of bureaucratic timidity, supported Sharp's request to "destroy in depth" all war-supporting industry and transportation targets in the Hanoi-Haiphong area. He also wanted authority to "close" Haiphong Harbor, through which more than a third of the North's imports passed, with air strikes and aerial mining.

On the other hand, Robert McNamara and his civilian staff at the Pentagon in their formal recommendations for 1967 had proposed "stabilizing" the bombing at a level of 12,000 sorties per month. Disillusioned by the statistical evidence of Rolling Thunder's lack of success, McNamara had also endorsed the anti-infiltration barrier as an alternative to the bombing. He and his staff warned especially about the danger of mining Haiphong Harbor, arguing that if a Russian ship were damaged, the situation could become "explosive." Even if Haiphong were closed, Pentagon analysts calculated that North Vietnam could maintain the war effort at its present level with supplies brought overland from China.

Although a Harris public opinion poll released on February 13 indicated that 67 percent of the American people backed the bombing, President Johnson moved cautiously. He opened up a number of the lesser-risk targets on the Joint Chiefs' list for the next month's Rolling Thunder program, most of them factories comprising the bulk of North Vietnam's fledgling industrial base. None, however, was inside the thirty-mile Hanoi restricted zone.

Johnson rejected Adm. Sharp's proposal to mine Haiphong but authorized him to begin aerial mine-laying operations against North Vietnamese rivers below the twentieth parallel to cut off waterborne coastal traffic. Johnson considered the increased pressure as necessary strategic persuasion in the test of wills between Hanoi and Washington. But his policy of bombing and bargaining was as much directed toward politics at home as it was toward Hanoi. For the next six months, he continued to dole out sensitive targets one by one to the generals, while at the same time trying to placate the doves with periodic cutbacks and half-hearted peace feelers. In the end, this erratic course satisfied no one and did little to alter the course of the war.

In March, during President Johnson's "little escalation," American pilots began pounding factories, power plants, rail lines, and switching yards around the periphery of Hanoi and Haiphong. They were knocking at the gates of

North Vietnam's strategic heartland—the Red River Delta—where Hanoi had prepared a deadly reception for their uninvited guests.

After two years of sustained bombing, North Vietnam had developed its air defenses into a sophisticated and well-integrated network of AAA, SAMs, and Migs patterned after the Soviet defense model. Thirty mobile SAM battalions, each with four to six launchers, constantly roamed the countryside. Each site had about 200 SA-2 missiles on hand and could draw on an estimated 2,000 to 3,000 more stockpiled around the country. Over 7,000 anti-aircraft guns crisscrossed the surrounding hills and flat, delta lowlands. They ranged in size from relatively small, optically aimed 12.7 and 37MM guns to longer-range, radar-directed 85 and 100MM weapons. Despite losing the 7 Mig-21s in January, the North Vietnamese air force kept its inventory of Migs at around 100 planes, thanks to Soviet and Chinese replacements.

The bulk of this vast array of air defense weaponry rested squarely in the Red River Delta around Hanoi and Haiphong. Colonel Jack Broughton, an F-105 flight leader at Takhli, described the area in his memoirs as "the center of hell with Hanoi as its hub."

Before each mission, Broughton consulted the huge map that hung in his office and ran through every detail of the operation in his mind. He knew every possibility had to be anticipated if he were to complete his mission and survive. During a typical mission he came in from the north along the thirty-mile buffer zone paralleling the Red Chinese border. Turning right he would lead his flight south along Thud Ridge. As the flight approached downtown Hanoi, the pilots started jinking and weaving to avoid the AAA gunfire and to throw off the aim of SAM radar operators. "If you dragged the force in too low, the ground fire got them. If you brought them in too high, where the Mig was in his preferred envelope, he could

*Reports in the New York Times in early 1967 that despite all efforts to avoid North Vietnamese population centers, civilians were sometimes inadvertent casualties of U.S. aircraft, created a sensation in the United States. Here, a woman bends over the body of her son, the casualty of a bombing mission in the Red River Delta in late 1966.*

force you to ... jettison your bombs. ... If you flew straight and level either in the clouds or in the clear ... the SAMs ... would gobble you up."

To a visiting reporter, David Schoenbrun, Hanoi resembled "an armed porcupine, with hundreds, probably thousands, of spiny, steel guns sticking out beyond the tops of the trees." The Pentagon estimated that North Vietnamese gunners were throwing 25,000 tons of flak and tracer bullets into the sky over Hanoi every month. Air Force Chief of Staff General John P. McConnell labeled it "the greatest concentration of antiaircraft weapons that has ever been known."

Many veteran pilots claimed they were encountering more flak than they had ever seen in World War II. In Germany, where the targets were more widely spread out, AAA defenses were concentrated around the most important areas. In North Vietnam, where all the strategic targets were clustered in the Red River Delta, Hanoi had the advantage of being able to concentrate its air defense in one area. In addition, AAA technology had advanced since World War II. "The flak up north is said to be worse than Germany's because it is ten times as accurate," said World War II veteran Olds. "You get more thrown at you in a shorter span of time and it's thrown at you on every mission up around Hanoi. ..."

Adding SAMs to the picture only made it worse. Equipping F–105s with ECM pods helped even the odds a bit, but as American pilots ventured farther into the Red River Delta, SAM operators began firing their missiles a dozen or more at a time. The bomber pilot's best ally remained the Wild Weasels in their F–105F Thunderchiefs.

## Just doing his job

The most important target on the list opened up by President Johnson was thirty-five miles due north of Hanoi and just east of Thud Ridge, a large industrial complex at Thai Nguyen. Manned by 14,000 technicians and workers, the complex housed a thermal power plant, chemical and steel barge assembly plants, and the country's only steel mill. Nearly $3 billion worth of steel had been manufactured at the plant in 1965, making it one of the bright successes in North Vietnam's embryonic industrial sector.

American fighter–bombers had been to Thai Nguyen before but only to hit the railroad yards that connected the plant with Hanoi. It had proved an unhappy hunting ground for the Americans, because Hanoi had ringed the complex with ninety-six AAA sites. SAM installations around nearby Hanoi covered the approaches to the plant, and Mig bases on either side provided additional coverage.

On the morning of March 10 Captain Merlyn Dethlefsen jockeyed his F–105F Wild Weasel into the number three spot in Lincoln flight after taking off from Takhli airfield. The four-plane formation of two twin-seat Wild Weasels and two single-seat F–105Ds was assigned to be the first flight over Thai Nguyen that day.

Two miles from the target, Lincoln lead brought the flight up to attack altitude. In the back seats of the lead plane and Dethlefsen's F–105F, two electronic warfare officers scanned scopes for their target, a SAM site located southeast of the complex. Locked onto the site's probing radar beam, Lincoln lead rolled his plane into a steep, diving attack with his wingman—Lincoln Two—in tow. Dethlefsen and Lincoln Four followed a mile behind.

As if a hornet's nest had suddenly been poked, the sky began buzzing with bursting shells and tracer bullets. In all his seventy-seven combat missions Dethlefsen had never seen so much flak. It was so intense that he lost sight of Lincoln lead in the swirl of colored flashes and drifting smoke. When he saw Lincoln Two suddenly break hard to the right, Dethlefsen followed suit.

Moments later beeping noises came over the emergency radio frequency, the sound of two rescue homing devices, which were automatically triggered once a pilot ejected. Lincoln lead had been hit and the two airmen had bailed out. Lincoln Two had also been hit—by flak from an 85MM shell. Captain Billy Hoeft gingerly coaxed the damaged F–105D back toward Thailand.

Assuming command of what was left of the flight, Dethlefsen decided to finish the job. The strike force had not yet arrived and the SAM site was still operating. Circling around the site, he studied the flak looking for an opening. "It wasn't a matter of being able to avoid the flak," Dethlefsen recalled, "but of finding the least intense areas."

On the first pass, Dethlefsen's back-seater, Captain Kevin Gilroy, got a fix on the site. Rolling in, Dethlefsen was just about to release one of his Shrike missiles when he spotted two Mig–21s bearing down on his tail.

Quickly firing the Shrike, he broke in a hard right turn just as one of the Migs fired a heat-seeking missile. Instead of jettisoning his remaining ordnance and punching in the afterburner to outrun the trailing Migs, Dethlefsen dove straight through the flak barrage. "Didn't think the Migs would want to follow me through that stuff," he thought to himself. "They didn't." With another high-G turn, he evaded two more Migs waiting to jump him on the other side of the site.

He had shaken off all four Migs but the flak had taken its toll. A 57MM shell had hit the Thud squarely in the fuselage and Dethlefsen could feel the slight drag caused by the hole. His left wing tip was riddled with bullet holes, probably from a Mig cannon. He was surprised to find all his systems still working.

By then, the strike force had completed its bombing run and was on its way back to Thailand. But Dethlefsen knew that the fighter–bombers would be back to hit Thai Nguyen the next day and his assigned SAM site was still operating. "I made up my mind to stay until I got that SAM site or they got me," he vowed.

149

Easing his plane down, Dethlefsen spotted the SAM site's radar control van. He rolled in and unleashed a string of bombs directly over the van. Although Major Kenneth Bell's plane was so damaged by flak that he could make only right turns, Lincoln Four followed his leader in on the attack. The two Thuds circled and bore in again with their 20MM cannons to deliver the knockout blow.

"All I did was the job I was sent to do," Dethlefsen later said. "I didn't consider the mission extraordinary. I had been up that way before and . . . I expected to get shot at a lot." Others had greater esteem for the Wild Weasel pilot's exploits that day over Thai Nguyen. Eleven months later, Dethlefsen was awarded the Medal of Honor.

On the same day that USAF Thunderchiefs hit Thai Nguyen, navy pilots aboard the U.S.S. *Bon Homme Richard* were preparing for a mission that was to revolutionize air warfare. Before the "Bonnie Dick" left California for

Yankee Station, her sailors had taken aboard a number of strange looking bombs. Known as Walleyes, these experimental 1,000-pound bombs were equipped with television cameras that could transmit a picture of what they saw to a pilot in the cockpit. With the Walleyes programmed to detect contrasts in light, all the pilot had to do was identify the target, lock the bomb's navigational system onto the selected aiming point, and punch the release button. The TV eye guided the bomb to the target.

Walleyes promised, in theory, increased accuracy. Designed to glide in on its target, it also allowed pilots to release from a safer distance, giving them a better chance to evade missiles and gunfire. Commander Homer Smith, skipper of Attack Squadron 212, was selected to find out if the Walleye lived up to its manufacturer's claims.

On March 11 Smith's Skyhawk catapulted off the Bonnie Dick with a single Walleye cradled underneath its fuselage. Accompanied by F-4 escorts, Smith bore in on

*Smoke billows out of the Thai Nguyen steel complex on April 23, 1967, after a strike by U.S. fighter-bombers.*

*Commander Homer Smith of Attack Squadron 212 talks with the maintenance crew aboard the U.S.S.* Bon Homme Richard *on April 24, 1967.*

the military barracks at Sam Son and released the 1,000-pound glide bomb without a hitch. The navy pilots watched as the Walleye flew straight through the window of one of the buildings and exploded inside.

The next day three more navy A-4s under Comdr. Smith's command, each carrying a single Walleye, tried their luck against the stubborn Dragon's Jaw Bridge at Thanh Hoa, now within the navy's assigned area of operation. Although all three glide bombs exploded on the bridge within five feet of each other, the Dragon's Jaw again refused to fall.

Although the results at Thanh Hoa were disappointing, navy pilots would claim a high success rate with the few experimental television glide bombs at their disposal. A total of sixty-eight Walleyes was employed during the *Bon Homme Richard*'s tour of duty at Yankee Station, sixty-five of them scoring accurate hits. Encouraged by the results, Pentagon experts and munitions manufacturers began developing more advanced "smart bombs" that would prove so effective later in the war.

## Turning the lights off in Hanoi

Following the month-long strikes against Hanoi's industrial sector, President Johnson released yet another plum to the Joint Chiefs on March 22. North Vietnam's electrical power plants had been high on the military's list of target requests since the beginning of Rolling Thunder. American planes struck the two main power plants in Haiphong and a transformer station in Hanoi in April. But it was not until May 19 that U.S. planes were allowed to hit the most important part of the power system, the 32,000-kilowatt thermal power plant in downtown Hanoi.

To reduce the possibility of damage to residential areas, Washington insisted that the mission be flown by navy planes using the Walleye bombs. Once again Cmdr. Homer Smith was tapped to head the strike force of just two A-4s. Six F-8E Crusaders went along to suppress AAA fire and provide fighter escort. Planes from the U.S.S. *Kitty Hawk* were to strike the Van Dien truck park, five miles south of the city, as a diversionary measure.

Crossing the coastline, the Walleye strike force sped north toward Hanoi. Weaving through a shifting barrage of AAA fire and snaking SAMs, Smith and his wingman, Lieutenant Mike Cater, popped up and rolled in low over the city toward the power plant. Locking their Walleyes onto the target, the two pilots punched their release buttons, pulled up, and headed for home. During the attack, two of their six Crusader F-8 escorts fell victim to Hanoi's air defenses. Homeward bound, the strike force was attacked by ten Mig-17s just outside the city. Within minutes the dogfight turned into the navy's largest air-to-air battle of the war up to then. Three Migs went plunging earthward in flames before the battle was over.

In Hanoi that afternoon, British consul John Colvin was sipping a drink underneath the overhead fan in his assistant's apartment when he heard the air raid sirens. During the past few months, Colvin had grown used to their high-pitched wail as American planes pounded targets in the surrounding countryside. But on this day, as he stepped out onto the balcony, Colvin had a bird's-eye view of the air war that had been raging around Hanoi. From out of nowhere, Smith's strike force shot across the sky, barely skimming the roof tops.

In a flash the planes disappeared behind the trees and buildings between the consulate and the power station a mile to the south, then could be seen climbing back into the sky. At that moment every light that was on in the apartment blinked out and the ceiling fan stopped turning. To the south, Colvin could see "a column of dust, smoke, and flame" rising from the direction of the electrical plant. Already falsely suspected of being an observer for the American bombers by North Vietnamese authorities, Colvin made it a practice to avoid being seen near the site of an air strike. Occasionally, angry North Vietnamese threw stones at Westerners walking in the streets. But this time curiosity overcame his usual sense of caution.

He traveled to the power station, where dust from fallen masonry choked the air and a few small fires remained burning. The plant's smokestacks had collapsed, and the 100-foot-tall building, riddled with gaping holes, appeared to be "listing drunkenly to one side," Colvin later wrote. The consul was surprised by the accuracy of the American bombers. He noted that "out of the complex of the fifty or so small private houses around the power plant, only three had been at all damaged, and those from the blast rather than direct hits."

The next day the air conditioner and ceiling fans in his office were silent as Colvin sat down in the stifling heat to draft a telegram to London concerning the air strike. He wrote that there seemed no possibility of restoring electrical power in the capital. He had just passed the cable to his assistant for encoding when the lights in the office came on and the fans overhead slowly began revolving. Colvin had no idea what had happened. A distant power station plugged in to fill the gap? Small diesel-powered

generators? Whatever the cause, the British consul was once again astonished by the North Vietnamese. He could not help but think of the dogged determination of his own countrymen during the German blitz. Colvin knew that "only continual air attacks of a kind Rolling Thunder had not yet initiated would surmount those qualities."

But in Washington, just the reverse was being pondered. Four days after the strike on the power plant, Adm. Sharp received word that no further targets would be authorized within the Hanoi prohibited zone. The internal debate over the course of the war had flared up once again.

## McNamara's "defection"

By mid-1967 civilian opposition to any further escalation of the war had hardened into a formidable counterpoint to the military's position. Nowhere was it more apparent than in the Department of Defense, where the lines between the generals and Pentagon bureaucrats were clearly drawn. Leading the skeptics were Deputy Secretary Cyrus Vance and Assistant Secretaries John McNaughton of International Security Affairs and Alain Enthoven of Systems Analysis, whose opposition was based on practical rather than moral grounds.

In response to Westmoreland's request for an additional 100,000 troops in April and Adm. Sharp's continuing calls for heavier bombing of the North, these midlevel skeptics initiated an unsolicited campaign to stabilize the war effort. A number of Enthoven's reports questioned whether raising U.S. troop levels above the half million mark would do any good. According to one report, "the size of the force we deploy has little effect on the rate of attrition of enemy forces," and the Communists had retained the initiative on the ground, engaging U.S. troops at times and places of their own choosing.

As for increasing the bombing, John McNaughton noted there were few significant targets left to hit. Those that remained were sensitive targets in the Hanoi-Haiphong area that involved "serious risks of generating confrontations with the Soviet Union and China." McNaughton argued that there was "no evidence" to suggest that hitting these targets would "change Hanoi's will," while there was considerable evidence that such attacks would have the opposite effect.

Robert McNamara, torn between his disenchantment with the progress of the war and his loyalty to the president, now called for de-escalation of the war. In a memo to the president on May 19, he rejected Westmoreland's call for more troops and recommended that the bombing be cut back to below the twentieth parallel and concentrated against North Vietnamese supply routes and activities in the panhandle. He believed this would give more direct support to Westmoreland in the South and, by relieving the pressure on Hanoi and Haiphong, possibly induce North Vietnam to negotiate as a "bonus" side effect.

McNamara was convinced that strategic bombing of North Vietnam's economic heartland had proved unsuccessful. It had become apparent that Hanoi was ready and willing to endure the bombing as long as there was hope of winning the war of attrition in the South. There seemed to be no other reason for the bombing than punishing the enemy, a rationale that McNamara saw as meaningless and in the long run counterproductive.

One pilot in every forty who ventured into the Red River Delta never returned, a loss ratio six times greater than that for missions below the twentieth parallel. McNamara found such figures "unacceptable and unnecessary." He believed escalating the bombing would only further harden Hanoi's stand while raising the costs and risks involved. Even more damaging was the growing "backfire of revulsion" to the bombing among American and foreign opinion. He wrote the president, "The picture of the world's greatest superpower killing or seriously injuring 1,000 noncombatants a week, while trying to pound a tiny, backward nation into submission on an issue whose merits are hotly disputed, is not a pretty one."

McNamara's "defection" from stated American policy aims in Southeast Asia elicited a "war on paper" in Washington, which divided the administration into two camps as the hawks and doves battled behind closed doors. McNamara had the backing of many midlevel civilian officials but found only lukewarm support among the administration's major policymakers. Assistant Secretary of State William Bundy and White House National Security Adviser Walt Rostow agreed in principle to the cutbacks in the bombing but held some reservations about the extent of McNamara's pessimism.

CIA Director Richard Helms wrote McNamara that neither his nor the Joint Chiefs' recommended bombing programs would have any substantial influence on the war. Helms, already on record against escalation, warned that North Vietnam's supply network below the twentieth parallel was protected by a "deep cushion" of alternate roads and waterways. Even if the bombing in the panhandle could destroy 50 percent of the routes, his analysts had estimated that the North Vietnamese would still be left with five times the capacity needed to supply the VC at the present level.

Strangely enough, the one adviser closest to the president who disagreed with McNamara was Dean Rusk. The secretary of state was now emerging as the leading hardliner in the administration, taking over the role McNamara had played previously. Rusk maintained vehemently that

*General William Westmoreland, at the White House on April 27, 1967, sells his request for additional troop deployments to President Johnson and his top advisers.*

U.S. credibility was at stake in Vietnam. "We are not prepared to stop half of the war," he told reporters in mid-July, "while the other half goes on unrestricted, unimpeded and with maximum violence."

Predictably, the JCS and Adm. Sharp condemned McNamara's recommendations as an "alarming" departure from stated U.S. objectives in Vietnam. They were particularly outraged at the suggestion to cut back the bombing. General Earle Wheeler warned that such an action would be interpreted by the North Vietnamese as a victory, "an aerial Dien Bien Phu."

There were rumors afoot that some of the Joint Chiefs were threatening to resign if Johnson agreed to McNamara's plan for a cutback in the bombing. The generals saw their role as the president's prime military advisers being undercut by a group of civilians they considered unversed in the harsh realities of war.

But President Johnson, haunted by the possible ramifications of unrestricted bombing, was determined to keep a tight rein on his generals. His most vivid fear of Soviet or Chinese intervention in response to bombing sensitive targets had come close to reality early in June. A flight of air force bombers, passing over the port of Cam Pha on June 2, was fired upon by gun batteries in the harbor. In retaliation the pilots strafed the antiaircraft emplacements.

Next day Moscow charged that the American planes had attacked one of their merchant ships, the *Turkestan*, killing one crew member and injuring several others. Washington denied the claims. Three weeks later, when President Johnson met with Soviet Premier Aleksei Kosygin for talks in Glassboro, New Jersey, he was presented with a 20MM slug with U.S. markings taken from the hull of the *Turkestan*.

Johnson had to worry not only about the reactions of Hanoi's allies but those of antiwar critics at home who were growing in numbers and influence. Rumors of dissent within the administration had boosted their hopes. While antiwar protesters and Congressional doves worried the president, they still represented a minority viewpoint. He was much more concerned about how a larger contingent of hawkish senators and congressmen would react to McNamara's de-escalation proposals. Johnson noted in his memoirs that "a unilateral bombing halt would run into fierce opposition from these powerful men on the Hill."

During the course of the debate, the president received an unsolicited letter from his former national security adviser, McGeorge Bundy. Now head of the Ford Foundation, Bundy noted that Hanoi's leaders appeared to be willing to continue the war no matter the costs until the elections in 1968, when a change of government in Washington might bring a more conciliatory American attitude. They had used the same tactic against the war-weary French in 1954. Bundy recommended that just enough pressure be kept on Hanoi to convince them of America's determination to stay the course without arousing the wrath of the doves and hawks at home.

Bundy's analysis confirmed the president's own views, and Johnson rejected both options presented by McNamara and the Joint Chiefs. Instead, he chose to continue on the same course. The new Rolling Thunder directive issued on July 18 included only sixteen new targets within the Red River Delta. None were authorized within the prohibited zones around Hanoi and Haiphong.

## The generals go to Congress

The Joint Chiefs were not at all satisfied with the piecemeal way in which the president was doling out strategic targets. Unlike their predecessors in the 1950s who tended to be politically naive professional soldiers, Johnson's top military advisers were hardened bureaucrats adept at political infighting. Perceiving the bombing campaign against North Vietnam as a symbol of the importance of air power itself, they thought that past failures and present restrictions threatened to undermine their credibility. Unless they were given the opportunity to demonstrate the full potential of U.S. air power, the armed services, particularly the air force and the navy, feared for their future roles and the size of their budgets. Fortunately for the generals, they had close ties with influential senators and congressmen who were sympathetic to their views.

On August 9 the Congressional hawks gave the generals the chance to air their grievances in public. The Senate Armed Services Committee, chaired by Senator John Stennis, a Democrat from Mississippi, opened hearings on the conduct of the air war. The odds were stacked in the generals' favor. Sitting on the committee were some of the most vocal hawks on Capitol Hill. Eleven military leaders involved with the bombing campaign were called to testify. Robert McNamara was the only civilian called before the committee and he was scheduled to appear last. It was obvious that the senators were out to crucify the secretary of defense.

In an effort to deflect the criticisms that would be leveled at his bombing policy, President Johnson authorized sixteen more targets the day before the hearings were to open, six of them within the "sacred" ten-mile Hanoi inner circle. The president's gambit failed to soften the tone of the committee or their star witnesses.

Appropriately, the first to testify was Adm. Sharp, who welcomed the sixteen new targets but indicated he would become "dissatisfied" if the pace did not continue. Sharp indicated that ninety-one "high-value" military targets located in the northeast sector had not yet been authorized for air strikes. In addition, he noted that authorization to restrike targets that had been repaired was often slow in coming. "Normally when I make a recommendation it is neither approved or disapproved," he told the senators. "I just don't hear anything about it for a while."

The antiwar movement heats up. Opponents of the war parade through Central Park on April 15, 1967, during an antiwar "be-in" that drew 200,000 people. On the other side of the political coin, prowar "hawks" stepped up their protesting on behalf of an expanded military effort.

Sharp maintained that the bombing had reduced infiltration into South Vietnam. But without hard-hitting air strikes against the supply sources in Hanoi and Haiphong, Sharp admitted, it was almost impossible to halt the flow. Increasing the "level of pain" on the Hanoi regime was the only way to bring the North Vietnamese to their knees, he asserted, reiterating his recommendation to strike targets within the Hanoi and Haiphong prohibited zones and to mine Haiphong Harbor. Any decision to reduce the bombing would only "result in increased infiltration and increased casualties" in the South. In closing, Sharp said, "I know that your feeling is the same as ours, that we must come out of this war as we have come out of all wars ... on top."

Subsequent testimony by the military leaders—including all five members of the JCS—reinforced Sharp's assertion that air power could be a decisive factor in ending the war if only the civilians would stop their meddling. Perhaps the most damning indictment of the restricted bombing strategy was voiced by Major General Gilbert Meyers, former deputy commander of the 7th Air Force. Meyers told the committee, "If I found my staff selecting the kinds of targets we were attacking, I would have fired them all."

By the time McNamara appeared, the senators were well armed. Using the arguments of the previous witnesses, they lashed into him for his failure to heed the military's advice. The secretary of defense was ready for them. He bluntly rejected the idea that unlimited bombing would win the war: "There is no basis to believe that any bombing campaign ... would by itself force Ho Chi Minh's regime into submission, short, that is, of the virtual annihilation of North Vietnam and its people."

McNamara took issue with the importance placed on the targets not yet authorized for air strikes. They included such insignificant targets as a warehouse that "wouldn't fill in the corner of a Sears, Roebuck district warehouse." The remainder were more politically sensitive targets, such as Mig airfields and port facilities, which he thought were not worth the risks involved.

McNamara went on to say that strategic bombing had little effect on the course of the war. North Vietnam had no real industrial base and what little there was had already been virtually wiped out with no evident results. Referring to the power plants hit earlier in the year, McNamara pointed out that the entire North Vietnamese system equaled less than one-fifth the capacity of the Potomac Electric Power Company's plant in Alexandria, Virginia.

Senator Jack Miller replied that although such a power system might be considered insignificant by American standards it would be "most meaningful" to an undeveloped country like North Vietnam. "It could be," retorted McNamara, "but it has not been, because it is out and we have not seen any noticeable effect."

Mining the North's major ports, as the Chiefs advised, would do little to stem the flow of supplies, according to McNamara. Beyond the obvious risks of confrontations with the Soviets, he argued that the North Vietnamese would be able to circumvent such actions by taking supplies ashore in small barges and relying more heavily on overland routes from China.

Keeping these supplies from reaching the Vietcong was the main task of Rolling Thunder. Yet the bombing had only been able to put a ceiling on the level of infiltration, not strangle it completely. McNamara indicated that, according to intelligence estimates, the VC needed only 15 tons per day of externally supplied materials to maintain their current level of combat activity. Yet the pipeline from North Vietnam down through the Ho Chi Minh Trail had an estimated capacity of over 200 tons per day.

As he had often argued, the secretary told the senators that all the bombing could do was force Hanoi to "pay a high price" for its "continued aggression" by making the infiltration of men and supplies "increasingly difficult and costly." The air war against North Vietnam was a "supplement" to the real battle in South Vietnam, McNamara argued, not a "substitute." He testified:

The tragic and long-drawn-out character of that conflict in the South makes very tempting the prospect of replacing it with some new kind of air campaign against the North. But however tempting, such an alternative seems to me completely illusory. To pursue this objective would not only be futile, but would involve risks to our personnel and to our nation that I am unable to recommend.

With the publication of large portions of the committee's testimony, the president could no longer hide the growing rift among his advisers. Although he greatly admired McNamara, Johnson was energetically intolerant of dissenters within his official family. According to Undersecretary of the Air Force Townsend Hoopes, the president felt that McNamara had "depreciated the bombing publicly in a way that increased Hanoi's bargaining power." Johnson compared himself to a man trying to sell his house while one of his sons was informing potential buyers that there were leaks in the basement.

In short, McNamara had become a liability to Johnson's administration. Not only had he alienated the military and many hard-line politicians, but he had lost the confidence of the president. In November Johnson announced that McNamara would take over as president of the World Bank at the end of the year. Replacing him as secretary of defense would be Washington lawyer Clark Clifford, a trusted confidant of the president and a man known for his hawkish views.

Once the energetic and resilient man with the answers, McNamara had now become President Johnson's scapegoat for the stalemate in Vietnam. A brilliant manager, he had tried to achieve U.S. policy objectives in Vietnam in a limited and cost-effective manner. But in the end McNamara found there were forces he just could not control.

## The Paul Doumer Bridge

At 10:00 A.M. on August 11, the Takhli air base commander received an urgent message from 7th Air Force headquarters. The scheduled mission of the 355th TFW that afternoon had been scrubbed, superceded by President Johnson's decision to give the generals more of the targets they had been clamoring for. The wing commander, Colonel John Giraudo, notified his men they were flying against the Paul Doumer Bridge near Hanoi.

Built at the turn of the century, the 5,532-foot-long bridge was the linchpin of the rail system conceived by one of the French governors general of Indochina, Paul Doumer, after whom it was named. It was the only bridge across the Red River within fifty kilometers of Hanoi and provided the sole rail entry to the capital for trains traveling south from China and east from Haiphong. On an average day, twenty-six trains carrying an estimated 6,000 short tons crossed the bridge. Besides its central rail track, the span also included two highways. Hanoi had surrounded the strategically important span with more than 100 antiaircraft guns.

Gen. Momyer had decided to launch a strike the moment he got the green light from Washington, thereby minimizing security leaks and allowing the Americans the element of surprise. But it left Col. Giraudo with only four hours to brief his pilots and ready planes for the changed objective. Remembering their earlier failures at trying to knock down the Dragon's Jaw at Thanh Hoa with medium-sized bombs, headquarters called for 3,000-pound bombs to be used against the Paul Doumer Bridge. This meant that ground crews at Takhli would have to remove all the bombs they had just loaded onto the F-105s and rearm each one with two of the larger bombs and a single, center-line fuel tank mounted under the fuselage. There were twenty planes to rearm, and takeoff time was set for 2:18 P.M. The task seemed impossible.

Sweating and straining in the ninety-three degree tropical heat, the 355th's ground crews worked frantically underneath the monstrous jets. Barracks and mess halls emptied as all available personnel lent a hand. Col. Giraudo took a calculated risk and waived the ban on loading fuel and bombs at the same time. By 1:30 P.M.—in three hours—the job was done, at the rate of eighteen minutes per plane instead of the usual hour.

After an abbreviated briefing, twenty pilots led by Giraudo's deputy, Colonel Bob White, hastily charted on their maps the strike plan passed down from headquarters. Intelligence officers passed on all the information they had on the bridge and its defense. "Expect the heaviest defenses yet encountered in the war," they told the pilots. The pilots donned G-suits, parachutes, and survival vests and headed for their waiting planes. One by one, the twenty-five-ton Thunderchiefs rolled down the runway.

Heading the pack were four Wild Weasels and another flight of four F-105s assigned as flak suppressors. Behind them came Col. White leading three flights of Thunderchiefs with their seventy-two tons of 3,000-pound bombs. An identical force of Thunderchiefs from the 388th TFW at Korat trailed a few miles behind. F-4 Phantoms, led by Col. Robin Olds, provided fighter escort and also carried heavy bomb loads.

As White's strike force streaked closer to Hanoi, the North Vietnamese came to life. Thirty miles from the city, seven SAMs arched upward toward the force, but the Americans adroitly evaded them. Lieutenant Colonel James F. McInerney and his flight of four Wild Weasels went to work. During the battle they eliminated two SAM sites and forced four more to launch their missiles only sporadically. At twenty miles out the expected Migs showed up, four of them, on a head-on intercept course with the Thunderchiefs. Realizing the importance of the mission, the pilots maintained their formation, refusing to jettison their bombs. But the Migs streaked by just 200 feet below the strike force, strangely without firing a shot.

Breaking into the open over the flat delta that led to Hanoi, White could clearly make out the bridge across the muddy Red River. The weather over Hanoi was good, "almost too good," noted White. "We could have used a few clouds to help us dodge the North Vietnamese gunners." To evade the barrage of red-hot steel that lay in front of them seemed impossible. One pilot likened it to "trying to run several blocks in a rainstorm without letting a drop hit you."

The first wave of Thuds hit the bridge. Following behind them in his F-4, Col. Olds dove headlong through the flak; he could see string after string of 3,000-pound bombs pound the bridge. Col. White's Thunderchiefs scored a perfect hit on the central span.

Nearly a hundred tons of high explosives dropped during the mission cut the Paul Doumer Bridge in half. Incredibly, only two planes were badly damaged and both pilots made it safely back to Thailand. That was the good news. The disappointing facts were that within two months the bridge was back in operation. Twice again, in October and December, air force pilots returned to knock out the bridge. Each time the North Vietnamese repaired it.

## The biggest shooting gallery in history

Loss-free missions, like the one against the Doumer Bridge, were a rarity. Thirty-nine American planes went down over North Vietnam in August, bringing to 649 the total of aircraft lost since the beginning of Rolling Thunder. Throughout the fall of 1967 the rate continued to climb as American planes began a concentrated effort to isolate Hanoi and Haiphong.

"We were losing men and airplanes at an alarming rate," wrote Captain Gene I. Basel. Eight of the fifteen other F-105 pilots that had shipped out with him to the

*North Vietnamese local militia haul away the wreckage of a U.S. Navy F–8 destroyed northwest of Hanoi in spring, 1967.*

345th TFS at Takhli had been shot down within months of their arrival. Air force headquarters in Saigon demanded an explanation for the "unacceptable" loss rate.

Basel and his fellow pilots stayed awake nights pondering the same question, trying to devise different ways to reduce their casualties. One of the problems was fatigue. They would fly at least one, sometimes two, missions per day, grab a few hours' sleep, and then get up and repeat the hellish sequence all over again. It would not have been that bad except for the fact that they were now flying virtually every mission near Hanoi.

Although President Johnson still allowed only sporadic strikes against targets within the ten–mile prohibited zone around Hanoi, air force Thunderchiefs were now hitting everything they could around the edges. If they were not allowed to hit Hanoi itself, air commanders had decided to try and isolate the city by cutting the transportation routes leading in and out of the capital. This meant

that while the Thunderchiefs were not actually hitting targets in the city, they were still exposed to Hanoi's air defenses.

Emphasis was placed on cutting the rail line connecting Hanoi with China. But with the thirty–mile restricted zone around the capital and the thirty–mile Chinese buffer zone, only a twenty–five–mile section of the rail line was open to attack. The North Vietnamese concentrated AAA along the short strip, creating a gauntlet of fire that U.S. pilots came to call "Slaughter Alley."

Navy losses also ran high as they faced the same problems in their efforts to isolate Haiphong. During August sixteen navy planes were shot down, six by SAMs. During the month nearly 250 missiles had been sighted in the air by navy fliers, 80 on a single day.

Hanoi's already awesome defenses improved daily as the air war dragged on. In November optical tracking devices were installed on SAM launchers. American elec-

# Boston Publishing Company, Inc.

314 Dartmouth Street, Boston, Massachusetts 02116
Telephone: (617) 267-8800 Telex: 940-568

*In mid–1965, pilots of the U.S. Air Force leave their F–100 Supersabres and carry their flight gear back to the hangar at the Da Nang airfield.*

(Larry Burrows, LIFE Magazine. © Time Inc.)

*October 31, 1968. President Lyndon Johnson announces to the nation that, after more than three years of steadily increasing bombardment, the United States will end all air strikes against North Vietnam. By then . . .*

> **. . . American aircraft have dropped 850,000 tons of bombs on North Vietnam, more than had been expended in the entire Pacific Theater in World War II;**
>
> **. . . total bomb tonnage dropped on both North and South Vietnam—nearly 2 million—has exceeded the total used by the Allies in Europe during World War II; and**
>
> **. . . the United States has lost nearly 2,500 fixed–wing aircraft and more than 2,000 helicopters over the skies of North and South Vietnam.**

*The bombing halt brings the Communists to the negotiating table. Yet the rain of bombs has neither dampened the Communists' will to fight nor softened their negotiating stance. And, although U.S. bombers have hit virtually every major North Vietnamese industrial site at least once, the bombing campaign has been deemed a strategic failure.*

*(turn inside please)*

Dear Reader:

Having served as a marine jet pilot in Vietnam, I am doubly proud of the book now before you, *Thunder From Above.* This is the first of two volumes that deal with the air war in Vietnam. In this volume, our editors describe the war in the skies over Southeast Asia through 1968, a dramatic story of a high-stakes strategy, dangerous missions flown into the heart of North Vietnam, and high–tech aircraft designed to cope with the risks of flying over the most heavily defended turf in history.

It is also the story of a government and people—the North Vietnamese—steeling themselves against the might of U.S. air power with the assistance of a highly advanced Soviet–supplied air defense system.

*Thunder From Above* also takes you into the sky over South Vietnam during bombing missions flown in support of U.S. and South Vietnamese "search and destroy" operations. These "close air support" missions often meant the difference between life and death for embattled soldiers and success and failure for the ground operations. You will also read about the role of the most vulnerable aircraft in the war, the Hueys, Sea Knights, Chinooks, and all the other helicopters that introduced a new concept in ground warfare—air mobility.

*A formation of supersonic F–102 Delta Dagger jets flies in support of an operation to rescue a downed American pilot.* (Larry Burrows, LIFE Magazine, © Time Inc.)

The focus on *Thunder From Above* is on Operation Rolling Thunder, the bombing of North Vietnam between 1965 and 1968, and the men and aircraft that carried it out. President Lyndon Johnson and his secretary of defense, Robert McNamara, reasoned that bombing the North would cause the Communists to give up their fight to take over all of Vietnam and sue for a negotiated settlement.

But America's leaders didn't bargain on the resolve and resourcefulness of the North Vietnamese. Nor did they initially realize the extent of the sophisticated air defense system provided North Vietnam by the Soviet Union, which made the sky over Hanoi—in one pilot's words—"the biggest shooting gallery in history."

*Thunder From Above* puts you in the cockpit to show you close up the dangers of the air war. In *Thunder From Above,* you will:

- take the controls of an F–105 Thunderchief for a typical"Thud" mission over the North;
- join the flight deck crew aboard the aircraft carrier U.S.S. *Coral Sea* as it launches a Rolling Thunder mission;
- follow downed U.S. airmen as they try to avoid Communist capture; and
- fly in a B–52 Stratofortress as it carries out an "Arc Light" strike in South Vietnam.

*The gun camera of a USAF F–105 Thunderchief flying a Rolling Thunder bombing mission northeast of Hanoi on June 5, 1967, records the death of a Communist Mig. At left, the Thunderchief, piloted by Major Ralph Kuster of St. Louis, Missouri, closes in on the Mig–17. The Mig's wing, hit by the Thunderchief's 20MM cannon fire, bursts into flame, center, and disintegrates, right.*

The volume presents fascinating analysis of the controversial air tactics employed by the U.S. Air Force as it tried to follow the strategic guidelines laid down by Washington. *Thunder From Above* also takes you back to the 1940s to witness the first American air operations in Vietnam—assisted by Ho Chi Minh—and traces the steps in the 1950s and 1960s that led to full–scale air war over Vietnam.

The second volume in our two–part coverage of the air war picks up the story with the election of President Richard Nixon. In part two, we detail the "secret" bombings of Laos and Cambodia, give you an airman's view of the war from the airstrip at Da Nang (which, at the height of the war, was busier than Chicago's O'Hare Airport), and recount the infamous Christmas bombing blitz over Hanoi, which ultimately caused North Vietnam to sign the Paris peace agreement. The second part will also focus on the air war in South Vietnam to show you the tension and relief both pilots and ground forces experienced during close air support missions.

The volume now before you, *Thunder From Above*, tells the story of the men that flew over North Vietnam in the war's early years. As one former Rolling Thunder pilot wrote about the volume, "It brought back the sweaty palms and knotted stomach" of flying in Vietnam. I agree, and think you will find *Thunder From Above* a gripping chapter in THE VIETNAM EXPERIENCE.

Sincerely,

Robert J. George
Publisher

tronic jamming and detection gear aimed against the missile's radar proved useless when the North Vietnamese operators relied solely on their optical sights.

North Vietnamese Migs were now fully committed to the air battle as the Americans threatened their capital once again. While Migs had accounted for 3 percent of the entire number of planes lost to North Vietnamese defenses in 1966, the figure climbed to 8 percent in 1967. By the end of the year, the Americans were losing one plane for every two Migs they shot down. The previous ratio had been four-to-one. By comparison, in Korea U.S. pilots had achieved a fourteen-to-one rate.

Alarmed by these rising loss rates, Washington agreed at last to a campaign to destroy Mig air bases. Sporadic attacks had been authorized against three of the five airfields in April and June. Beginning with the strike on the largest airfield at Phuc Yen on October 25, each of North Vietnam's major air bases were now hit repeatedly during the fall. Gia Lam, which also doubled as Hanoi's international commercial airport, was the only exception.

Cratered runways were quickly repaired, however, and planes destroyed on the ground were replaced by the Soviets and Chinese. Many of the Migs were moved to Gia Lam or sent to operate out of airfields in southern China, where U.S. fighters were forbidden to follow. During the first three months of 1968, Migs accounted for 22 percent of all American planes shot down over the North, a startling increase that threatened to refute U.S. claims to superiority in the skies over North Vietnam.

The bulk of U.S. losses, however, continued to come from conventional antiaircraft fire. Thud Ridge, once a safe haven, now bristled with AAA guns. With the help of Soviet helicopters, the North Vietnamese had solved the problem of getting their guns atop the craggy peaks. The one relatively undefended route into the Red River Delta was now closed. Hanoi itself seemed to sprout new gun emplacements every day. "The city and surroundings were wall-to-wall guns," recalled Gene Basel, and he felt that flying over Hanoi was like "being a target in the biggest shooting gallery in history."

Despite the increasing losses, American bombers were getting through. Daily air strikes were taking their toll, severely straining North Vietnam's already impoverished economy. But as long as victory in the South appeared within their grasp, Hanoi's leaders found it possible to persevere. Prime Minister Pham Van Dong, who had taken over the day-to-day running of the government because of the failing health of Ho Chi Minh, vowed that their comrades in the South would strike "terrible blows against the American and satellite troops to avenge Hanoi every time the bombers hit our city." And in the South, the Communists continued to hold the initiative.

*On October 25, 1967, U.S. bombs fall toward the Phuc Yen Mig airfield, previously off-limits to American aircraft.*

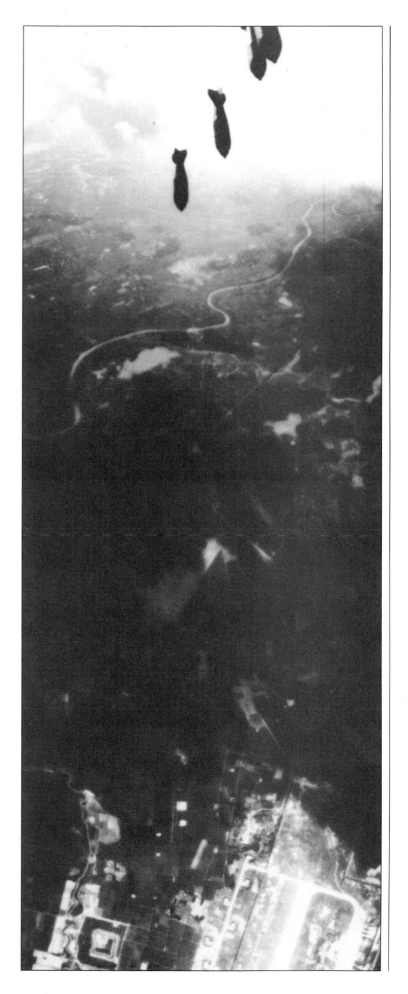

# Life in the Hanoi Hilton

A few days after being shot down on June 14, 1965, air force Major Larry Guarino was ushered into his new quarters at Hao Lo Prison in the center of downtown Hanoi. It was a dark, dank cell, sixteen feet long and seven feet wide with a single barred window. Ordered to strip, he was handed a pair of blue and white striped cotton pajamas and a small can for a toilet. Besides a metal cot, there was a concrete slab with a set of rusty leg stocks, relics of the days when the prison had been the main penitentiary of the French colonial regime.

That night, Guarino was taken to a large room where an English-speaking officer began interrogating him. Guarino refused to give more than his name, rank, and serial number. When the North Vietnamese incorrectly told him that U.S. B–52s had bombed North Vietnam two days after his capture and asked why this had occurred, Guarino answered: "That's a retaliatory raid." "What for?" the officer asked. "You shot me down," he responded. "They are not going to let you get away with that." The North Vietnamese officer landed a blow to Guarino's head that knocked him to the floor.

Continuing his defiance, Guarino had his rations cut after two days. Instead of the usual meal of soup, bread, three slices of pork, and vegetables, he was given a bowl of watery soup and a bowl of stale rice covered with dirt. He refused to eat it. The next day in the interrogation room, a North Vietnamese officer told Guarino: "You must understand that your position here is and will always be that of a criminal. You are not now or ever going to be treated in accordance with the Geneva agreements, because this is an undeclared war. Sooner or later you are going to denounce your government. You are going to beg our people for forgiveness!"

But Guarino continued to refuse to eat or cooperate and ended up doing a two-week stint in the stocks, during which he was allowed out of the stocks for only ten minutes each day to empty his waste bucket in the latrine area. On these trips he passed by another larger cell where he heard four voices calling his name. One was that of a squadron mate, Captain Carlyle Harris, and another belonged to Lieutenant Robert Peel. The other two, Lieutenant Commander Robert Shumaker and Lieutenant Philip Butler, were navy men he did not know. Shumaker had earlier contacted Bob Peel by scratching a note that read, "Welcome to the Hanoi Hilton!" The name stuck. But Guarino refused to acknowledge them or answer the notes they scratched on toilet paper and left hidden for him in the latrine. Smelling their food and hearing them talk and laugh, Guarino thought they had sold out to the enemy.

On July 20 Guarino made contact with navy Commander Jeremiah Denton, who had been captured the day before and placed in a cell nearby. After a few days, Denton answered the other POWs' notes, despite Guarino's warnings. As Denton suspected, the North Vietnamese had put the men together to try and weaken the morale of the other prisoners by making them think togetherness was a reward for cooperating. In fact, all four had done stretches in solitary confinement for trying to contact Guarino.

The ability to communicate was to be the key to sustaining the POWs' morale. After a number of written messages were intercepted, Shumaker and Harris devised a code using taps on the cell walls. The tap code provided the American POWs with a means of exchanging information and developing organized resistance.

By the fall of 1965, the North Vietnamese had begun extracting from the POWs "confessions," which could be broadcast to the world or used to persuade other POWs to cooperate. When softer methods of persuasion—such as the promise of better treatment—failed, the North Vietnamese turned to physical torture.

Many prisoners avoided torture, but new arrivals, who had not yet been contacted by other POWs; senior officers, whom the North Vietnamese considered the key to organized resistance; and defiant prisoners could count on it. The North Vietnamese singled out Lt. Col. Robbie Risner, who had received international publicity in an April 1965 *Time* magazine cover story. Risner was the senior ranking officer (SRO) at the "Zoo," another POW camp fifty-five kilometers west of Hanoi. There Risner had established policy and behavior guidelines for the POWs.

When guards discovered one of Risner's directives, he was bound and gagged and taken back to Hao Lo Prison. For thirty-two days, Risner remained in leg irons in solitary confinement on a diet of bread and water but refused to reveal anything about the POWs' resistance organization or communications network. Finally, he was introduced to the ropes.

Each of his arms was wrapped tightly from wrist to shoulder with tight half hitches. Both arms were then pulled behind his back and lashed together from the elbows up toward the shoulders. Tying his ankles together, the guards tied a rope around his neck and attached it to his feet, pulling it as taut as a bowstring. His right shoulder popped out of its socket, and he could feel his ribs separating from his breastbone. Risner later remembered the pain:

I was hollering. . . . I was in such pain that I knew that I couldn't last much longer. . . . I had been reduced to a mass of rope and sheer pain. . . . Finally, I hollered "Okay, I'll talk." The minute it came out I felt miserable. . . . I had agreed to go against all I had believed in, but it was not enough. They simply let me continue screaming.

Not until the next morning, after he agreed again to write a "confession" of his "crimes" against the Vietnamese people, were the ropes loosened.

By the end of 1968, more than 400 Americans, most of them pilots, were incarcerated in seven separate prison camps in North Vietnam. Although conditions varied, for the most part two men shared a small, dirty cell infested with roaches, mosquitoes, and sometimes rodents. The prisoners were usually fed two meager meals a day. Despite the threats and beatings, the POWs, who would rally behind each other, continued to try to resist.

In mid-1968, when the POWs were told of the bombing halt and the subsequent peace negotiations in Paris, rumors of their impending release spread through the camps. But it was to be another three years before they would see America. For some that was too late.

# Arc Light Mission Over Khe Sanh

Preceding page. A B-52 Stratofortress takes off from Guam on an Arc Light mission to Khe Sanh in January 1968. The 6,000-mile round-trip flight took twelve hours, but once they reached their target the huge bombers faced no opposition.

Above. Captain Robert Grabstald and his B-52's six-man crew synchronize their watches during the preflight briefing.

Left. An M-904 nose fuse is fitted into a Mark 82 500-pound bomb before it is loaded aboard the B-52, which will weigh over 220 tons when armed and fueled. The red safety pin and attached streamer will be removed just before takeoff.

Right. Ordnance personnel attach a rack of six 500-pound bombs to one of the four bomb stations under the B-52's wings. The plane's internal bomb bay holds another eighty-four 500-pound bombs.

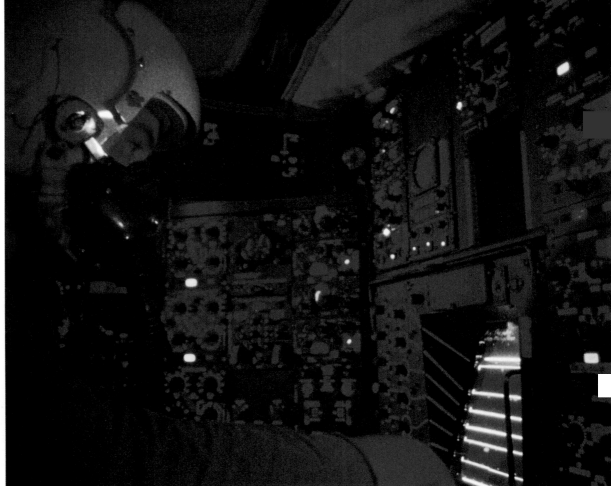

Above. Captain Grabstald and his copilot, First Lieutenant Dennis W. Mack, check their instruments after takeoff. B–52s flew their missions at 35,000 feet, so high their crews never saw the targets.

Right. The Electronic Warfare Officer watches his controls, which he uses to monitor and jam enemy radar.

Above. The navigator plots the jet's course on his route chart.

Left. Beads of sweat form on Grabstald's brow as he maneuvers the B–52 behind a KC–135 refueling tanker. Aerial refuelings were perhaps the riskiest moments in Arc Light strikes until B–52s flying against the Red River Delta in 1972 first faced the North's defenses.

Above. In flight, the navigator (left) peers at his instrument panel while the radar navigator looks through the peroscopic bomb sight. To their left are indicator lights and switches used to monitor the twenty-two-ton bomb load.

Left. The radar navigator's thumb is poised above the D-2 bomb release switch as he awaits the order to send the bombs earthward toward the enemy surrounding the U.S. Marine base at Khe Sanh.

Right. One by one, bombs drop from the bomb bay. Stratofortresses dropped as much as 90,000 tons of bombs during the seventy-seven day siege of Khe Sanh. Between April 1965, when they were first used in Vietnam, and December 1968, B-52s dropped 886,000 tons of bombs in Southeast Asia, more than the total amount dropped by allied aircraft during the Korean War.

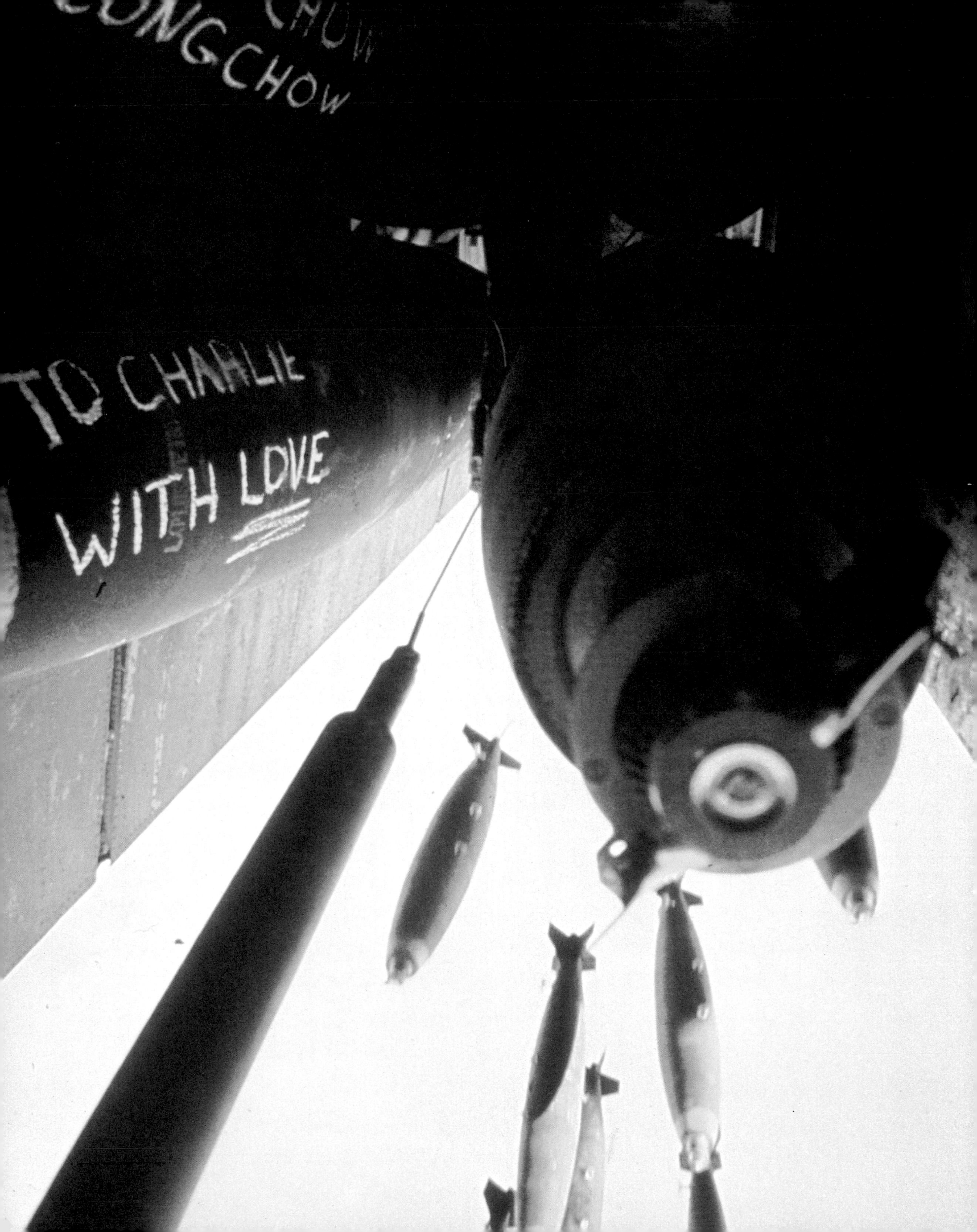
TO CHARLIE
WITH LOVE

# Failure of a Strategy

Circling high above the South Vietnamese countryside two F-100 pilots watched as thousands of feet below them a tiny O-1 Birddog pulled over in a steep dive. From under the FAC's left wing, a smoke rocket flashed toward the ground, bursting in a white cloud near a cluster of huts alongside a canal. "Target fifty feet at six o'clock from smoke burst," the FAC radioed. "Hut at edge of garden."

Maneuvering in a wide, sweeping turn, the two fighter pilots lined their jets up with the marker smoke. Straightening out in a shallow dive, the Supersabres skimmed over the canal at 450 knots. Seconds before they reached the cluster of huts, a pair of aluminum canisters detached themselves from underneath each plane's fuselage and tumbled end over end toward the ground. The first two failed to explode, but the second pair erupted on impact, engulfing two of the huts in a crimson fireball of napalm.

Pulling back into the sky, the two Supersabres looped back around for a second run. They delib-

erately aligned their planes with the target once again. There was no need to rush. They had not drawn any return fire from the suspected Vietcong encampment.

Bearing in once more, the Supersabre pilots opened up with their 20MM cannons, sending a stream of bullets ripping through the thatched huts. Again they encountered no resistance. Having exhausted their supply of ammunition, the two jets checked in with the still-orbiting FAC and headed for home.

This was the air war for a jet jockey in South Vietnam. No SAMs streaking skyward to cut a plane in two. No Migs hiding behind the clouds, waiting to pounce. No clouds of flak filling the view from the wind screen. Only an occasional burst of tracer bullets and small-arms fire. "One pass and haul ass," the cardinal rule for Rolling Thunder pilots, did not apply to pilots flying missions over South Vietnam.

Although at worst they occasionally hit pockets of heavy automatic-weapons fire, they usually encountered only small-arms fire. If a pilot strayed in too low, it was possible that a lucky hit from a single bullet could disable one of the vital internal mechanisms in his multimillion dollar jet and send it crashing to the ground. But fixed-wing aircraft losses in the South were nowhere near the rate of losses suffered over the North. By the end of 1967, 223 planes had been shot down over South Vietnam, 681 over the North. Even if a pilot were shot down, his chances of being rescued were high. For many pilots, missions over the South seemed no more dangerous than flying target practice back in the United States.

The result was a highly impersonal war for the jet pilots flying missions in the South. They aimed at little puffs of marker smoke in the jungle, dropped their bombs, and headed back to an air-conditioned officers' club or the wood-paneled wardroom aboard an aircraft carrier. Rarely did they see the enemy or the effects of their air strikes.

Lieutenant Frank C. Elkins, a navy A-4 pilot who was later killed in action over North Vietnam, flew his first combat mission over South Vietnam on June 30, 1966, in support of 1st Air Cav soldiers fighting the VC forty-five miles northwest of Saigon. His four-plane formation blanketed a patch of jungle near the troopers with 250-and 500-pound bombs, Bullpup missiles, and napalm. The next day the navy received word that 600 Vietcong bodies had been uncovered in the area.

"It never occurs to you while you're flying that there are people down there," Elkins recorded in his diary the night after the mission.

The real shame that I feel is my own lack of emotional reaction. I keep reacting as though I were simply watching a movie of the whole thing. I still don't feel that I have personally killed anyone. Somehow the whole experience remains unreal.

For another kind of aviator the war in the South hit closer to home. Army and marine helicopter pilots, hugging the terrain in their slow-moving, thinly armored ships (some jet pilots thought of Hueys as "10,000 pieces of equipment flying in loose formation"), saw the war from a totally different perspective. While jet pilots like Lt. Elkins could only imagine what attacks left on the ground below, chopper pilots saw it vividly.

Robert Mason, a Huey pilot with the 1st Air Cav, recorded in his memoirs a harrowing heliborne assault during Operation Masher/White Wing in early 1966. Mason's chopper was the fortieth in a string of about one hundred carrying soldiers to a landing zone named Dog in the Bong Son Valley in II Corps.

Constantly bunching up, the ships were able to maintain an air speed of only twenty knots as they skimmed over paddies, dotted occasionally with small villages known to be populated by VC sympathizers. Mason could hear pilots ahead of him calling that they had been hit. "Below us, the villagers were having a picnic, shooting at a lot of helicopters flying low and slow," he wrote. "I couldn't see any guns, just women and children and men watching the helicopter parade."

Just as the ship in front of him was hit, Mason spotted a VC gunner. He had set up right in the center of a crowd of villagers. Mason ordered his door gunner to spray the ground in front of the villagers to scare them away. As the bullets ripped through the muddy paddies, Mason expected to see the men, women, and children scatter.

"When the bullets were smashing fifty feet in front of them, I knew they weren't going to move," he recorded. "They threw up their arms as they were hit and whirled to the ground." Finally, the bullets smashed into the gunner. When it was all over, Mason counted a dozen people lying around the gunner.

Twenty ships were damaged and five shot down during the approach to the landing zone that day. Four men were killed. The actual assault at LZ Dog proved anticlimactic, as the choppers met little resistance. That night Mason could not keep from replaying the grisly scene in his mind.

"Why didn't they duck?" he wondered out loud.

"The VC forced them to stand there," replied his copilot. "Obviously they were more afraid of him than they were of us."

Not all the landings were as uncontested as the one Mason flew to LZ Dog that day. Another 1st Cav chopper crewman, Chief Warrant Officer Sidney Cowan, recalled the tension aboard the Hueys as they moved in closer toward a landing zone they knew to be "hot." He could see it in the faces of the men they ferried: "They know Charlie is waiting."

*A UH-1B of the 1st Air Cavalry fires its 2.75-inch rockets near An Khe during Operation Pershing in May 1967.*

The key to survival was getting in and out of the LZ as quickly as possible. Sitting out in the open, a helicopter was a fat target. Seconds seemed like hours as the familiar sound of bullets piercing the ship's aluminum hull echoed throughout the chopper. As the last man scrambled out the door, the pilot revved the engine and pulled up the collective control stick to get the ungainly looking bird into the safety of the sky. Then it was back to the staging area to pick up more men and repeat the process.

## Search and destroy

After the 1st Air Cavalry's impressive showing in the Ia Drang Valley in late 1965, helicopter assaults became the mainstay of American tactics in South Vietnam. Not only did they allow the Americans to react quickly to guerrilla attacks, but they added a potent offensive capability as well. Operating from their enclaves along the coast, U.S. troops had during 1966 gradually enlarged the areas under government control. By combining their new-found air mobility with ground sweeps, they managed to break the VC's control of the rich, rice-growing coastal plains.

Spoiling attacks relying heavily on air strikes against the guerrillas' base camps in the central highlands and in the remote western border areas managed to keep the Communists off balance. Improved intelligence had produced encouraging results from interdiction bombing. The introduction of the Combat Skyspot bombing system in July 1966, in which ground control radar units directed B–52s to their targets, allowed the U.S. to maintain the pressure even during bad weather.

The number of jet aircraft available for operations in South Vietnam had nearly doubled by 1967, to twenty-eight tactical fighter squadrons of roughly twenty-four aircraft each based in the country. On any given day the 7th Air Force could manage about 300 preplanned sorties. Another 40 aircraft were usually on alert and scrambled three or four times a day in answer to calls for close air support of ground troops. In I Corps, the marines averaged 200 sorties per day and the South Vietnamese air force another 100 daily. On a typical day, 750 to 800 combat sorties supported ground troops. In addition, Westmoreland could draw upon over 3,000 army and marine helicopters.

Air power had also proved effective in the vital area of logistics. Transports of the air force's Military Airlift Command shuttled troops and supplies from the U.S. to Southeast Asia via bases in Japan, Okinawa, and the Philippines. Seven major air bases in South Vietnam, as well as four more in Thailand, were upgraded to accommodate the ever-increasing volume of traffic flowing through the 16,000-kilometer pipeline. Critical supplies, such as spare parts for combat equipment, came in via a continuous airlift called the "Red Ball Express."

By the end of 1966, after over a year of build-up and consolidation of American forces, Gen. Westmoreland felt a "genuine optimism" about the progress of the war. Bolstered by a solid working base of nearly 400,000 troops, the logistics to maintain them, and added firepower and mobility, Westmoreland was ready to initiate major offensive operations.

In the Combined Campaign Plan for 1967, South Vietnamese troops got the task of securing and pacifying areas under their control while U.S. forces carried the bulk of the fighting against the Communists. The aim was to destroy the enemy's close-in base areas and push them farther away from the cities with large-scale, combined air and land offensives.

Operation Cedar Falls, mounted in January 1967 against the Communist stronghold northwest of Saigon called the "Iron Triangle," was one of the first of these sweeping "search and destroy" actions. U.S. troops cordoned off the area to block any escape routes. Armored cavalry units and air assault teams, supported by fighter-bombers, then swept through the Iron Triangle, ferreting out guerrilla units and destroying their installations.

During the operation nearly 750 Vietcong were killed in skirmishes with ground troops or as a result of supporting air strikes. Another 280 prisoners, 540 deserters, and 512 suspects were taken into custody. Large amounts of enemy equipment were captured or destroyed as well as numerous bunkers and tunnels. The entire civilian population of Ben Suc, a village considered the hub of VC activity in the area, was evacuated to government resettlement camps in order to establish the Iron Triangle as a "free fire zone" so that attacks by U.S. bombers could discourage the guerrillas from returning.

Encouraged by the results of Cedar Falls, American commanders turned their attention to War Zone C, a 2,600-square-kilometer area wedged between the Iron Triangle and the Cambodian border. The area had been under Communist control for over twenty years. Through-

*The free fire zone that was Ben Suc. The former VC-dominated village located in South Vietnam's Iron Triangle was razed in January 1967 during Operation Cedar Falls.*

*Men of the U.S. 2d Battalion, 503d Infantry, 173d Airborne Brigade, stream toward the CH-47 Chinooks that will take them into battle during Operation Junction City in February 1967.*

out the dense jungles and forests, the guerrillas had developed an extensive system of tunnels and bunkers. Housed in these camps were the 101st NVA Regiment and the 9th VC Division. U.S. intelligence also believed that the Communist Central Office for South Vietnam was hidden somewhere in War Zone C. COSVN controlled all VC political and military activities in the South. Feeling that this tempting prize was within his grasp, Westmoreland told the planners to "think big."

The result was the most ambitious operation the Americans had yet undertaken in the war; its plan called for 35,000 U.S. and ARVN soldiers divided into two forces. One was to form a horseshoe-shaped cordon around the northwestern portion of War Zone C while the others drove up the horseshoe, forcing the VC into the open where they could be hit by air strikes. For air support, General Momyer allocated 200 sorties per day to the operation, an incredible amount considering 7th Air Force aircraft based in the South were averaging only 300 sorties per day through all of South Vietnam. To avoid getting caught short elsewhere, Momyer requested and received authority to use air force F-105s based in Thailand and navy aircraft if necessary. Before D-Day, Arc Light mis-

sions saturated areas that radio intercepts had indicated might be the location of COSVN.

On February 22, Operation Junction City swung into action. Eight infantry brigades were airlifted into blocking positions along the Cambodian border. Wave after wave of helicopters touched down in their assigned landing areas, which had been softened up by rocket and machine-gun fire from low-flying jets. Fourteen C-130s dropped 845 paratroopers of the 173d Airborne Brigade in the only U.S. combat parachute assault of the Vietnam War. No contact was made with the enemy during the airdrop.

For A Platoon from the 1st Infantry Division, led by Lieutenant David Cejka, part of the force sweeping up the horseshoe, it would be a different story. Walking down a dirt trail toward the Cambodian border, one sergeant whispered: "I can smell Charlies all around us." As they entered a bamboo thicket, Cejka's platoon ran into a hail of automatic-weapons fire which pinned them down.

*Newsweek* correspondent François Sully, who had accompanied the platoon, could see a B-52 strike ripping apart the jungle in the distance. "Why don't we get any air support?" he muttered to himself. Half an hour later, Sully heard the machine guns of army helicopters, rattling "like Spanish castanets," rake the brush nearby. He wrote in his notebook: "12:30 P.M. The jets are here."

First the dart-shaped Supersabres zoom in at treetop level, so fast that I cannot photograph them. They unload their pointed fragmentation bombs, and the precision is amazing. Between passes of the screaming jets, I can swear I hear North Vietnamese voices.

Four B-57 bombers followed the F-100s with napalm runs, creating an inferno directly in front of the platoon. Some of the canisters landed a bit too close for comfort, splattering the trees and shrubs nearby as Cejka's men hit the dirt. Sully wiped a sticky droplet that failed to ignite off a cactus plant. "It smelled like the rubber cement at the office," he wrote.

On the first day of the operation, air force planes flew 180 close air support sorties but soon were scaled back to 100 sorties per day because the Vietcong refused to commit themselves to battle. The first phase of Junction City proved "very disappointing" according to Gen. Momyer. U.S. and ARVN troops captured large quantities of arms, ammunition, and rice but made only sporadic contacts with the enemy.

During the second phase, which began on March 18 and consisted of sweeps through the eastern portion of War Zone C, the Vietcong decided to counterattack. But instead of the big battle that the Americans had hoped for, the guerrillas concentrated on hitting isolated landing zones and firebases.

Early on the morning of March 21, the Vietcong attacked Fire Support Base Gold near the town of Suoi Tre and threatened to overrun the camp. An O-1 Birddog raced to the scene to coordinate air support. But after the pilot directed the first air strike, heavy machine-gun fire ripped through the fragile plane. It crashed to the ground, killing both the pilot and observer.

Two more O-1s were scrambled to Suoi Tre. Additional F-100s from Bien Hoa and F-4 Phantoms from Cam Ranh Bay were also sent. By 9:00 A.M. more than eighty-five fighters had been committed to the battle, including an AC-47 gunship. Combined with the arrival of a relief column, the air strikes broke the back of the attack. The defenders suffered 31 dead and 109 wounded and later counted 647 VC bodies around the firebase.

By the time Junction City ended, air force F-100s and F-4Cs had flown more than 4,000 sorties in support of the nearly two-month long operation. The 1st, 11th, and 145th Aviation Battalions had ferried 9,518 combat troops into War Zone C along with fifty tons of supplies per day.

But Junction City was far from the decisive victory the Americans claimed. Although the sweep had rooted the guerrillas from War Zone C, it failed to deliver the crushing blow that had been intended. For all their superior weaponry, the Americans had been forced to fight the guerrillas on their own terms, and soon the enemy was seen returning to War Zone C.

Although large-scale heliborne assaults supported by artillery and air strikes initially demoralized the enemy, the VC quickly developed tactics to counter the Americans' mobility and firepower. One Communist strategist noted, "Success or failure in war is dictated by the human factor, not weapons."

Before an operation the Americans usually laid down a barrage of air and artillery fire to "prep" an LZ, giving the guerrillas advance warning of an assault. The prelanding barrage was usually targeted for landing zone areas, which the guerrillas would avoid during the bombing. After the barrage ended they often moved back into the bombed area to set an ambush for the incoming landing teams. They engaged the Americans at close quarters so they could not use supporting fire.

If the odds were stacked too heavily against them, the Vietcong simply withdrew deeper into the jungle or crossed the borders into Cambodia or Laos where the Americans could not follow. There they would wait until U.S. troops were withdrawn, then reoccupy the same piece of real estate. According to one North Vietnamese leader, the American large-scale offensive sweeps were like "stabbing the water, because when the sword has been pulled out of the water, the water remains unchanged."

## Operation Neutralize

During the spring of 1967 the Communists decided to shift their strategy to a three-phase, "coordinated struggle." By mounting assaults from their sanctuaries in phase one, the Communists hoped to draw U.S. troops away from the populated areas along the coast and in the South. The second phase was to be a "general uprising" of the people of South Vietnam against their government, led by the Vietcong with attacks against the major cities. Finally, Hanoi hoped a decisive battle in the northern provinces would seal the victory.

North Vietnamese General Vo Nguyen Giap set the plan in motion by deploying thirty-seven battalions—18,000 men—along the DMZ. Heavy artillery pieces, up to 152MM in size, were brought up and dug into fortified bunkers protected by antiaircraft guns. The heavily armed and well-trained conventional force represented a much more sophisticated and dangerous enemy threat than ever before thrown at the South.

On March 20 the North Vietnamese opened phase one. Over 1,000 rounds of mortar, rocket, and artillery fire rocked U.S. Marine positions at Con Thien and Gio Linh, the northernmost outposts in a string of bases just below the DMZ. Throughout the summer, marine units near the border endured constant North Vietnamese attack. Westmoreland was forced to call in army units from II and III Corps as reinforcements, but the pounding continued.

To break the back of the North Vietnamese onslaught,

*U.S. soldiers of the 2d Battalion, 503d Infantry, parachute from a C–130 into War Zone C in South Vietnam.*

U.S. forces launched Operation Neutralize, which employed a new concept for marshaling American firepower. Dubbed SLAM (seek, locate, annihilate, and monitor), the plan called for coordinating an intensified air campaign with artillery and naval gunfire to wipe out enemy positions along the DMZ. Gen. Westmoreland gave Gen. Momyer full authority over the 7th Air Force and navy and marine air to coordinate the operation. A combined intelligence center, set up at Momyer's headquarters in Saigon, analyzed and pinpointed suitable targets.

It was extremely difficult to locate the North Vietnamese guns because they were hidden by ingenious camouflaging techniques and well dug-in bunkers. Some were "actually kept in caves, rolled out to be fired, and then rolled back in," Momyer said. Because electronic intelligence equipment proved less effective than he had hoped, Momyer relied mainly on aerial photo reconnaissance.

For forty-nine days, starting on September 11, air force, navy, and marine fighters pounded North Vietnamese positions in and across the DMZ. More than 3,100 sorties were flown during the SLAM operation, some of them di-

rected by F-100s serving as FACs because they were less vulnerable to the intense ground fire than slower O-1s. B-52s flew an additional 820 sorties, making their first appearance over North Vietnam since their attempt in April 1966 to close the Mu Gia Pass.

Slowly, the volume of Communist artillery fire dwindled away to almost nothing. America's overwhelming advantage in aerial firepower had proven the decisive factor, killing or wounding an estimated 2,000 NVA soldiers. Back in Washington in November, Gen. Westmoreland expressed his confidence in a speech to the National Press Club. He said that the Communists had not won a "major victory" in over a year. "Whereas in 1965 the enemy was winning," he said, "today he is certainly losing." At the close of the year, however, new intelligence reports were to cast a dark shadow over his optimistic claims.

Around the new year, a recently installed American electronic monitoring system along the DMZ and in Laos, part of the electronic infiltration barrier called "McNamara's Fence," indicated a flurry of activity along the Ho Chi Minh Trail. CIA and MACV intelligence reports con-

*An NVA rocket explodes an ammunition dump at the U.S. Marine base at Khe Sanh in early 1968.*

firmed that a huge build-up was in progress. It was obvious that the North Vietnamese were preparing to launch a major offensive. The mystery was where it would come.

## Another Dien Bien Phu?

Early in January of 1968 marine patrols from Khe Sanh, the westernmost outpost in the chain of U.S. bases along the DMZ, ran into heavily armed NVA troops. Since the base was located close to the Laotian border near a spur of the Ho Chi Minh Trail, such contacts had occurred before. But this time the North Vietnamese were not just passing through. They were staying.

Three NVA divisions, an estimated 20,000 men, soon surrounded Khe Sanh. One of the divisions was the battle-hardened 304th Home Guard that had won its fame at the battle of Dien Bien Phu. They were heavily supported by long-range howitzers, mortars, rocket launchers, anti-aircraft artillery, and Soviet-built PT-76 tanks.

Gen. Westmoreland believed the build-up around Khe Sanh was the opening move in another Communist attempt to seize control of South Vietnam's two northernmost provinces. Sending reinforcements to bring the garrison's strength up to 6,000 men, Westmoreland ordered the marines to "dig in." Westmoreland's decision to hold at Khe Sanh was controversial. Many observers pointed to the similarities between the marines' situation at the outpost and that of the French at Dien Bien Phu fourteen years earlier. Like Dien Bien Phu, Khe Sanh was surrounded by a vastly larger force. The Communists had cut all the land routes to the base, making it entirely dependent on aerial resupply. With the northeast monsoon season in full swing, air operations would be severely hampered by fog and low clouds.

But there were crucial differences as well, and Westmoreland was quick to point them out. At Dien Bien Phu, the Vietminh had held the hills overlooking the French camp; the only high ground, to the west of Khe Sanh, had been turned into hilltop outposts by U.S. Marines. In addition, unlike the foreign legionnaires trapped inside Dien Bien Phu, U.S. forces held a distinct edge in artillery in and around the marine base. But the most telling difference was the vast reserve of air power the marines had at their disposal.

The French air force had been able to put only 200 fighters and bombers in the air each day to support the garrison at Dien Bien Phu. The Americans could draw on an armada of 2,000 fixed-wing aircraft and 3,300 helicopters based throughout Southeast Asia, including B-52 Stratofortresses. All-weather attack planes, such as the A-6 Intruder, and radar-controlled bombing techniques could overcome most any weather conditions. Also, nearly 250 American cargo planes could theoretically deliver six times as much as the smaller French transports had been capable of carrying.

No one was more concerned with the possibility of history repeating itself than Lyndon Johnson, who requested daily briefings on Khe Sanh. But Westmoreland was firmly convinced that he could hold Khe Sanh. His gamble was soon put to the test. Just after midnight on January 21, 300 North Vietnamese regulars blasted into the American outpost on Hill 861. Counterattacking marines drove the intruders back after hand-to-hand fighting. A few hours later, the main base was rocked by an intense artillery barrage. One helicopter parked on the airstrip was left a blazing wreck and five others were damaged; well-placed rounds blew up the main ammo dump. The siege of Khe Sanh had begun.

The keys to the survival of Khe Sanh were its 3,900-foot runway, the transport planes of the 834th Air Wing, and marine cargo helicopters. Without them there would be no way to provide the vast quantities of ammunition, food, and medical supplies to sustain the base. Knowing this the North Vietnamese had brought as many antiaircraft guns as they could haul over the mountain and jungle trails from Laos, placing them directly underneath the flight path leading to Khe Sanh's runway. "They had the glide slope zeroed in with .50-caliber machine guns," said one marine pilot. "They'd just listen for you and start laying fire down the glide slope. If you were on it you were drilled."

Landing at Khe Sanh was no easy task, even without having to run a gauntlet of enemy ground fire. Low clouds combined with fog forced most pilots to rely on their instruments at least 40 percent of the time. Once on the ground the huge air force cargo planes were easy targets for the NVA guns, which pounded the base daily. "Every inch of the runway was zeroed in," said a pilot. "They just walked artillery rounds right up the center line." Enemy gunfire became so synchronized to the landings that the marines sardonically referred to the transports as "mortar magnets."

To minimize the time the transports were on the ground, crewmen shoved pallets of supplies mounted on rollers through the rear cargo doors and onto the runway while the plane was still moving. Rushing out from behind sandbagged bunkers, ground crewmen scooped up the pallets with fork lifts. Incoming reinforcement troops jumped out of the still moving planes while outgoing casualties were loaded aboard. The odds finally caught up with the transports on February 10, when a marine C-130 carrying fuel was riddled by machine-gun fire just before it touched down. The two pilots managed to escape the burning plane, but seven crewmen died in the ensuing explosions.

Two days later Gen. Momyer ordered all C-130 landings at Khe Sanh suspended. The newest and largest transports in the air force's inventory, the C-130 was in limited supply, and Momyer did not want to risk losing any more at Khe Sanh. C-123K Providers, which needed only half the distance the larger C-130s took to take off and land, were assigned to the task, with smaller C–7A Caribous as back-ups.

The C-130s continued to drop supplies by parachute and also experimented with two new low-level delivery systems. Flying in only a few feet above the runway with their rear cargo doors open, pallets of supplies mounted on rollers would be dragged out by a parachute electrically triggered open by the pilot. But the heavily loaded pallets sometimes careened dangerously across the runway before stopping and gouged deep scars in its surface. Another system, in which C-130 pilots snagged a cable stretched across the runway with a hook attached to the supply pallets, worked much better. In one instance a load containing thirty dozen eggs was delivered without cracking a single one.

Supplying the nearly 1,200 marines dug in on the hills northwest of the main base posed an even more hazardous task. The outposts were too small and the terrain too steep for accurate parachute drops. Direct helicopter landings were the only answer. Marine CH-46 Sea Knights were the primary aircraft used on these shuttle runs between the main base and the hill outposts.

Lieutenant Colonel David Althoff, executive officer of marine Medium Helicopter Squadron 262, described the missions as "pure hell." North Vietnamese mortar crews had every inch of flat ground on the hills zeroed in. Once they saw the choppers approaching they would open up. So damaging was the enemy fire that less than a month into the siege, more than half the CH-46s in Althoff's squadron had been lost to enemy fire. Huey gunships escorting the Sea Knights did not have the firepower to neutralize the North Vietnamese guns. The marines came up with the idea of running the choppers in small convoys called "Super Gaggles" under the cover of A-4 Skyhawks. The A-4s neutralized enemy gun sites with bombs, napalm, and tear gas and laid down a smoke screen for the choppers, which lumbered into the outposts with 4,000 pounds of supplies slung in cargo nets underneath each of them. Super Gaggles proved the turning point in the battle to maintain the hill outposts. Only two Sea Knights were lost during the system's period of operation.

## Operation Niagara

While the transports and cargo helicopters kept Khe Sanh supplied, U.S. jet fighters and bombers made life miserable for the North Vietnamese. Gen. Momyer finally had the opportunity he had been waiting for—large concentrations of Communist troops in a remote, sparsely populated area with no restrictions on bombing missions. "We never let up," said Momyer. Khe Sanh had first priority on close air support. All available aircraft in South Vietnam and some usually used over the North were at the marines' disposal for what Gen. Westmoreland named Operation Niagara. On an average day 350 tactical fighters, 60 B–52s, 10 RF–4C reconnaissance jets, and 30 O–1 and O–2 Birddogs operated over the base.

Layers of orbiting planes, waiting for their assignments, reached upward of 35,000 feet. Coordinating the gigantic armada became a taxing problem. "You had FACs working down low and the B–52s up high, with a mixed bag of air force, navy, and marine fighters in between," one fighter pilot said. "The controllers had to be on their toes."

As Westmoreland's deputy for air operations, Gen. Momyer was given responsibility for coordinating Operation Niagara. From the outset he ran into problems with the marines. They were reluctant to relinquish their authority to an air force general. Momyer's two predecessors had wrestled with the same issue—whether there should be a single commander for air operations throughout South Vietnam.

Marine doctrine emphasized the close coordination of their air and ground units. Since Khe Sanh was a marine operation, they maintained that all air assets employed in close air support of the base should be under their control. They even suggested that only marine aircraft be allowed to operate in the immediate area around the camp.

Momyer protested that the marines did not have sufficient resources. Marine air capabilities were traditionally devoted to supporting amphibious operations, not prolonged air offensives covering wide areas. Westmoreland endorsed Momyer's request that he be made single air manager for Khe Sanh. "To have several tactical air systems functioning in the same confined region was simply too ponderous, too extravagant with resources, [and] . . . too conducive to errors," he reasoned.

Although the single air manager made sense to Westmoreland, it sparked a bitter debate among the Joint Chiefs. Marine Corps Commandant General Leonard F. Chapman, Jr., strongly objected to the proposal, worried that it would set a precedent leading to the marines' losing command of their own air power. Even Army Chief of Staff General Harold Johnson hesitated to support Westmoreland. He feared a single air manager might hand over control of the army's helicopters to the air force. A majority of the JCS decided, however, not to interfere with Westmoreland, who had gone so far as to threaten resignation over the issue. So for the first time in the Vietnam War air operations were placed firmly—if only temporarily—under the control of a single manager, and Operation Niagara swung into high gear.

Tactical fighters were sent in to support the base. Controlling them were marine airmen operating the Direct Air Support Center located in a heavily bunkered trailer inside the base. The DASC also was responsible for coordinating air strikes with artillery fire from Camp Carroll to the east. Above the camp an air force C-130 acted as an airborne control center. Both assigned incoming strike aircraft to targets called in by ground troops and marked by FACs.

*An F-8 Crusader fires on enemy positions near Khe Sanh in February 1968.*

When weather conditions made FAC-directed air strikes impossible, the fighter-bombers were guided to their targets by the marine TPQ-10 radar station within Khe Sanh or one of the many air force Combat Skyspot MSQ-77 radar stations located across the country. Using the coordinates provided by the DASC, the radar operators programmed their computers to calculate the coordinates of the target, wind currents, air speed, altitude, heading, and the exact point of bomb release. This information was relayed to the strike aircraft by a pencil-thin radar beam. Once the plane was over the target, the controller would call "Mark!" to the pilot who then released his bombs.

Outside the immediate area around the base, B-52 Stratofortresses struck nearby North Vietnamese troop concentrations, staging areas, and supply lines in Laos. A formation of three B-52s took off from bases in Guam, Okinawa, and U Tapao, Thailand, every ninety minutes enabling the B-52s to maintain a constant presence over the area.

Lieutenant General Robert E. Cushman, commander of the 3d Marine Amphibious Force, concerned that a slight miscalculation might cause a B-52 to hit his own men, asked that the giant bombers be restricted from operating within a two-mile radius around the main base and the surrounding hill outposts. Taking advantage of this safety zone, the North Vietnamese moved their bunker and trench systems as close to the marines as possible.

Gen. Momyer, confident that the B-52s could hit with precision targets within three-quarters of a mile of friendly positions, asked that the safety zone be reduced. A test run by a single Stratofortress on February 26 proved his point, and close-in B-52 strikes soon became routine.

Statements from prisoners and deserters confirmed the devastating effects of these Arc Light strikes. One reported that three-quarters of an entire regiment was lost in one raid alone. North Vietnamese soldiers would be found wandering around in a daze after the raids, bleeding at the nose and mouth from concussions.

"The tonnage of ordnance that has been placed in a five-mile circle around that arc is unbelievable," reported the vice commander of an F-100 squadron operating over Khe Sanh. "The jungle has literally been turned into a desert. There is hardly a tree standing. . . . It is just a landscape of splinters and bomb craters."

By March 12, the fourteenth anniversary of Gen. Giap's victory at Dien Bien Phu, the long-anticipated final assault on Khe Sanh had still not materialized. Toward the end of

# Laos: Battling the Ho Chi Minh Trail

The Communists' ability to operate freely from their sanctuaries in Laos proved extremely frustrating to the U.S. military effort in Vietnam. General William Westmoreland had recommended several plans for cross-border operations into the Laotian panhandle. However, civilian officials in Washington shuddered at the thought of openly committing U.S. combat troops to Laos, fearing escalatory countermoves by Hanoi or involvement of the Soviets, who had cosigned with the U.S. the 1962 Geneva accords guaranteeing Laotian neutrality. Instead, Washington centered its efforts on backing the Royal Laotian Army in its struggle against North Vietnamese–supported Pathet Lao guerrillas who controlled large portions of the northeast section of the country. The CIA also recruited Meo hill tribesmen into counterguerrilla units operating behind Pathet Lao lines.

Limited air operations in the early 1960s by the Laotian air force, with advisers and aircraft supplied secretly by the USAF and CIA, hardly dented NVA activities in Laos. By the end of 1964, the southern panhandle adjacent to the Vietnamese border had been transformed into a vast supply corridor to support Vietcong military operations in the South. At its heart was the Ho Chi Minh Trail.

With the Laotian government unable and unwilling to divert any of its meager resources against the trail, President Johnson committed U.S. aircraft to combat operations in Laos. In December 1964, U.S. aircraft began flying limited strikes against Communist supply lines along Laos's northeastern border in Operation Barrel Roll. U.S. air operations in Laos soon expanded into a full-fledged bombing campaign. On April 3, 1965, LBJ authorized Operation Steel Tiger, designed to interdict traffic on the Ho Chi Minh Trail. By midyear, U.S. planes were flying 1,000 sorties per month over the trail.

Conditions for bombing operations in Laos were less than ideal. From the air, there were few landmarks for pilots to use as navigational guides in Laos's tropical rain forests and triple-canopied jungle. Although some of the larger roads were discernible, the vast network of smaller roads and trails was virtually invisible.

Photo reconnaissance was only marginally effective under these conditions. Since the North Vietnamese moved 90 percent of their supplies at night, strike aircraft were forced to rely on flare drops to locate enemy truck convoys. During the day, they concentrated on roads, narrow mountain passes, and other "choke points" to create traffic jams in an attempt to expose the elusive trucks.

To improve its intelligence, the army, under the aegis of MACV's Study and Observation Group, began sending in small recon teams to monitor enemy traffic patterns. Information also occasionally came from CIA teams operating behind enemy lines. Aerial reconnaissance improved considerably with the introduction of air force RF-4Cs and army OV-1 Mohawks equipped with infrared detection devices and side-looking radars. Also, FACs sometimes used hand-held Starlight scopes, which magnified existing star and moonlight up to 50,000 times.

Because the targets were usually moving vehicles, rapid reaction was essential. Once spotted, a target was called in to an orbiting C-130. The C-130 then assigned strike aircraft to a FAC in the area. Initially, fast moving aircraft, like the F-105 and F-100, were employed. But since there was little opposition along the trail, B-57 Canberras, AC-47 gunships, and World War II vintage A-26 Invaders took over as the primary strike aircraft.

But the Communists' camouflage techniques and countermeasures severely limited the success of these missions. Usually the best pilots could hope for would be to catch a few trucks rumbling along on the open road. Many times they would find nothing and would merely dump their bombs on a strip of road in a random effort to block it. Truck parks and supply depots were rare finds.

In addition, a web of overlapping command structures plagued U.S. air operations in Laos. General William Momyer, commander of the 7th Air Force, was responsible for coordinating the interdiction campaign. But the CIA, which had been running clandestine paramilitary operations in Laos for years, often demanded specific air strikes or asked that others be canceled at the last minute because, unknown even to other U.S. agencies, it had men in the area. Complicating matters, late in 1965 Gen. Westmoreland was granted authority over the portion of the panhandle directly adjacent to South Vietnam as part of the "extended battlefield." While operations north of the seventeenth parallel continued to be coordinated by Momyer, those south of that line were now named Tiger Hound and came under MACV jurisdiction.

But final approval for targets recommended in both areas had to be obtained from the U.S. ambassador to Laos, William Sullivan. From his embassy office in Vientiane, Sullivan had the unenviable task of juggling often conflicting demands of the CIA, air force, and army, while simultaneously holding down the bombing to a level that would not shatter the thin façade of Laotian neutrality. He also had to follow strict guidelines set down by the Laotian government to avoid bombing of civilians.

All strikes not flown in free fire zones specified by U.S. and Laotian officials had to be cleared personally by the U.S. ambassador or by Laotian observers who accompanied FACs. Sullivan also ordered that pilots flying armed reconnaissance could not fire at targets more than 200 yards off the roads. The enemy responded by moving truck parks and supply depots outside the 200-yards limit.

The restrictions were gradually loosened, and by 1967 U.S. planes were flying more than 3,000 sorties per month over the Ho Chi Minh Trail. USAF B-52 bombers were also employed that year, flying 1,718 sorties. In November electronic sensors were planted along the trail to help monitor NVA traffic under the code name Igloo White, part of U.S. Secretary of Defense McNamara's electronic barrier concept.

Despite the increased effort, the combination of politically imposed restrictions and the resourcefulness of the North Vietnamese left American air power with little room to maneuver and produced, at best, only fair results. And the Communists were able to send men and supplies down the Ho Chi Minh Trail into South Vietnam at an ever-increasing pace.

the month the NVA began withdrawing from around the marine base. During the first week in April, Operation Pegasus, spearheaded by 1st Cavalry Division helicopter assault teams, cleared the roads leading to the base to end the siege seventy-seven days after it began. History had not repeated itself at Khe Sanh.

In quantity, Operation Niagara had lived up to its name. Nearly 100,000 tons of ordnance had been expended during almost 25,000 sorties by marine, navy, and air force aircraft between January 8 and April 8. According to Gen. Westmoreland the spectacular display of aerial firepower was "the key to our success at Khe Sanh." The statistics on the amount of supplies flown in to Khe Sanh were also staggering. Over 15,000 tons of "beans, bullets, and bandages" had been delivered, surpassing the total airdropped to troops in the field across all of Vietnam to that date.

But any comfort drawn from the outcome at Khe Sanh was darkened by the second phase of Hanoi's combined struggle strategy. While the Americans were preoccupied with the siege at a remote northern outpost, the Vietcong launched a country-wide offensive that was to alter the course of the war.

# Tet

January 31 began like any other night for civilian air controller Richard O. Stark on duty in the tower at the Tan Son Nhut heliport. Being the last day of a thirty-six-hour Tet holiday cease-fire, it seemed even quieter than usual at the sprawling air base located on the northern outskirts of Saigon.

At 3:15 A.M. Stark received a call from an aircraft orbiting the field reporting what was thought to be enemy activity in the area. Stark had noticed sporadic tracer fire to the northwest but was not much alarmed. Minutes later a C-47 that had just taken off drew heavy ground fire. Stark realized the firing was not just "nervous guards, but actual enemy contact."

All at once, incoming mortar rounds began exploding amid the hangars, barracks, headquarters compounds, and around the flight line. Guerrillas were swarming through the base's western perimeter. Pilots and ground crewmen grabbed rifles and pistols to help security forces and MPs repel the assault. They managed to stop the guerrillas just 210 meters from the flight line in fierce, close-in fighting. Helicopter gunships and AC-47 Dragonships got into the air and joined in the counterattack.

Operations at the air base ground to a halt. It was not until later that morning that U.S. and ARVN troops arrived to drive the Vietcong back across the wire. By then the full extent of the Communist onslaught had become apparent. Tan Son Nhut had been merely one incident in the largest series of coordinated attacks the VC had ever mounted. Vietcong units had taken advantage of the Tet truce to in-

filtrate men and arms into the major population areas. Within forty-eight hours they had launched attacks against thirty-six provincial capitals, five major cities, twenty-three airfields, and numerous district capitals.

With the guerrillas occupying buildings in the hearts of the cities, American firepower was virtually neutralized. Realizing that any attempt to dislodge them with bombs or rockets would result in the destruction of homes as well as the deaths of civilians, the 7th Air Force Command dictated that close air support missions would be authorized only if the situation were "desperate." As the well-entrenched guerrillas began inflicting heavy casualties in house-to-house urban fighting, American and Vietnamese aircraft were called in more and more often, in spite of the risks.

Ground troops ferreted out pockets of resistance, then backed off while helicopter gunships blasted the buildings with rockets. In Saigon, low-flying planes strafed a VC staging area near the Phu Tho Racetrack, and Vietnamese Skyraiders bombed a low-income housing complex where a VC battalion had taken refuge. Heavy artillery and air strikes destroyed large portions of My Tho, a city of 70,000 south of Saigon. Sixty city blocks in the city of Ban Me Thuot were razed by air and armor strikes, leaving 16,000 homeless.

Hardest hit was the Imperial City of Hue, one of the few places where North Vietnamese troops fought alongside the guerrillas. The Communists succeeded in capturing most of the city and the Citadel, the walled-in section of the city that formerly housed the emperors of Vietnam. While most of the Tet offensive attacks were quelled by the second week of February, fighting in Hue continued for twenty-five days.

During the battle for Hue, air units used everything from bombs to napalm to root out the stubborn Communists. More than half of the ancient Imperial City was reduced to smoking ruins. Nearly 2,000 civilians were killed in the fighting and an estimated three-fourths of Hue's population was left homeless.

Hard-line anti-Communist Hue residents saw the bombings as justified; some of their family members had been assassinated in an apparent massacre carried out by the Communists during their occupation of Hue. Others were hostile to their U.S. and ARVN liberators. One resident told a *Newsweek* correspondent: "We understand why you had to do it but we can never forgive you for it—all the destruction and death you caused."

Once the last remnants of resistance had been mopped up and the cities were firmly back under government control, Gen. Westmoreland told reporters that the VC had "paid dearly." MACV officials claimed that 15,000 Communist soldiers had been killed in the first week of the fighting alone. The American commander claimed the battle had been a convincing U.S. "victory."

Although the Communists had admittedly failed to

*A section of Hue lies in ruin in the aftermath of the battle for the city during Tet, 1968.*

achieve their goal of a general uprising against the government, they had, it turned out, delivered a stunning psychological defeat. The inability of South Vietnamese forces to secure the urban areas had shattered confidence in the Saigon government. Pacification efforts, aimed at reducing the Vietcong's grip in the outlying countryside, suffered severe setbacks as South Vietnamese troops were pulled back to restore order in the cities.

## From hawks to doves

Tet was also a severe shock to the U.S. people, a majority of whom had believed the optimistic reports emanating from South Vietnam. Instead of seeing the "light at the end of the tunnel" they had been promised, they were barraged with unrestricted television coverage of the massive Communist assault during Tet. Somehow the sight of Gen. Westmoreland making optimistic statements to reporters while standing in front of the battle-scarred U.S. Embassy in Saigon was not very reassuring.

The administration put on a brave face. The president tried his best to rally support for the war, portraying the Communist offensive as yet another challenge in the test of

wills between America and North Vietnam. LBJ's key advisers, including National Security Adviser Walt Rostow and Secretary of State Dean Rusk, remained adamantly convinced that the U.S. was on the right course. Many officials within the administration, however, privately questioned whether the war could ever be won. At the Department of Defense there were signs of deep discouragement with U.S. policy in Vietnam, which quickly became apparent to the new secretary of defense, Clark Clifford.

President Johnson had selected Clifford, a close personal friend, because he felt he could rely on him to defend his policies. Clifford's first assignment, however, as chairman of an interagency task force to consider military recommendations in response to the Tet offensive, caused him to change quickly from hawk to dove.

The task force had been assembled to evaluate a request made in late February by General Earle Wheeler, chairman of the JCS, and Westmoreland that 206,000 more troops be sent to Vietnam. In reaction to Tet, the JCS also recommended bombing in the Chinese buffer zone, reducing the prohibited zones around Hanoi and Haiphong, and closing Haiphong Harbor with air strikes and mining. The Joint Chiefs were supported by CINCPAC Adm.

Sharp, who called for lifting the restrictions on Rolling Thunder so he could strike back against the "source of aggression in North Vietnam."

Clifford's task force began its deliberations on February 28. It was the opportunity that administration dissenters had been waiting for. In a flood of memos, position papers, and personal conversations with the new secretary of defense, task force members and other officials voiced their objections to continuing a strategy they considered bankrupt.

Undersecretary of the Air Force Townsend Hoopes pointed out the force requests would place a heavy strain on air force resources. According to the Joint Chiefs, seventeen additional tactical fighter squadrons would be needed to provide air support for the increased ground forces. With thirty squadrons operating in the country, "a number of professional airmen considered South Vietnam already saturated with allied air power," Hoopes said.

There was also the question of where the fighter squadrons would come from. In response to the seizure of the U.S.S. *Pueblo* on January 23 by the North Koreans, the air force had dispatched 150 aircraft to South Korea. Additional planes and pilots for Vietnam would either have to be taken from NATO forces in Europe or created by activating reservists, a long and costly process. The question of how they would be used was even more controversial.

Neither Gen. Westmoreland's search and destroy strategy, which relied heavily on heliborne assaults supported by aerial firepower, or interdiction bombing by air force B-52s, had been able to neutralize the Vietcong. The Communists' manpower pool never seemed to run dry despite the statistical claims of MACV officials. American units were just drawn farther away from the populated areas in their offensive sweeps, many of which ended in dubious victory. Either the VC would reoccupy the areas once the Americans withdrew, or thousands of South Vietnamese were left homeless or sent to government resettlement camps so the air force could create free fire zones.

Bombing operations against North Vietnam had also apparently failed to influence the course of the war in the South. One of the most telling lessons of the Tet offensive was the inability of Rolling Thunder and the air interdiction campaign in Laos to reduce significantly the flow of men and materiel from North Vietnam to the battlefield in the South. In fact the Communists had been able to launch a nationwide offensive in spite of three years of sustained bombing.

America was relearning the lessons of the Korean War all over again according to Paul Warnke, who had replaced John McNaughton as assistant secretary of defense for international security affairs. He noted, "A relatively underdeveloped Asian country with a surplus of men can stand an awful lot of bombing without saying 'uncle.' " By diverting manpower from the fields and factories to run and maintain the supply network, Hanoi had been able to

keep the pressure on in the South despite the bombing. Ironically, it was the Americans who found themselves paying the higher price.

By the end of 1967 Rolling Thunder had inflicted $370 million worth of damage in North Vietnam. But the effort was costing Washington billions of dollars in operational expenses, ordnance expended, and aircraft losses. As Deputy Secretary of Defense Paul Nitze pointed out, "it takes maybe twenty tons of bombs to destroy one ton of material coming from the North to the South."

Meanwhile, the Chinese, Soviets, and Eastern Europeans had poured more than $1.5 billion into the North Vietnamese war effort. This external support was the bête noire of America's air strategy in North Vietnam. "Unless we were prepared to bomb the Chinese and Russian cities where the war supplies were in fact manufactured," said Paul Warnke, "we couldn't destroy the war-making potential of the other side."

After reading reams of briefing papers and enduring late night discussions at the Pentagon, Clifford concluded that after more than three years America's strategy had failed to produce any results. To him, the generals—who admitted the war could last at least another four to five years—did not seem to have a plan to win the war, and the American public saw only the rising casualty rates and increased costs. It had become clear to the new secretary of defense that "the military course we were pursuing was not only hopeless but endless."

## A halt to the bombing

Clifford's conclusions were only the beginning of a difficult month for the president. On March 12, the Senate Foreign Relations Committee opened hearings on military assistance funds for South Vietnam. Senator William Fulbright, now a leading critic of the war, used the hearings as a public forum on U.S. policy in Vietnam.

Another blow came later that day when the results of the Democratic presidential primary in New Hampshire were announced. Senator Eugene McCarthy, whose campaign had been based on his opposition to the war, had only narrowly lost to the president. Four days later, Senator Robert Kennedy, another war critic, declared his candidacy.

Besieged from within and without, Johnson continued to stand firmly behind his policy in Vietnam. In truculent speeches to the nation, the president reminded the public of America's deep responsibilities in Vietnam. Clifford faced an uphill battle as he tried to impress upon the president that any further escalation of the war was pointless. Trying to find ways to persuade Johnson, he proposed a meeting of the president's "senior informal advisory group." Comprised of a number of well-respected men from the Johnson administration and preceding ones, the so-called "wise men" had endorsed U.S. policy in Vietnam as recently as November of the previous year. But Clifford suspected that their support had begun to waver.

The group met with the president on March 26. The change in their findings was as dramatic as Clifford's had been. As Arthur Dean, the chief U.S. negotiator during the Korean War peace talks, noted, "All of us got the impression that there [was] no military conclusion in sight. We felt that time [was] running out."

Surprised by his "wise men's" reversal, a troubled Lyndon Johnson set to work on what he hoped would be a decisive speech to the nation. He wrangled with his circle over the tone and content of the speech. Clifford hoped an unconditional deescalation of the bombing would result in negotiations while Dean Rusk pointed out that if the Communists again failed to respond with their own peace gesture, Johnson might expect increased public support for continuing the war. Also, as Rusk pointed out, bad weather was likely to ground many bombing missions that spring. With all his advisers—save Walt Rostow—in favor of a bombing cutback Johnson agreed to halt the bombing above the twentieth parallel. He had already decided against approving Gen. Westmoreland's troop requests, believing that South Vietnam was already too dependent on American military protection.

Only a handful of his most trusted aides knew that he also intended to say more in that talk to the nation. This was to be the last major decision Johnson would make concerning the war, the final effort to induce an honorable settlement. On March 31, Lyndon Johnson informed the American people and the world of his decisions and his refusal to run again for president.

Much to Washington's surprise, three days after the partial bombing halt went into effect Hanoi announced its willingness to open talks with the United States. American and North Vietnamese representatives met in Paris throughout the summer to iron out the details. After exhaustive diplomatic wrangling the two sides agreed in late October to a format for negotiations involving the U.S., South Vietnam, North Vietnam, and the National Liberation Front. With the discussions ready to commence, President Johnson announced on October 31 that as of 8:00 A.M., Washington time, on November 1, the United States would end all air strikes against North Vietnam.

Just ninety minutes before Johnson's directive was issued, Major Frank C. Lenagan of the 8th Tactical Fighter Wing flew his F-4D over Dong Hoi in the last Rolling Thunder mission over North Vietnam. Four days later Richard Nixon won the presidential election, becoming heir to the helm of U.S. policy in Vietnam.

Instead of increased pressure it was, ironically, a bombing halt that had brought Hanoi to the bargaining table. But this step was, at best, only a partial one; it was hardly a North Vietnamese delegation begging for mercy that sat opposite the Americans in Paris. The bombing had not weakened the will of North Vietnam to wage war, nor had it lessened the Communists' war-making capabilities.

The strategy of a gradually escalating bombing campaign—with its limited goals—had been based on a rational assumption: the application of increasing increments of strength and the threats of more to come would eventually force Hanoi to abandon its aggressive aims or risk total destruction. The strategy might be said to have worked before, against the Russians during the Cuban missile crisis and earlier during the blockade of Berlin.

What American officials had failed to realize, however, was the hardship North Vietnam was willing to endure to reunify Vietnam under its leadership. Each time Washington escalated the bombing, Hanoi dug its heels in deeper. By 1968 Washington planners found themselves committing more money, men, and resources to the conflict than they had ever intended or could afford.

Throughout, the military had criticized the Johnson administration's bombing policy. The generals had at first been uneasy about the limited strategic goals—that stopped short of defeating the Communists—although they had grown accustomed to them. But they never accepted the tactical restrictions placed on the bombing. "Once the decision has been made to wage war, that leadership must permit the war to be engaged expeditiously and full bore, not halfway," Adm. Sharp said later. "The pilot hit by a surface-to-air missile whose site he was not permitted to bomb does not fall halfway out of the sky or spend seven years as a limited prisoner of war."

Johnson's decision to halt the bombing was greeted dimly by the military's top brass, many of whom still held out hope for unrestricted bombing. But by 1968 the generals' claims that massive bombing could break Hanoi's will had been found invalid. The U.S. had hit virtually every major target in North Vietnam during Rolling Thunder. American planes had dropped more bombs on the tiny nation than had been expended in the entire Pacific theater of operations in World War II. The total tonnage dropped in both North and South Vietnam surpassed that expended in the entire European theater. All that seemed to remain was targeting population centers to inflict a terrible toll in lives and property, something that Lyndon Johnson and his advisers thought too dangerous and too inhumane even to consider.

Although Johnson's suspension of the bombing campaign against North Vietnam had finally brought Hanoi to the bargaining table, negotiations in Paris soon bogged down. The new Nixon administration continued the search for an "honorable settlement," in both public and private talks with Hanoi, but the war dragged on. U.S. planes continued bombing operations in South Vietnam and over the Ho Chi Minh Trail in Laos, and in 1970 the conflict would spill over into neighboring Cambodia. And ultimately, three years after the bombing halt, U.S. bombers would return to the skies over Hanoi as another president turned to air power to influence the course of the war.

*A U.S. soldier leans over the center of a bomb crater in the A Shau Valley, South Vietnam, in 1968.*

# Bibliography

## I. Books and Articles

Addington, Dr. Larry H. "Antiaircraft Artillery Versus the Fighter-Bomber." *Army* (December 1973).

"Air: The Essential Element in Vietnam." *Air Force* (June 1966).

"Air Power—What it is Doing in Vietnam." *U.S. News & World Report*, May 9, 1966.

"Air War in Vietnam—The Statistical Side." *Air Force* (March 1968).

Althoff, Lt. Col. David L. "Helicopter Operations at Khe Sanh." *Marine Corps Gazette* (May 1969).

Ashmore, Harry S., and William C. Baggs. *Mission to Hanoi*. Putnam, 1968.

Austin, Anthony. *The President's War*. Lippincott, 1971.

Ball, George. *The Past Has Another Pattern*. Norton, 1982.

Basel, Gene I. *Pak Six*. Assoc. Creative Writers, 1982.

Birdsall, Steve. *The A-1 Skyraider*. ARCO, 1970.

Blair, Ed. "A Man Doing His Job." *Airman* (April 1969).

Bowers, Ray L. "Americans in the Vietnamese Air Force: The Dirty Thirty." *Aerospace Historian* (September 1972).

Broughton, Col. Jack. *Thud Ridge*. Lippincott, 1969.

Brownlow, Cecil. "B-52s Prove Tactical Value During Siege of Khe Sanh." *Aviation Week & Space Technology*, May 13, 1968.

Burchett, Wilfred G. *Vietnam North*. International Publishers, 1967.

Butz, J.S. "Those Bombings in North Vietnam." *Air Force* (April 1966).

Cagle, Vice Adm. Malcolm W. "Task Force 77 in Action Off Vietnam." *U.S. Naval Institute Proceedings*, May 1972.

Cameron, James. *Witness*. Gollancz, 1966.

Carter, Gregory A. *Some Historical Notes on Air Interdiction in Korea*. Rand Corporation P-3452, September 1966.

CBS News. "Air Rescue, Part II—Vietnam." Broadcast January 9, 1966. Transcript.

———. "LBJ: The Decision To Halt the Bombing." Broadcast February 6, 1970. Transcript.

Charlton, Michael, and Anthony Moncrieff. *Many Reasons Why*. Hill & Wang, 1978.

Chen, King C. "Hanoi's Three Decisions and the Escalation of the Vietnam War." *Political Science Quarterly* (Summer 1975).

Clifford, Clark. "A Viet Nam Reappraisal." *Foreign Affairs* (July 1969).

Colvin, John. "Hanoi in My Time." *The Washington Quarterly* (Spring 1981).

Cooper, Chester. *The Lost Crusade*. Dodd, Mead, 1970.

Cowan, Sidney C. "Ride a Slick Ship to Hell and Back." *U.S. Army Aviation Digest* (June 1966).

"Death of a Mig." *Airman* (May 1967).

Denton, Jeremiah A. *When Hell Was in Session*. Robert E. Hopper & Assoc., 1982.

Dickson, Paul. *The Electronic Battlefield*. Indiana Univ. Pr., 1976.

Drendel, Lou. *Air War Over Southeast Asia. A Pictorial Record*. Vol. 1, *1962-1966*. Vol. 2, *1967-1970*. Squadron/Signal Publications, 1982, 1983.

Duiker, William J. *The Communist Road to Power in Vietnam*. Westview, 1981.

Eisenhower, Dwight D. *White House Years*. Doubleday, 1963.

Elkins, Frank C. *The Heart of a Man*. Norton, 1973.

Enthoven, Alain, and K. Wayne Smith. *How Much is Enough?* Harper & Row, 1971.

Evans, Rowland, and Robert Novak. *Lyndon B. Johnson: The Exercise of Power*. NAL, 1966.

Everett, Capt. Robert P. "Destroy the Doumer Bridge." *Airman* (March 1968).

Fenn, Charles. *Ho Chi Minh: A Biographical Introduction*. Scribner, 1973.

"Full Story of Lyndon Johnson's 'World War III' Remark." *U.S. News & World Report*, May 29, 1967.

Gallucci, Robert L. *Neither Peace Nor Honor*. Johns Hopkins Univ. Pr., 1975.

Gelb, Leslie H. *The Irony of Vietnam: The System Worked*. The Brooking Institution, 1979.

George, A.L. *Some Thoughts on Graduated Escalation*. Rand Corporation RM-4844-PR, December 1965.

Gerassi, John. *North Vietnam: A Documentary*. Bobbs-Merrill, 1968.

Goulden, Joseph C. *Truth is the First Casualty*. Rand McNally, 1969.

Goulding, Phil G. *Confirm or Deny*. Harper & Row, 1970.

Graff, Henry. *The Tuesday Cabinet*. Prentice-Hall, 1970.

Gravel, Sen. Mike, ed. *The Pentagon Papers*. 5 vols. Beacon Pr., 1971.

Greenhalgh, William H., Jr. "AOK Airpower over Khe Sanh." *Aerospace Historian* (March 1972).

Hai Thu. *North Vietnam Against U.S. Air Force*. Foreign Languages Publishing House, 1967.

Halberstam, David. *The Best and the Brightest*. Random, 1972.

———. *The Making of a Quagmire*. Random, 1964.

Harvey, Frank. *Air War—Vietnam*. Bantam, 1967.

Haugland, Vern. "Airborne Ordnance." *Ordnance* (March-April 1967).

Herring, George C. *America's Longest War*. Wiley, 1979.

Hilsman, Roger. *To Move a Nation*. Doubleday, 1967.

Ho Chi Minh. "President Ho Chi Minh Answers President L. B. Johnson." Foreign Languages Publishing House, 1967.

Hoeffding, Oleg. *Bombing North Vietnam: An Appraisal of Economic and Political Effects*. Rand Corporation RM-5213-1-ISA, December 1966.

Hoopes, Townsend. *The Limits of Intervention*. David McKay Co., 1969.

Hubbell, John G. *P.O.W.: A Definitive History of the American Prisoner-of-War Experience in Vietnam, 1964-1973*. Reader's Digest, 1976.

Hymoff, Edward. *The First Cavalry Division, Vietnam*. M. W. Ladd, 1966.

Johnson, Lyndon Baines. *The Vantage Point*. Holt, Rinehart & Winston, 1971.

Kasler, Col. James H. "The Hanoi POL Strike." *Air Univ. Review* (November-December 1974).

Kearns, Doris. *Lyndon Johnson and the American Dream*. Harper & Row, 1976.

Kennedy, Col. Thomas B. "Airlift in Southeast Asia." *Air Univ. Review* (January-February 1965).

Kinnard, Maj. Gen. Harry O. "A Victory in the Ia Drang: The Triumph of a Concept." *Army* (September 1967).

———. "Battlefield Mobility of the New U.S. 1st Air Cavalry Division." *NATO's Fifteen Nations* (April-May 1966).

Kipp, Robert M. "Counterinsurgency from 30,000 Feet." *Air Univ. Review* (January-February 1968).

Kraslow, David L., and Stuart Loory. *The Secret Search for Peace in Vietnam*. Random, 1968.

LeMay, Gen. Curtis E. *America is in Danger*. Funk & Wagnalls, 1968.

———. *My Story*. Doubleday, 1965.

Littauer, Raphael, and Norman Uphoff, eds. *The Air War in Indochina*. Beacon Pr., 1972.

McArdle, Maj. Frank H. "The KC-135 in Southeast Asia." *Air Univ. Review* (January-February 1968).

McGarvey, Patrick J. *Visions of Victory: Selected Vietnamese Communist Military Writings, 1964-1968*. Hoover Inst. Pr., 1969.

McLaughlin, Maj. Gen. Burl W. "Khe Sanh: Keeping an Outpost Alive." *Air Univ. Review* (November-December 1968).

Mason, Robert. *Chickenhawk*. Viking Pr., 1983.

Mataxis, Brig. Gen. Theodore C. "A Product of Necessity: Operational Coordination." *Army* (October 1965).

———. "War in the Highlands: Attack and Counter-Attack on Highway 19." *Army* (October 1965).

Mersky, Peter B., and Norman Polmar. *The Naval Air War in Vietnam*. The Nautical and Aviation Publishing Co., 1981.

Meyers, Maj. Gen. Gilbert L. "Why Not More Targets in the North?" *Air Force* (May 1967).

Mikesh, Robert C. *B-57 at War, 1964-1972*. Scribner, 1980.

Nalty, Bernard C. *Tigers Over Asia*. Talisman/Parrish Bks., 1978.

Nalty, Bernard C. et al. *An Illustrated Guide to the Air War in Vietnam*. ARCO, 1981.

Nguyen Cao Ky. *Twenty Years and Twenty Days*. Stein & Day, 1976.

Nguyen Nghe. *Facing the Skyhawks*. Foreign Languages Publishing House, 1964.

O'Gorman, Maj. John P. "Battles are Bloody Maneuvers From the Cockpit." *Air Univ. Review* (September-October 1967).

Olds, Brig. Gen. Robin. "Forty-Six Years a Fighter Pilot." *American Aviation Historical Society Journal* (Winter 1968).

———. "How I Got My First Mig." *Air Force* (July 1967).

———. "The Lessons of Clobber College." *Flight International*, June 26, 1969.

Outlaw, Adm. Edward C. "An Admiral Speaks His Mind." *New York Times*, April 8, 1971.

Parks, W. Hays. "Rolling Thunder and the Law of War." *Air Univ. Review* (January-February 1982).

Patti, Archimedes. *Why Vietnam? Prelude to America's Albatross*. Univ. of California Pr., 1981.

"Pilot Report From Vietnam." *Aviation Week & Space Technology*, October 24, 1966.

Plattner, C.M. "Tactical Raids by B-52s Stun Viet Cong." *Aviation Week & Space Technology*, November 29, 1965.

Poole, Gordon L. "Dirty Thirty." *Airman* (October 1963).

Rausa, Rosario. *Skyraider: The Douglas A-1 "Flying Dump Truck."* The Nautical and Aviation Publishing Co., 1982.

Raymond, Jack. "The Pilots of Danang Aren't Flyboys." *New York Times Magazine*, August 15, 1965.

Risner, Gen. Robinson. *The Passing of the Night*. Random, 1975.

Robbins, Christopher. *Air America*. Putnam, 1979.

Roberts, Charles. *LBJ's Inner Circle*. Delacorte Pr., 1965.

Rostow, Walt W. *The Diffusion of Power*. Macmillan, 1972.

Roth, Capt. Michael J.C. "Nimrod—King of the Trail." *Air Force* (October 1971).

Salisbury, Harrison E. *Behind the Lines: Hanoi*. Harper & Row, 1967.

Sams, Kenneth. "The Fall of A Shau." *Air Force* (June 1966).

———. "Tactical Air Support—Balancing the Scales in Vietnam." *Air Force* (August 1965).

Schoenbrun, David. "Report From Hanoi." *Newsday*, October 1967.

Scholin, Allan R. "An Airpower Lesson for Giap." *Air Force/Space Digest* (June 1968).

Scutts, J.C. *F-105 Thunderchief*. Scribner, 1981.

Secord, Capt. Mack D. "The Viet Nam Air Force." *Air Univ. Review* (November-December 1963).

Shaplen, Robert. *The Lost Revolution*. Harper & Row, 1965.

_____. *The Road From War: Vietnam 1965-1970.* Harper & Row, 1970.
Sharp, Adm. U.S. Grant. "Air Power Could Have Won in Vietnam." *Air Force* (September 1971).
_____. *Strategy for Defeat.* Presidio Pr., 1979.
Shepard, Elaine. *The Doom Pussy.* Trident Pr., 1967.
Simler, Maj. Gen. George B. "North Vietnam's Air Defense System." *Air Force* (May 1967).
Simon, Lt. Col. William E. *Coercion in Vietnam?* Rand Corporation RM-6016-PR, May 1969.
Stanton, Shelby L. *Vietnam Order of Battle.* U.S. News Books, 1981.
Stoner, Lt. Col. John R. "Air Force Support." Air Force briefing at the annual meeting of the Association of the U.S. Army, Washington, D.C., October 10, 1966.
_____. "The Closer the Better." *Air Univ. Review* (September–October 1967).
Sturm, Ted. R. "Battle at the Bridge." *Airman* (December 1968).

Taylor, John W.R., ed. *Jane's All the World's Aircraft, 1964-1965.* McGraw-Hill, 1965.
Taylor, Maxwell D. *Swords and Plowshares.* Norton, 1972.
Thies, Wallace. *When Governments Collide: Coercion and Diplomacy in the Vietnam Conflict, 1964-1968.* Univ. of California Pr., 1980.
Thompson, James Clay. *Rolling Thunder: Understanding Policy and Programming Failures.* Univ. of North Carolina Pr., 1980.
Thompson, W. Scott, and Donaldson D. Frizzell, eds. *The Lessons of Vietnam.* Crane, Russak & Co., 1977.

Van Dyke, Jon M. *North Vietnam's Strategy for Survival.* Pacific Bks., 1972.
Van Tien Dung. "People's War Against Air War of Destruction." *Vietnamese Studies* 20 (1968).
Vo Nguyen Giap. *People's War Against the U.S.: Aero-Naval War.* Foreign Languages Publishing House, 1975.
_____. *Vietnam's People's War Has Defeated U.S. War of Destruction.* Foreign Languages Publishing House, 1969.
Vu Van Thai. *Fighting and Negotiating in Vietnam: A Strategy.* Rand Corporation RM-5997-ARPA, October 1969.

Wei Wei. "Even Planes Fear the Militia." *Chinese Literature* 8 (1966).
Westmoreland, Gen. William C. *A Soldier Reports.* Dell, 1980.
Windchy, Eugene G. *Tonkin Gulf.* Doubleday, 1971.
Witze, Claude. "Interdiction: Limited But Effective." *Air Force/Space Digest* (May 1967).
Wolfe, Tom. "The Truest Sport: Jousting With Sam and Charlie." In *Mauve Gloves & Madmen, Clutter & Vine,* Farrar, Straus, & Geroux, 1976.

## II. Government Publications
BDM Corporation. *A Study of Strategic Lessons Learned in Vietnam.* National Technical Information Service, 1980.
Berger, Carl, ed. *The United States Air Force in Southeast Asia, 1961-1973.* Office of Air Force History, 1977.
Buckingham, William A., Jr. *Operation Ranch Hand. The Air Force and Herbicides in Southeast Asia, 1961-1971.* Office of Air Force History, 1982.
Burbage, Maj. Paul et al. *The Battle for the Skies Over North Vietnam, 1964-1972.* Vol. 1, Monograph 2, USAF Southeast Asia Monograph Series, 1976.

Corum, Col. Delbert et al. *The Tale of Two Bridges.* Vol. 1, Monograph 1, USAF Southeast Asia Monograph Series, 1976.

"Fifty Days." *Sea Breeze,* U.S.S. *Coral Sea.* 16, no. 1 (March 1965).
Fox, Roger P. *Air Base Defense in the Republic of Vietnam, 1961-1973.* Office of Air Force History, 1979.
Futrell, R. Frank, and Martin Blumenson. *The United States Air Force in Southeast Asia: The Advisory Years to 1965.* Office of Air Force History, 1980.
Futrell, R. Frank et al. *Aces and Aerial Victories: The United States Air Force in Southeast Asia, 1965-1973.* Office of Air Force History, 1976.

Hurley, Col. Alfred F., and Maj. Robert C. Ehrhart, eds. *Air Power and Warfare. Proceedings of the 8th Military History Symposium USAF Academy, 1978.* Office of Air Force History, 1979.

Momyer, Gen. William W. *Air Power in Three Wars.* United States Air Force, 1978.
_____. *The Vietnamese Air Force, 1951-1975. An Analysis of its Role in Combat.* Vol. 3, Monograph 4, USAF Southeast Asia Monograph Series, 1975.

Nalty, Bernard C. *Air Power and the Fight for Khe Sanh.* Office of Air Force History, 1973.

Rogers, Lt. Gen. Bernard W. *Cedar Falls—Junction City: A Turning Point.* Department of the Army, Vietnam Studies Series, 1974.

Schneider, Maj. Donald K. *Air Force Heroes in Vietnam.* Vol. 3, Monograph 9, USAF Southeast Asia Monograph Series, 1979.
Scott, Journalist 2-C, and Lt. (j.g.) Manuel Perez. *The Story of a Carrier West, 1964-1965.* U.S.S. *Coral Sea.* CVA-43, 1965.
Sharp, Adm. U.S. Grant, and Gen. William Westmoreland. *Report on the War in Vietnam.* GPO, 1969.
Shore, Capt. Moyers S., II. *The Battle for Khe Sanh.* Historical Branch, United States Marine Corps, 1969.

Tilford, Earl H., Jr. *Search and Rescue in Southeast Asia, 1961-1975.* Office of Air Force History, 1981.
Tolson, Lt. Gen. John J. *Airmobility, 1961-1971.* Department of the Army, Vietnam Studies Series, 1973.

U.S. Congress. Senate. Committee on Armed Services. *Air War Against North Vietnam.* Hearings before the Preparedness Subcommittee. 90th Congress, 1st sess., August 1967.
_____. *Investigation of the Preparedness Program; Report . . . on U.S. Navy and U.S. Marine Corps in Southeast Asia.* 90th Congress, 1st sess., 1967.
U.S. Congress. Senate. Committee on Foreign Relations. *Bombing as a Policy Tool in Vietnam: Effectiveness.* Staff Study. 92d Congress, 2d sess., 1972.
_____. *The Gulf of Tonkin, the 1964 Incidents.* Parts I & II. 90th Congress, 2d sess., 1968.
U.S. Department of Defense. *United States-Vietnam Relations, 1945-1967.* (Pentagon Papers.) GPO, 1971.
U.S. Department of State. *Department of State Bulletin.* 1964-1968.
_____. *Foreign Relations of the United States, 1952-1954.* Volume 13, Indochina, Part 1. GPO, 1982.
U.S. Military Assistance Command, Vietnam. *Monthly Summaries.* USMACV, 1967-1968.
_____. *1968 Summary.* USMACV.
U.S. Strategic Bombing Survey. *Over-All Report (European War).* GPO, 1945.
_____. *Summary Report (Pacific War).* GPO, 1946.

## III. Unpublished Government and Military Reports
Allen, Capt. Ben H., Jr. Personal Diary, August–September 1965.
Alsperger, Maj. E.J. *Unclassified Southeast Asia Glossary 1961-1971.* Project CHECO Report, HQ. PACAF, Directorate of Operations Analysis, CHECO/CORONA HARVEST Div., February 1, 1971.

CINCPACFLT. *The U.S. Navy in the Pacific, 1965.* Serial No. 1/00847. July 18, 1967.
Combat Operations After Action Reports:
Mongilardi, Cmdr. Peter M., Jr. "The Dong Hoi Strike on February 7, 1965." Attack Squadron 153, Air Wing 15, U.S.S. *Coral Sea.*
Pleiku Campaign, Pleiku Province. 1st Cavalry Division (Airmobile), October 23–November 26, 1965.
Stafford, Lt. Cmdr. Kenneth B. "Dong Hoi Strike–February 7, 1965." Fighter Squadron 154, Air Wing 15, U.S.S. *Coral Sea.*

Dean, Lt. Col. Orien G., Jr. "Measuring the Effectiveness of Airpower Employed Against North Vietnam, February–September 1965." Air War College, Air University, Report No. 2995. January 1966.

Fitzgerald, Oscar. *History of U.S. Naval Operations in the Vietnam Conflict.* Vol. 3, *1965-1967.* Department of the Navy, Office of the Chief of Naval Operations, February 1971.
"563d Tactical Fighter Squadron History, Southeast Asia." April 8–August 16, 1965.

Miller, Rear Adm. Henry L. Daily Diary, October 18, 1965–February 16, 1966.
_____. *History of Task Force 77, September 2, 1964–March 17, 1965.* Deployment Report, Serial No. 0014. March 29, 1965.

Seventh Air Force In-Country Tactical Operations. Air War College, Air University, Maxwell AFB, Alabama. March 20, 1968.

U.S. Department of Defense. *United States-Vietnam Relations, 1945-1968.* Section 6. C., "Settlement of the Conflict. History of Contacts. Negotiations."
U.S. Seventh Fleet. *Monthly Reports, 1965-1966.* Serial No. 0011623.
U.S.S. *Midway.* CVA-41, Cruise Report, 1965. Chapter 11, Attack Carrier Wing Two.

Youngblood, Lt. Col. Russell W. "Observations—Airpower Strategy in North Vietnam." Research Monograph, U.S. Army War College, Carlisle Barracks, Pennsylvania. March 12, 1973.

## IV. The author consulted the following newspapers and periodicals:
*Newsweek,* 1964-1968; *New York Times,* 1964-1968; *Pacific Stars and Stripes,* 1964-1965; *Time,* 1964-1968; *U.S. News & World Report,* 1964-1968; *Washington Post,* 1964-1968.

## V. Archival Sources
Lyndon Baines Johnson Library, Austin, Texas:
Declassified and sanitized documents from the Presidential Papers of Lyndon B. Johnson
Meeting Notes File
National Security File
Country File, Vietnam
Memos to the President
International Meetings and Travel File
NSC History Files, Vietnam
NSC Meeting Notes File
Office Files of the President
Jack Valenti, Notes Taken at Various Meetings, 1965-1966
White House Aides File
White House Central File
Countries, 312 (Vietnam)
Oral History Interviews: William P. Bundy, Clark M. Clifford, Chester L. Cooper, Alain Enthoven, Lyndon B. Johnson, Gen. John P. McConnell, Paul H. Nitze, Benjamin H.

Read, Harrison Salisbury, Gen. Maxwell D. Taylor, Paul C. Warnke, Gen. William C. Westmoreland, Gen. Earle G. Wheeler

John F. Kennedy Library, Boston, Massachusetts:
Declassified and sanitized documents from the Presidential Papers of John F. Kennedy
National Security File, Meetings and Memoranda Series:
NSC Meetings, 1961–1963
NSC Meetings on Vietnam, August 24, 1963–November 2, 1963
Staff Memoranda–Walt Rostow
National Security Memoranda
National Security File
Country File, Vietnam
Hilsman Papers

U.S. Air Force, Office of Air Force History, Bolling AFB, Washington, D.C.
Oral History Program: Lt. Gen. Albert P. Clark, Maj. Gen. Edward Lansdale, Col. Robert L.F. Tyrell
U.S. Naval Institute, Annapolis, Maryland
Oral History Project: Adm. Harry D. Felt, Rear Adm. Henry L. Miller, Adm. U.S. Grant Sharp
U.S. Navy, Naval Historical Division, Washington Navy Yard, Washington, D.C.

**VI. Interviews**
Capt. Ben H. Allen, USAF (Ret.), former F-105 pilot, 562d TFS, 23d TFW, Takhli AFB, Thailand and Out-Country Planning Officer for Brig. Gen. George B. Simler, Director of Operations, 2d Air Division, Saigon.
Lt. Col. Kile D. Berg, USAF (Ret.), former F-105 pilot, 563d TFS, 23d TFW, Takhli AFB, Thailand. (Former prisoner of war.)
Col. Ronald E. Byrne, USAF (Ret.), former F-105 pilot, 67th TFS, 18th TFW, Korat AFB, Thailand. (Former prisoner of war.)
Maj. Martin V. Case, USAF (Ret.), former F-105 pilot, 36th TFS, 6441st TFW, Korat AFB, Thailand in 1964 and 563d TFS, 23d TFW, Takhli AFB, Thailand in 1965.
Col. James P. Coyne, USAF, former F-4 pilot and aide to Maj. Gen. Gilbert L. Meyers, Vice Commander, 2d Air Division, Saigon.
Col. William B. Craig, USAF (Ret.), former F-105 pilot and commander, 44th TFS, 18th TFW, Korat AFB, Thailand.
U.S. Senator Jeremiah A. Denton, Jr., former A-6A pilot, VA-75, Air Wing 7, U.S.S. Independence. (Former prisoner of war.)
Capt. William N. Donnelly, USN (Ret.), former F-8 pilot and commander, VF-154, Air Wing 15, U.S.S. Coral Sea.
Col. Peter M. Dunn, USAF, Chief of Tactical Control Team, Udorn AFB, Thailand in 1965 and EB-66 Navigator, 41st TRS, Takhli AFB, Thailand in 1966.
Rear Adm. Henry P. Glindeman, Jr., USN (Ret.), former commander, Air Wing 15, U.S.S. Coral Sea.
Col. Carlyle S. "Smitty" Harris, USAF (Ret.), former F-105 pilot, 67th TFS, 18th TFW, Korat AFB, Thailand. (Former prisoner of war.)
Col. William J. Hosmer, USAF (Ret.), former F-105 pilot, 12th TFS, 18th TFW, Korat AFB, Thailand.
Col. Richard P. Keirn, USAF (Ret.), former F-4 pilot, 47th TFS, 15th TFW, Ubon AFB, Thailand. (Former prisoner of war.)
Adm. Wesley L. McDonald, USN, former A-4 pilot, Commander of VA-56, U.S.S. Ticonderoga in 1964 and Commander of VA-153, Air Wing 15, U.S.S. Coral Sea in 1965.
Gen. Robinson Risner, USAF (Ret.), former F-105 pilot and Commander, 67th TFS, 18th TFW, Korat AFB, Thailand. (Former prisoner of war.)
Commodore Robert H. Shumaker, USN, former F-8 pilot, VF-154, Air Wing 15, U.S.S. Coral Sea. (Former prisoner of war.)
Capt. Kenneth B. Stafford, USN (Ret.), former F-8 pilot, VF-154, Air Wing 15, U.S.S. Coral Sea in 1965. Staff Operations Officer, Air Wing 5, U.S.S. Ticonderoga in 1966.
Capt. Frank Tullo, USAF (Ret.), former F-105 pilot, 12th TFS, 18th TFW, Korat AFB, Thailand.
The author would also like to thank the following individuals who provided accounts of their experiences in Vietnam: Gene I. Basel, Rick Curtin, Vernon D. Ellis, Donald L. Ismari, Col. Ralph L. Kuster, Archie T. Lorentzen, Col. Harrison Matthews, Frank N. Moyer, Roger Nelson, Col. Jose Olvera, John Ruffo, Tony Semenov, Frosty Sheridan, Richard S. Skeels, Billy Sparks, J. Frank Street, William Wirstrom, Jack Woodul and other veterans of the Vietnam War who wish to remain anonymous.

# Acknowledgments

The author would like to acknowledge the kind assistance of the following people: Col. Raymond Powell (Ret.), U.S. Marine Corps, who read the manuscript; Charles W. Dunn, professor and chairman, Department of Celtic Languages, Harvard University; William Heimdahl, Office of Air Force History, Bolling AFB, Washington, D.C.; David Humphrey, LBJ Library, Austin, Texas; Col. John McMerty, Commander, and the men of the 184th Tactical Fighter Group, U.S. Air National Guard, McConnell AFB, Wichita, Kansas; Jack Mason, U.S. Naval Institute, Annapolis, Maryland; Edward Marolda, Operational Archives Branch, Naval Historical Center, Washington, D.C.; John Piowaty, President, Patti Sheridan, Executive Secretary, and the members of the Red River Valley Fighter Pilot's Association; Maj. Earl H. Tilford, Jr., USAF, Associate Editor, Air University Review, who read parts of the manuscript; and William Tuchrello, Southeast Asia Division, Library of Congress, Washington, D.C.

The index was prepared by Elizabeth Campbell Peters.

# Photography Credits

**Cover Photograph**
Camera Press Limited

**Chapter 1**
p. 5, R.T. Smith. p. 6, National Archives. pp. 7–8, AP/Wide World. p. 9, Daniel Camus–Paris Match. p. 11, Library of Congress–U.S. News & World Report Collection. p. 13, ©Larry Burrows Collection. p. 15, U.S. Army. pp. 16–7, Larry Burrows–LIFE Magazine, ©Time Inc. p. 18, UPI. p. 19, James Pickerell–Black Star. p. 21, Y.R. Okamoto, courtesy LBJ Library.

**Chapter 2**
p. 23, Larry Burrows–LIFE Magazine, ©1971, Time Inc. p. 25, Ngo Vinh Long Collection. p. 27, U.S. Navy. p. 28, Jerry Rose–LIFE Magazine, ©1964, Time Inc. p. 29, Cecil Stoughton, courtesy LBJ Library. p. 31, AP/Wide World. p. 32, U.S. Army. p. 33, Sovfoto. pp. 34–5, ©Larry Burrows Collection. p. 37, James Pickerell–Black Star. p. 38, Pictorial Parade. p. 39, AP/Wide World.

**On Line at Yankee Station**
pp. 42–3, ©Tim Page Photography. p. 44, top, Harry Redl; bottom, Harry Redl–LIFE Magazine, ©Time, Inc. pp. 45–6, Harry Redl. p. 47, Harry Redl–LIFE Magazine, ©Time Inc. pp. 48–9, Harry Redl.

**Chapter 3**
p. 51, AP/Wide World. pp. 52–3, ©Larry Burrows Collection. p. 54, Harry Redl. p. 55, U.S. Navy. p. 57, William Donnelly Collection. p. 59, top, U.S. Air Force; bottom, AP/Wide World. pp. 60–1, Roger Pic. p. 63, Bill Eppridge–LIFE Magazine, ©1965, Time Inc.

**Arsenal of the Sky**
pp. 65–71, Illustrations by Lou Drendel.

**Chapter 4**
p. 73, UPI. p. 75, U.S. Navy. p. 76, Arnold Noble. pp. 77–80, U.S. Air Force. p. 81, AP/Wide World, courtesy Life Picture Service. pp. 84–5, Matthew Meselson. pp. 86–7, U.S. Air Force. p. 89, AP/Wide World. p. 93, Larry Burrows–LIFE Magazine, ©1966, Time Inc. p. 95, AP/Wide World.

**Chapter 5**
p. 97, Camera Press Ltd. p. 99, Lee Lockwood–Black Star. pp. 100–1, Camera Press Ltd. p. 102, INTERFOTO MTI + Hungary. p. 103, Camera Press Ltd. p. 104, Dick Swanson–LIFE Magazine, ©1966, Time Inc. p. 109, Frank Tullo Collection. p. 110, UPI. p. 111, U.S. Air Force. p. 113, Owen–Black Star.

**Chapter 6**
p. 115, UPI. p. 117, U.S. Navy. p. 118, Y.R. Okamoto, courtesy LBJ Library. p. 119, Owen–Black Star. pp. 120–1, UPI. p. 122, ©1966, Universal Press Syndicate. Reprinted with permission. All rights reserved. p. 127, AP/Wide World. pp. 129–30, U.S. Air Force. p. 131, Camera Press Ltd. p. 133, Lee Lockwood–Black Star.

**The Struggle To Survive**
pp. 134–5, Lee Lockwood–Black Star. p. 136, Roger Pic. pp. 137–9, Marc Riboud. p. 140, Lee Lockwood–Black Star. p. 141, Marc Riboud.

**Chapter 7**
p. 143, Camera Press Ltd. p. 145, U.S. Air Force. p. 147, Roger Pic. pp. 148, 150, U.S. Air Force. p. 151, U.S. Navy. p. 153, Frank Wolfe, courtesy LBJ Library. p. 155, Burt Glinn–Magnum. p. 158, Roger Pic. p. 159, U.S. Air Force.

**Arc Light Mission Over Khe Sanh**
pp. 161–6, top, Co Rentmeester–LIFE Magazine, ©Time Inc. p. 166, bottom, Co Rentmeester–LIFE Magazine, ©1972, Time Inc. p. 167, Co Rentmeester–LIFE Magazine, ©Time Inc.

**Chapter 8**
p. 169, UPI. p. 171, U.S. Army. pp. 172–3, Dick Swanson–LIFE Magazine, ©Time Inc. p. 175, Co Rentmeester–LIFE Magazine, ©1967, Time Inc. p. 176, Robert Ellison–Black Star. p. 179, Dave Powell–UPI. p. 182, John Stewart–UPI. p. 185, Philip Jones Griffiths–Magnum.

# Map Credits

All maps prepared by Diane McCaffery. Sources are as follows:

p. 36—pp. 157, 181, Raising the Stakes, Terrence Maitland and Stephen Weiss, a volume in "The Vietnam Experience," Boston Publishing Company.

pp. 41, 106, and 125—Air Power in Three Wars, William W. Momyer, Office of Air Force History.

p. 126—Copyright ©1966/67/73 by The New York Times Company. Reprinted by permission.

# Index

## Allied Military Units

(See note below)

**U.S. Air Command Structure:** Fighters and fighter-bombers of the USAF's Tactical Air Command were organized into tactical fighter wings. Each wing, commanded by a colonel, consisted of a headquarters staff, supply squadron, engineering squadron, a medical unit, and three tactical fighter squadrons of about twenty-five aircraft each. Commanded by a lieutenant colonel, each squadron was manned by 300 enlisted airmen and forty officers, of whom thirty-five were pilots. They were further divided into four flights of five or six aircraft and seven or eight pilots, each commanded by a major. Tactical reconnaissance, early warning radar, ECM, transport, and other support aircraft were organized in their own independent wing and squadron structures. All units based in South Vietnam and Thailand were under the operational control of the 2d Air Division, later designated the 7th Air Force.

The USAF's Strategic Air Command, which retained control of its B-52 bombers, aerial refueling tankers, and long-range reconnaissance jets employed in Southeast Asia, and the Military Airlift Command, whose long-range transports ferried supplies and personnel from the U.S. to bases in Southeast Asia, were also organized into wings, squadrons, and flights.

The navy organized its aircraft into carrier air wings, self-contained units that were each based aboard an attack aircraft carrier. Each air wing contained approximately seventy-five aircraft, depending on the size of the carrier to which it was assigned. The wing was divided into eight squadrons. Wings usually consisted of two fighter squadrons and four attack squadrons of twelve aircraft each. Two smaller squadrons of reconnaissance and early warning aircraft rounded out the rest of the wing. Marine aircraft, based aboard carriers and on shore, followed a similar organizational pattern.

U.S. Army aircraft were organized at the battalion and company level. Each infantry division had its own aviation battalion and could also draw upon the assets of independent aviation battalions in-country. Airmobile divisions, such as the 1st Cavalry, possessed their own organic aviation battalions and companies.

# Names, Acronyms, Terms

**AAA**—antiaircraft artillery.

**AFB**—air force base.

**Alpha strike**—a preplanned Rolling Thunder mission against a specific target in North Vietnam.

**armed reconnaissance**—missions flown against specified areas in which it was expected that pilots would discover and bomb enemy targets.

**ARVN**—Army of the Republic of Vietnam. The army of South Vietnam.

**attack aircraft**—aircraft designed for delivering air-to-ground ordnance.

**CAP**—combat air patrol. Assignment of fighter aircraft in which they provide cover for strike aircraft.

**CIA**—Central Intelligence Agency.

**CINCPAC**—Commander in Chief, Pacific. Commander of American forces in the Pacific region, which includes Southeast Asia.

**close air support**—air action against enemy positions in close proximity to friendly forces.

**COMUSMACV**—Commander, U.S. Military Assistance Command, Vietnam.

**COSVN**—Central Office for South Vietnam. Communist party headquarters in South Vietnam, overseen by Hanoi.

**DIA**—Defense Intelligence Agency. Intelligence arm of the Joint Chiefs of Staff (JCS).

**Dixie Station**—cruising area for U.S. Navy carriers in the South China Sea 100 miles southeast of Cam Ranh Bay.

**DMZ**—demilitarized zone. Area dividing North Vietnam from South Vietnam along the seventeenth parallel.

**DRV**—Democratic Republic of Vietnam. North Vietnam.

**ECM**—electronic countermeasures. Equipment employed to identify and nullify enemy radar and radar-directed weapons systems.

**element**—USAF term for the basic fighting unit of two aircraft.

**FAC**—forward air controller. Pilot who controls strike aircraft engaged in close air support of ground troops or flying against other targets.

**fighter**—aircraft designed for maneuverability and speed used primarily for air-to-air combat.

**fighter/bomber**—fighter aircraft which could double as an attack bomber.

**flak**—antiaircraft fire; short for German *Fliegerabwehrkanonen*.

**flight**—USAF tactical fighter unit, usually consisting of four aircraft.

**G-pressure**—the force exerted upon a pilot and his aircraft by gravity or a reaction to acceleration or deceleration during a change of direction.

**GVN**—U.S. abbreviation for the government of South Vietnam, the Republic of Vietnam.

**gunship**—fixed-wing aircraft or helicopter equipped with rapid-firing guns or cannons to provide close air support for troops in battle.

**Iron Hand**—code name for a U.S. aircraft with special ordnance and electronic equipment with the mission of finding and destroying enemy SAM and radar-directed AAA sites.

**JCS**—Joint Chiefs of Staff. Consists of chairman, U.S. Army chief of staff, chief of naval operations, U.S. Air Force chief of staff, and marine commandant. Created in 1949 to advise the president, the National Security Council, and the secretary of defense.

**JGS**—Joint General Staff. South Vietnamese counterpart to MACV.

**KIA**—killed in action.

**lead**—the first aircraft in a flight.

**LOCs**—lines of communication. Land, water, and air routes along which supplies and reinforcements move from rear bases to troops in the field.

**Mach**—a designation for the speed of sound.

**MACV**—Military Assistance Command, Vietnam. U.S. command over all military activities in Vietnam.

**MIA**—missing in action.

**MIG**—name for Russian-built fighter aircraft developed by designers Mikoyan and Gurevich.

**MIGCAP**—combat air patrol directed against MIG aircraft.

**napalm**—incendiary used in Vietnam by French and Americans both as a defoliant and antipersonnel weapon.

**NLF**—National Liberation Front, officially the National Front for the Liberation of the South. Formed on December 20, 1960, it aimed to overthrow South Vietnam's government and reunite the North and the South.

**NVA**—North Vietnamese Army.

**OSS**—Office of Strategic Services (1942-1945). Precursor of the CIA.

**pickle**—slang for a pilot releasing his aircraft's bomb load by depressing the button atop his control stick.

**POL**—petroleum, oil, and lubricants.

**POW**—prisoner of war.

**prohibited zone**—the areas encircling Hanoi by ten nautical miles and Haiphong by four nautical miles in which U.S. aircraft were forbidden to strike unless specifically authorized.

**pylon**—a projection under an aircraft's wing from which ordnance, fuel tanks, or ECM pods could be suspended.

**recon**—reconnaissance. Also referred to as recce.

**restricted zone**—the areas encircling Hanoi by thirty nautical miles and Haiphong by ten nautical miles in which U.S. aircraft were restricted from striking unless specifically authorized or unless fired upon by North Vietnamese AAA or SAM sites located in the zone.

**Rolling Thunder**—code name for U.S. air campaign against North Vietnam conducted from March 2, 1965, to October 31, 1968.

**Route Package**—one of seven geographic divisions of North Vietnam established to divide areas of responsibility for air operations between U.S. Army, Air Force, and Navy.

**SAC**—Strategic Air Command. Branch of the USAF designed for sustained long-range air operations against vital target systems to destroy an enemy's ability or will to wage war.

**SAM**—surface-to-air missile.

**sortie**—a single aircraft flying a single mission.

**TAC**—Tactical Air Command. Branch of the USAF designed for air operations in coordination with ground forces against enemy combatants.

**TACC**—Tactical Air Control Center. The joint U.S.-VNAF center at Tan Son Nhut responsible for control of all air operations in South Vietnam and 7th Air Force operations over North Vietnam and Laos.

**TFS**—tactical fighter squadron.

**TFW**—tactical fighter wing, which consisted of three tactical fighter squadrons.

**USAF**—United States Air Force.

**VC**—Vietcong. Derogatory reference to a member of the NLF, a contraction of Vietnam *Cong San* (Vietnamese Communist).

**Vietminh**—coalition founded by Ho Chi Minh in May 1941 and ruled by DRV. Absorbed by the Lao Dong party in 1951.

**VNAF**—South Vietnamese Air Force.

**Wild Weasel**—twin-seated USAF F-100F and F-105F aircraft equipped with electronic detection gear and antiradiation missiles enabling them to home in on SA-2 (SAM) radar guidance systems.

**wingman**—pilot (or aircraft) who flies at the side and to the rear of an element leader. In a flight of four, the pilot of number two aircraft is wingman to the lead, or number one, aircraft while number four is wingman to number three.

**Yankee Station**—cruising area located 100 miles east of Da Nang in the South China Sea for Task Force 77 carriers flying Rolling Thunder missions against North Vietnam.